—— A ——
PROPHETIC
CALENDAR

THE FEASTS OF ISRAEL

JILL SHANNON

DESTINY IMAGE® PUBLISHERS, INC.
P.O. Box 310, Shippensburg, PA 17257-0310

"Speaking to the Purposes of God for this Generation and for the Generations to Come."

This book and all other Destiny Image, Revival Press, Mercy Place, Fresh Bread, Destiny Image Fiction, and Treasure House books are available at Christian bookstores and distributors worldwide.

For a U.S. bookstore nearest you, call 1-800-722-6774.

For more information on foreign distributors, call 717-532-3040.

Or reach us on the Internet: www.destinyimage.com

ISBN 10: 0-7684-2827-0
ISBN 13: 978-0-7684-2827-8

For Worldwide Distribution, Printed in the U.S.A.

1 2 3 4 5 6 7 8 9 10 11 / 13 12 11 10 09

Acknowledgments

My deepest thanks to my Father in Heaven, the Lord Yeshua, and His Spirit, for initiating this book. He has daily carried me through the writing of this intense body of teaching and revelation and has so accelerated its completion that I am stunned. The Lord's co-authorship is so tangible to me that I believe this is *His* book. Lord, You are too good to be true, but You *are* true!

Thank you to my awesome family for their love and constant generosity with my time: Dear Dror, Larry, Raviv and Amber, Keren, and Ariela—I have become who I am because of you!

To my angelic sister in the Lord, Cathy Minnick: I cannot even dream up a friend who could believe in my creative work as you have, or could so extravagantly support me through prayer and encouragement. In addition, you are a priceless editor! Thank you, dearest friend.

To my generous and affirming pastors, John and Sandra Shantz, and my dear brothers and sisters at Spring City Fellowship: you have been so patient with my many words and have never failed to show me the Lord's welcome and love.

To Pastors Curt and Anita Malizzi: I bless and thank you for your pivotal role in the birthing of this book. Because you opened a door of utterance to me concerning the Feasts of the Lord, this teaching reached the ears of Destiny Image! You also commissioned the writing of my new Passover Haggadah, which will bless so many for years to come.

To my awesome sister Ronda Ranalli, who knew about this book before it existed; to my precious brother Jeff Newcomer, who first invited me; and to my dear family at Destiny Image: I cannot imagine the world of Christian publishing without your courage, vision, and integrity. I am so honored to be a part of you.

To my anointed brother, David Michael: When you opened your mouth and blessed me, I never dreamed what heavenly plans would be set in motion by the Lord's response! Twelve hours later, this blessing was released. May the Lord prosper your weighty destiny for His Kingdom. I am honored to call you my friend.

To Tanya: You are an exuberant encouragement to me in my writing and music, but even more so, in my teaching ministry. Not only do you hear what the Lord is saying, but you immediately put it into practice; this is precious in His sight.

To Karalice: You read this book in its infancy and embraced these revelations with extraordinary openness. You have modeled intimacy with the Lord to me and have overcome much pain with dignity and courage.

To Danielle: I thank you for meticulous editing, reading, and caring about the smallest detail made perfect. Fly into the Son, little butterfly, for you have received your white wings!

I bless Brian and Kathy and Jeff Banashak at Gazelle Press for your friendship and professional support with *Coffee Talks With Messiah*. You have laid my literary foundations, from which this book arises. May the Lord enlarge the place of your habitation and bless all that you undertake.

I am particularly indebted to the ministries and prophetic visions of Sid Roth and Dr. Robert Heidler, and to the outstanding scholarship of Kevin Howard and Marvin Rosenthal. These worthy ones have plowed before me and have written on this subject so well that I hesitated to write another book on the Feasts. But the Lord made it clear that I must dive yet deeper into these living waters, and so I have cited their quality work with my love and gratitude.

In addition, I wish to thank the following teachers and ministries, who have enlarged my heart of understanding: Neville Johnson, Sadhu Sundar Selvaraj, Choo Thomas, Dr. Bill Hamon, Nita Johnson, Robert Stearns, Lance Lambert, Carol Levergood, Paul Keith Davis, Dan Juster, Rick Joyner, Mike Bickle, Lars Enarson, Reuven Doron, and David Dolan.

I honor the memory and Jewish heritage of my parents, Irv and Mitzi

Sher, who gave me their very best. I love you, and hope you would be proud of me.

To my dear Lyn, who gave me the greatest gift of all: the knowledge of Yeshua's gift of eternal life. May the Lord reward you for patiently leading me into His Kingdom!

I praise You, Lord God of Abraham, Isaac, and Jacob. I could not bear to live one day on this earth without Your unfailing love.

Endorsements

One group of Christians believes God is finished with the feasts. Another group believes that your salvation is dependent on observing the feasts. They are both wrong. Jill Shannon's book tells us God's position and unlocks ancient mysteries of blessing.

SID ROTH
Host, *It's Supernatural!* TV

Our dear sister Jill Shannon has honored the Lord Jesus in this book, full of the treasures the Lord God has hidden in His biblical feasts. Those who read this book will be drawn closer to the Lord's heart and will be enriched to understand His prophetic calendar.

SADHU SUNDAR SELVARAJ
Jesus Ministries

Jill helps the reader see Jesus and His purpose for the feasts of Israel. I taught the Pentateuch for five years in Bible College and wrote a college course on the Tabernacle and the feasts. Every New Testament truth can be found in the Tabernacle and feasts that God had Moses establish in Israel. The reader will be greatly enlightened and blessed by the truth found in this book.

DR. BILL HAMON
Bishop of Christian International Ministries Network (CIMN)
Author, *The Eternal Church* and many other major books

A Prophetic Calendar deliberates well beyond academic excellence of truth and history. Filled with amazing revelation, this book is a deep drink from the well of Living Waters for the Church. It is a refreshing and intimate gaze into our Father's heart of love and fellowship for Jewish and Gentile believers alike.

As I read Jill's book, my heart was dramatically increased and transformed. I was awakened to richer knowledge and a fuller understanding of our biblical appointments with the Lord from His very own calendar, which has been preserved by Jewish tradition throughout the years. Allow the Lord to draw you even closer to His heart as you read about and enter into these set-apart times.

The King of kings has prepared a banqueting table for us, and His banner over us *is* love! As He invites us to remember Him and even longs for our intimate fellowship with Him through the biblical feasts, how can we say no?

RONDA RANALLI
Acquisitions Editor, Destiny Image Publishers

You can feel the love flowing from Jill's heart for Yeshua and His children as you let these words touch your own heart. Jill is filled with compassion for Christ and His Bride, and her teachings and writings are gentle encouragements to embrace all that brings hearts to a deeper understanding of Yeshua. Our spirits were renewed as we were reminded of the deep roots of our faith, and we were refreshed with hunger to understand more.

Also regarding our Jewish brothers and sisters, gratitude filled our hearts for their persevering faithfulness to protect God's Word. *This is a book of revelation that brings the holy feasts alive in our daily lives. This book is an unspeakable wealth of insight, and you will want to have your Bible nearby in order to make notes.*

Shalom, PASTORS JOHN AND SANDRA SHANTZ
Pastors, Spring City Fellowship, Spring City, PA

I am delighted to see more and more people recognizing the beauty and significance of the Feasts of the Lord. I encourage everyone to avail themselves of this informative resource.

ROBERT STEARNS
Executive Director, Eagles' Wings Ministries
Co-chairman, The Day of Prayer for the Peace of Jerusalem

Jill's timely and lively words are sound instruction to us, with touches of humor injected by her transparent and down-to-earth style. Jill continually labored with the Spirit to bring to birth His appointment for Jew and Gentile to come together as "One New Man in Messiah."

Through the most complete insights ever given in this one-of-a-kind book on the Feasts of the Lord, I tasted and experienced the feasts as I am certain He has intended. I promise, as you take time to read this meaty book, Yeshua will envelop you within the fringes of His wings as you soak up these most important truths of His Living Word, which endure forever!

CATHY MINNICK
Royersford, PA

As a Spirit-filled believer and a born teacher, Jill has been blessed with the anointed gift of being able to take a complex subject and break it down into easily digestible morsels of truth.

Her desire in writing this book was to capture the heart of God and impart it in such a way that every believer would be intrigued to pursue intimacy with God through His feasts. She has indeed been faithful to the call.

DANIELLE NIEMCZUK
Royersford, PA

Table of Contents

Foreword

Many Christians feel a hunger to understand the Feasts of the Lord in a way that makes it practical and exciting for them to celebrate these biblical holidays. They sense that there must be something more than church traditions, which have not brought the manifest presence of God.

These precious believers know that God's covenants, promises, and blessings are not only for the Jewish people, because Jesus (Yeshua) the Messiah has opened the way for all the nations, all the Gentiles, to receive these blessings. They want to understand the biblical calendar and God's appointed festivals because they *know* God is inviting them to His table! But they are not sure how or where to begin.

There is a great need in the Church for a book that presents these Feasts in the same way that the Spirit of God offers them: as a banquet for all the nations to taste and celebrate. If you desire intense biblical knowledge about God's heart in these holidays, prophetic revelation, and much practical help in one resource, *A Prophetic Calendar: The Feasts of Israel* will accelerate your heart knowledge and cut through years of hard-to-grasp mysteries.

In her first book, Jill wrote about Jews and Gentiles coming together as One New Man in Messiah Jesus—the foundation for the next end-time move of God's Spirit. In this book, she builds on this foundation and shows us how the glorious last-days' Church will restore God's calendar and celebrate in unity, both Jew and Gentile. Our Father is giving a banquet, and all are welcome. These feasts are a rehearsal for the Wedding Supper of the Lamb! Taste and see that the Lord is good!

SID ROTH
Host, *It's Supernatural!* TV

Introduction

This book was not birthed out of human desire or ambition. I had not thought to take on such a project. After all, other fine teachers have written on this subject, and I therefore considered another book to be redundant and unnecessary.

I was surprised when Destiny Image Publishers approached me with the request to write this book on the Feasts of the Lord, which is an intimate invitation for the Body of Messiah to understand and celebrate the feasts.

I prayed about this request each day for a week, asking the Lord to confirm to me that it was truly His desire for me to step into this great task. On the seventh day of prayer, the Lord reminded me of a peach I had eaten in His presence during a three-day period of seclusion with Him during the fall feasts of 2007 (this was a different "three days" than the one I recorded in *Coffee Talks With Messiah*). All I can say about this unforgettable peach is that eating it produced a heavenly ecstasy within me that was unlike any pleasure on this earth, and that no normal peach could *ever* produce, no matter how perfect a peach it might be!

As I remembered this supernatural encounter with the Lord, He then asked me, *"Do you know how disappointed you feel when you bite into a dry and mealy peach?"*

In confirming that He wanted me to write this book, the Lord compared it to the peach "encounter," which took place during the fall feasts. This book would be sweet and juicy, creating an atmosphere of intimacy in the feasts, and inviting His Beloved to a desirable banquet table. The Lord commissioned me with this and other kind encouragements, to help His flock to find His heart in His own feasts. All are welcome to celebrate them with the Lord Himself in the room, as the most welcomed and beloved Host of the Banquet.

As will become abundantly clear throughout the book, the seven festivals God laid out on Israel's yearly calendar *all* foreshadow the life and ministry of Jesus the Messiah, past, present, and future. For the most part, I will often refer to the Lord Jesus by His true Hebraic identity throughout the book. The name His parents gave to Him was Yeshua, in obedience to the angel who announced His conception. It is the Hebrew word for "Salvation."

One of the primary purposes of this book is to restore to the Gentile church a deep understanding of her foundations in the everlasting covenants given to Israel. This includes the restoration of the Lord's original Hebraic identity to the Church, although He will respond to His Name in any language, when it is uttered by a sincere heart. These ancient roots are infinitely precious, but they have been largely removed from the Church's vision by historical events and religious decisions that strayed from the rhythms of God's heartbeat.

One of the most unique aspects of this book is that it combines in-depth biblical teaching with fresh prophetic revelation from the Lord's heart on each holiday. As I began the writing, scriptural teaching was interwoven with practical tips and experiential struggles; to this I added the stark passion of Yeshua's love and sacrifice, giving the reader intimate whispers of Love's reality, which must be discovered within the words in our Bibles.

When I finished the second chapter on Passover, I sat before the Lord and asked Him if I had found His heart in the Passover. In response to my question, He astonished me by immediately "downloading" to me four separate prophetic words from His heart concerning Passover. I was to insert these words, written in italics, into the Passover chapter at the appropriate places. These words completed and complemented the teaching material I had already written.

Greatly encouraged by His generosity to me and to the reader in the Passover chapter, I began asking the Lord if I had found His heart after finishing each chapter. The Holy Spirit has been kind and faithful to give me a word for all seven biblical festivals, which are recorded at the right place in each chapter. True to His character, the Lord then continued to give me His word for the remaining four chapters. Some of these words are encouraging and corrective, both to the Jewish people and to the Church. Some contain exhortations to be obedient in finances, or in cultivating intimacy with the Lord. One was a creative word, as if a page from the "diary of a Hebrew wanderer." Several contain serious warnings, both to the Jewish people and the Church, about the troubles ahead; some are hard to bear. The words in the Passover chapter seem more focused on Jewish attitudes, while the Sabbath word is directed to Gentiles and those who struggle with sexual issues. Most are for His Church in general.

It took courage and faith for me to record these words as I received them, knowing the high accountability of publishing words attributed to the Lord. As with all extra-biblical prophetic words, I understand that the accuracy of these words are not to be compared with the trustworthiness and authority of the Scriptures, which are my foundation for objective truth. All words must be tested by Scripture for content and character; test them and see if they are consistent with the Bible. If I did not think they were, I would not have included them.

This book is truly a marriage of the Word and the Spirit. It contains the nourishing fruit of biblical understanding, combined with the pleasurable juice of fresh revelation, and in the center of it all, the Seed of God's own heart.

May you find your Bridegroom's heart in these chapters. May you be inspired to see the calendar through a new lens, through the heavenly eyes of your Bridegroom, who has prepared a banquet for all nations. May the Lord beckon you into the intimacy of sharing a meal with Him. If you open the door of your heart, the Lord Jesus will come in and eat with you. He promised it in Revelation 3:20!

My love and blessing go out to every reader who hungers for intimacy with the Lord; you *will* be satisfied!

PART I

THE SPRING FEASTS OF THE LORD

Chapter 1

THE BIBLICAL CALENDAR

Like an apple tree among the trees of the forest is my lover among the young men.
I delight to sit in his shade, and his fruit is sweet to my taste.
He has taken me to the banquet hall, and his banner over me is love (Song of Songs 2:3-4).

Our loving Father has set a place for us, even prepared a table for us in the presence of our enemies. He has spread the wing of His garment over us and covered us with a bridal canopy of unfailing love. As we sit under His shade, we enjoy the choice fruits of summer, the delight and refreshment of a perfect peach.

Here I am! I stand at the door and knock. If anyone hears My voice and opens the door, I will come in and eat with him, and he with Me (Revelation 3:20).

Out of all the promises the Lord Jesus could have given to His Church, He promised to come in and eat with us. The Lord must consider the fellowship of a shared meal very precious and one of the most intimate offers He could make.

When all worries about rules, legalism, and bondage have finally been put to rest, we may see that our Father designed the biblical feasts to be opportunities for Him to commune with His children in intimate dining and the sweetest form of friendship.

If your king invited you to a banquet, or your president or senator invited you to a state dinner, wouldn't you think twice before telling him you were too busy to attend? Would you really tell him you couldn't get off from work that day? Will your culture, your boss, or your teacher punish you for attending the king's feast?

When an individual or family attempts to live out the biblical calendar in a western nation, they come into conflict with the culture and calendar of that nation. It feels like an uphill battle to maintain an atmosphere of consecration and to dedicate these days and seasons to the Lord. He is actually the One who has requested our presence at a feast that He is hosting each year. What if all those who love the Lord thought about it this way?

At the beginning of each year, people often hang a calendar on the wall with all twelve months laid out for them. It is helpful to mark appointments, holidays, festive dinners, vacation slots, and the days and weeks in which the children are off from school. In fact, the designer of that calendar has already inserted national and religious holidays, such as President's Day, Easter, Independence Day, Thanksgiving, and many other such dates.

A calendar captures a yearly snapshot of how a society lives, works, celebrates special days, and remembers heroes and victories from our history. The calendar reveals much about the values and priorities of a given nation, tribe, or culture. In fact, it could be said that the calendar speaks volumes about what a society holds closest to its heart.

THE JEWISH CALENDAR

Since the first century, the Jewish people have been dispersed throughout the nations of the earth and have successfully assimilated into these diverse cultures. This assimilation includes language, education, business, agriculture, and other cultural norms of the nations in which they live. However, their neighbors in these countries have noticed that they observe a distinct calendar of biblical origin, despite being a part of their national culture.

For those readers who have friendships with Jewish people, you might have noticed that they celebrate Jewish holidays that do not fall on the same date every year, according to our normal calendar. Many people have heard of Rosh HaShannah and Yom Kippur, which take place in the fall, as well as Passover in the spring.

While we normally think of these as Jewish holidays, the Lord actually refers to them in Scripture as "the Lord's feasts" or "My appointed times" (see Lev. 23:1-2). It is true that they were originally given to Israel, but if they are truly His feasts and not merely Israel's holidays, then all of the Lord's children would greatly benefit to know what was in God's heart when He defined these times and seasons.

In Hebrew, there are three words used for our special days. One is *mo'ed*, which means a season or an appointed time. Just as the Creator made the sun, moon, and stars for times and seasons (see Gen. 1:14), He also pinpointed times on the calendar when His people must set time apart with Him, away from the normal business of life. It is interesting that in Daniel 7:25, it is prophesied that the antichrist will "speak against the Most High and oppress His saints, and *try to change the set times and the laws.*" Paul calls this man the "lawless one," a man without God's law in his arrogant heart (2 Thess. 2:8).

The second word used in Scripture is *mikrah*, which is a holy convocation, a sacred assembly, or even a rehearsal of God's past, present, and future acts. As we study these celebrations, we will see that each one is remembering or foreshadowing an aspect of Messiah's ministry. They represent His sacrifice, resurrection, the gift of the Holy Spirit, the Bride's preparedness for the rapture, and Messiah's return to earth to establish His Kingdom and to "tabernacle" with us forever (see Ezek. 43:7).

The third word is *chag*, which simply means a festive celebration.

Surely, if these feasts testify of Messiah, they belong to all who love Him. And if they are really about intimacy with the Lord, why shouldn't all believers have the opportunity to learn more about their significance and how easy they are to celebrate? Perhaps a stirring and desire will arise in your heart as you read this book. If nothing stirs, then perhaps the Lord is not directing you to celebrate them at this moment, and there is no moral failing, guilt, or obligation laid upon you by Him or by any other person. His love is unconditional and unwavering.

All of these biblical celebrations contain deep treasures of understanding. They unveil the Lord's intense desire for fellowship with His people, as living parables. They paint a prophetic picture of the Lord Yeshua's eternal redemptive purposes on the earth.

On the road to Emmaus, we see that the risen Lord Yeshua opened all the Scriptures to the two disciples, and explained everything to them which was written about Him in the Law and the Prophets (see Luke 24:13-32). Much of what Moses and the prophets wrote about Him was hidden in the feasts and their symbolism. It is no coincidence that the disciples did not recognize Yeshua until they sat down together for a meal and He broke bread and blessed it. We know the Lord through the fellowship of sharing a meal with Him. *The feasts of the Lord point to Yeshua, and they give us specific wisdom into what He has done for us, a unique revelation that becomes visible only through the lens of these holy festivals.*

THE ROMAN CALENDAR

Most nations operate on a Gregorian calendar, introduced by Pope Gregory XIII in 1582. This was a corrected form of the Julian calendar, as regulated by Julius Caesar. Obviously, both of these calendars are of Roman origin. Therefore, it is not surprising that many of the names of our weekdays and months are the names of Roman gods or Caesars (who were also considered gods). For example, the month of March is named after the god Mars, and January for the god Janus; Wednesday is named for Woden, the chief Teutonic god, and Thursday is for Thor, the old Norse god of thunder. Saturday is named after the god of agriculture, Saturn, and Sunday was named "the Venerable Day of the Sun" by Constantine in A.D. 321. Monday is the "Moon's Day." Why are we uttering the names of foreign gods every time we name a day of the week or a month? (See Exodus 23:13.)

One thing that seems perplexing about our adherence to the Roman calendar is that America was founded on Judeo-Christian values and principles. Wouldn't that suggest that our calendar should reflect these beliefs and priorities? Shouldn't our days, months, and holidays be of biblical origin, as defined by God? The Lord's appointed times were also followed by Jesus and His Jewish apostles in the New Testament (see John 7:1-14; Mark 14:12).

If we love the Lord and wish to honor Him in our lives and calendars, is there anything we can do to align ourselves with His appointed times, days, seasons, and festivals? Is it possible to take a fresh look at our customs and celebrations, despite the longstanding and pervasive cultural acceptance of an unbiblical calendar all around us?

If there were not wonderfully encouraging answers to these questions, there would be no point in writing this book. We can, indeed, align ourselves with God's heart. It is not too difficult, it is not religious, and it is not done out of guilt or fear. Our Lord has made a way for us to join with Him in the intimate fellowship of His appointed times and seasons. If this sounds exciting to your heart, then this was written just for you!

THE CHURCH'S CALENDAR

According to the Gospels and Acts, the Lord Yeshua and His apostles were Jewish. The only holidays celebrated and cited in any of the New Testament writings were the biblical feasts observed by the Lord and the apostolic community (see John 10:22; Luke 22:7-8; Acts 20:6; 1 Cor.16:8). The apostle Paul made plans during his missionary journeys to observe the biblical calendar when he could arrange it, and to return to Jerusalem in time for the Feast of Weeks, also called Pentecost (see Acts 20:16). Pentecost was one of the three pilgrimage festivals in which the Lord God had commanded all Israelite men to come up to Jerusalem to worship the Lord and present offerings (see Deut. 16:16-17).

After Paul left Ephesus and arrived in Jerusalem, the apostles joyfully informed him that myriads (tens of thousands) of Jews had believed and were zealous for the Law of Moses, which certainly included the biblical feasts. They also convinced Paul that he must disprove the rumors that were spreading, which claimed that he was teaching Jewish believers to apostasize, or turn away from Moses (see Acts 21:20-26). There is abundant biblical and historical evidence that the early church was Jewish and kept the feasts of Israel. There is also much documentation that shows that until the fourth century, much of the Gentile Church followed the biblical calendar, as it had been observed by the Jewish apostles.

During the second and third century, the original Jewish apostolic community died, and the Gentile church was growing in numbers and influence. Sadly, several historical factors combined to create a version of Christianity that began to be cut off from the roots of the faith that had been delivered by the apostles.

One of these factors was the Roman hatred and persecution of the Jews, due to the fierce resistance they displayed against the Roman occupation of Israel during the first and second century. The great Roman army was humiliated and infuriated by the Judeans' ability to drive back their assaults on Jerusalem, despite being an occupied people who had been starved out by Roman siege.

Under Rome's watchful eye, it became dangerous for Gentile Christians to continue to associate with the synagogues or Judaic practice. To protect themselves from Roman retaliation, they began to distance themselves from all things Jewish and thus avoided being associated with the zealots.

A second factor was the influence of Greek thought and religion, which were very different from Hebraic thought. Greek philosophies tended to separate spirit from body—elevating the spirit, punishing the body, and denigrating human emotions. The Hebrew view of man was holistic and allowed for mourning, joy, feasting, and worshiping a unique and utterly holy God. Even complaints could be poured out before the Lord, as to a friend who cared, just as David expressed in his psalms. The Lord's feasts were meant to be experienced with our senses, rather than merely understood with our minds.

When a Greek thinker read the Hebrew Scriptures, he would read it as a spiritual allegory, as wisdom literature with a deeper meaning. A Hebrew would read the Scriptures as a communication from the unique and holy Creator God; he would also read it as a literal and historic document, rather than as a mystical saying.

The Greek mindset was very influential in the early Gentile church and in the development of non-Hebraic theologies. It caused the Church to move further away from the biblical foundations, calendar, and teachings of the Lord Yeshua and His Jewish apostles. Two of the influential church fathers who absorbed and disseminated Greek thought, merging them with Christianity, were Origen (185-254) and Augustine (354-430).

The third and most decisive factor was the "conversion" of Constantine to Christianity in A.D. 312, although he continued to worship Mithras, the sun god, for the remainder of his life. While his adherence to a form of Christianity eliminated the cruel persecutions of the Roman emperors before him, much compromise and whoredom in the professing Church ensued. The darkness and idolatry worsened over the next ten centuries, until the light of the Reformation dawned.

Constantine merged Christianity with Roman culture and religion, and under his rule, a growing bias against Jewish practices evolved. The biblical feasts and calendar were deliberately and systematically cancelled and replaced. These changes took place through a series of councils and edicts issued by Constantine to the churches.

Much has been written about the history of the early church, and it is not the purpose of this book to document this history thoroughly. For those readers who wish to study the full path of this tragic abnormality in church history, I highly recommend Dr. Robert D. Heidler's book, *The Messianic Church Arising!* This clearly written book is well-researched, tracing this journey of ignorance and its destructive consequences on the reality of a living faith in Messiah Jesus.

I will now only briefly summarize these laws and deliberate changes to the biblical calendar imposed on all Christians during the fourth century. I believe the Lord wants me to move quickly into helping His flock to find His heart of intimacy in each feast, rather than duplicating the excellent teachings that have been admirably covered by Robert Heidler, Sid Roth, Michael Brown, and other fine scholars.

A Prophetic Calendar: The Feasts of Israel

In A.D. 189, the churches in Asia Minor fasted in memory of Yeshua's suffering and broke their fast by celebrating the Passover Seder. These Christians righteously observed the resurrection in connection with the Hebrew calendar and the Feast of Passover. However, the other churches throughout the Roman Empire had already declared the resurrection to be on a particular Sunday, pertaining to the vernal equinox, and not connected to the date of the Jewish Passover. This doctrinal disagreement became a great controversy between these two communities.

In A.D. 325, the Council of Nicaea changed the date of Easter. Emperor Constantine declared Easter Sunday to be the only acceptable day to observe the resurrection. He stated that the Christian celebrations must be independent from Jewish dates on the calendar, due to the defiling and detestable sin of the Jews. The word *Easter* is of pagan derivation, from the fertility goddess "Ishtar" or "Asherah" found in biblical accounts of Canaanite idolatry. It should not be associated with the Lord Yeshua's resurrection from the dead.

Between A.D. 343 and 381, the Council of Laodicea forbade Christians to observe the seventh-day Sabbath. Any Christian who continued to observe the Jewish Sabbath would be *anathema*, which means "accursed," to Christ. Up until the time of this edict, many Gentile Christians continued to observe this day.

These edicts became law, and over the following centuries, they were enforced with excommunication and death. Anti-Semitism increased, and the Jews of the medieval world were blamed for every ill of society, including the bubonic plague!

The Jewish community kept the Law of Moses, which included the safe and hygienic disposal of human waste. Therefore, while European streams were contaminated with raw sewage and infected rats, the Jews were largely protected from the contamination and the fleas that lived on the rats. Because they did not contract the plague, the "Christian" society accused them of causing the plague by evil practices.

The "church" became one of the vilest persecutors of the Jewish people. Of course, the people who did this were not walking with Yeshua's heart or in His Spirit. They were the professing church, but not the Bride. For more detailed research on "Christian" anti-Semitism, read *The Race to Save the World* by Sid Roth and *Our Hands Are Stained With Blood*, by Dr. Michael L. Brown.

As for Christmas, during the first and second centuries, Messiah's birthday was not celebrated, since the exact date of His birth remained unknown. His resurrection was the primary day of celebration. By the fourth century, many groups were celebrating His birth on various dates, ranging from January 6 in the East, to December 25 in the West. Other dates were also used. In A.D. 350, Pope Julius declared December 25 as the official date.

The English Puritans and Reformed Protestants rejected the December 25 celebration as pagan, and it was banned in England in 1644. However, King Charles II, upon taking the throne, reinstated it. American Puritans continued not to recognize this date, but by the 1830s, New England had moved away from Puritanism, and New Englanders were celebrating Christmas as we do today, with decorated trees, parties, and gift-giving.

WHAT DOES YESHUA SAY ABOUT CHRISTMAS?

Once I was praying with a troubled heart about the Lord's birthday. Because I am a Messianic Jewish Bible teacher, I had been teaching for many years that the Lord Yeshua was not born on December 25 (although I had not judged Christians who celebrated this day). There is strong biblical evidence that the Lord was born at the time of Tabernacles, which will be fully explained in Chapter 8.

However, after teaching this for many years, I read a testimony that seriously shook my theology. After reading the true testimony of Choo Thomas in her book, *Heaven Is So Real!*, I became confused by one of her testimonies, in which the Lord Jesus appeared to her in elegant robes on Christmas Eve, clearly celebrating His birthday. I wrote to Sister Choo and respectfully asked her if the Lord had specifically told her that He was born on this day, or if He had only said that He was celebrating with His people.

Before I received an answer from Choo, I was asking the Lord about it. I told Him that I did not want to be a false teacher, and that if this date was truly His birthday, I would repent publicly and never repeat this error again in my teaching ministry.

I asked Him, "If You were born on a certain date on the Hebrew calendar, which would fall on a different Roman date each year, why would You visit Choo on the Roman date of December 25?"

I felt the Lord answer me in my spirit:

The Roman calendar is the only one available to many nations, including your own culture. I chose to be born in the midst of the Roman Empire, and its influence and calendar are still with us. It is important for My people to have historical dates to link with the critical events in My ministry on earth: My birth, My crucifixion, and My resurrection. Since these dates are the only ones they know, I honor these days with My people if they are honoring Me in their hearts. I love them and want to be in fellowship with them as they celebrate Me. [In hearing this word, I sensed that the Lord was saying that the fact that He entered human history was more important than the accuracy of the date of His birth.]

Soon after receiving this word from the Lord, I received a helpful answer from my dear Sister Choo, which very much lined up with what I believe the Lord showed me. She was very kind to respond to my question, stating that the Lord told her He was not born on that day, but that He chose to celebrate it with His people on the day they were celebrating.

Therefore, the Lord does not disdain these sincere expressions, even if the dates were given through errors or sins committed by past political and church leaders. We are in a most exciting moment in history, when the Lord is restoring all things (see Acts 3:21), and this includes the restoration of His true biblical calendar and appointed times to His people.

SOME PRACTICAL PROBLEMS

In recent years, I have noticed that some public schools located in regions with significant Jewish populations will close school on some of these holidays, out of respect for the Jewish students. I have heard parents complain about these school closings, which seem inconvenient to the majority of the population, which does not observe these special days. While I truly understand their complaint, I'd like to share the other side of the matter, from the perspective of a Messianic Jewish family.

When our children were little, my family lived in Israel, where these holidays were a natural part of the culture and the calendar, even for Israelis who were not particularly religious. Businesses and schools in Israel were closed, and all students were exempt from their normal schoolwork. It was comparable to our American culture, where all the students have a week off for Christmas vacation. Since no schoolwork or homework takes place, no one is required to make up for lost time.

When we moved back to the United States with three young children, they began attending public school. My husband and I believed that these biblical feast days were created by God and that we would be disobeying Him to do our ordinary work on these days. It would be hypocrisy for us to send our children to school to do their normal work and homework.

I wrote notes to their teachers every year, as these feasts would come along very soon after school started in the fall, and then again in the spring. In middle school and high school, I was writing notes to five or six teachers for each holiday. While they were excused from school, it was hard for them to make up the work they had missed. As they got older, the workload increased, and the deadlines were often in conflict with keeping these days "set apart."

There were years when I wrestled with guilt and confusion, as the children would explain the difficulty, sometimes the impossibility, of missing school on those days. It was a terrible conflict for them to be forced to choose between missing school work and violating their heritage. Sometimes, in a weary spirit of sympathy and compromise, I would let them go to school.

I realize that many people would enjoy their day off, using the time to pursue their own desires or entertainment. When I was a child, I loved having the day off. I went to synagogue but didn't think about God for the rest of the day. When I fasted on Yom Kippur, all I could think about was when I could eat again! But now that we are more mature, will we treasure this separate space with our Beloved and put aside all distractions for Him?

There is a big difference between taking a day off from school or work and having a "date day" with the living God, our Maker and Husband (see Isa. 54:5).

Following the biblical calendar in our culture creates scheduling conflicts. This theme will be expanded in Chapter 11, concerning the observance of the Sabbath. Friends and family do not always understand why you might not wish to help them move on that day, go to a birthday party or school sports event, or buy things at the mall. It never fails. Someone will always schedule an event you "must" do on that very day.

One day when the children were young, one of my daughters received an invitation to a birthday party in the mail. I was so excited and opened it. As my eyes scanned the date and time, my heart sank, and great conflict arose in my mind. The birthday/swim party was on Yom Kippur (which fell on a Saturday that year), a day of fasting and the holiest day on the Jewish calendar. She would be expected to celebrate, eat cake and ice cream, and swim at the YMCA. I couldn't bear to disappoint my daughter, so I began to plead and negotiate with the Lord.

"Lord, she's only seven. You know she hardly ever gets invited to parties. Can't she go? Wouldn't it be OK?"

It was rare in those days for me to hear answers from the Lord, but this one came swiftly and unmistakably.

> "The nations make their plans and calendars with no regard for My times and seasons and set-apart days. Do you want to be just like them?"

I crumpled in shame and answered, "No, Lord. Of course I don't want to be just like them." I knew what I had to do and prayed that He would give my daughter grace to accept my decision. When she came home from school, I showed her the invitation and explained to her why she could not go. She immediately accepted this without sadness, and a week later, she was invited to another party. How the Lord honored and blessed our decision!

On "that day," He is requesting the honor of your presence at the

Wedding Supper of the Lamb (see Isa. 25:6-9; Rev. 19:6-9). None of us want to miss that appointment. Until that glorious day, He has appointed holy rehearsals on earth for intimate dining with our most generous Host.

Surely we are not too busy for our King. In the Lord's chilling parable of Luke 14:16-23, a great man gives a banquet and sends out many invitations. When the guests make excuses about needing to tend to business, property, and personal commitments, the host becomes angry. He declares that these unworthy guests will never taste his banquet. Instead, he invites the poor and unworthy to attend, so that his dinner and hospitality will not go to waste.

It is true that this parable is not specifically about the feasts of the Lord but is rather about the invitation into the Kingdom of God through radical commitment to Jesus, at any cost. However, it is still important to consider our Father's feelings about these events on His calendar. If He desires to commune with all of His children at these holy parties and not merely with observant Jews and Messianic Jews, then we would not wish to inadvertently hurt the Master of the banquet, even if our attendance is costly.

Interestingly, I was once threatened with losing my corporate position because I requested a day off on a particular feast day. This day happened to be inconvenient for my department's schedule, and I hated asking. I prayed to the Lord for favor during this uncomfortable confrontation. As I respectfully held to my convictions, my boss looked at me intently, possibly weighing the consequences of exercising the full measure of his authority to dismiss me. He was not an unkind man, and after some tension, he permitted me the day off. I was relieved and grateful but realized it could have turned out badly.

Nehemiah asked his boss, the king of Persia, for some time off from his job as cupbearer to the king. He needed to go to Israel in order to rebuild the walls and gates of Jerusalem, which had been broken and burned by the Babylonians. Though he was afraid, he prayed for favor during this confrontation, and his boss gave him some time off, as well as many supplies and legal papers. Nehemiah was gone for twelve years! However, he faithfully returned to Persia and continued to find favor with the king (see Neh. 2:4-5).

A Prophetic Calendar: The Feasts of Israel

The Restoration and the Motivation

The Lord Yeshua has taken a Bride for Himself from all the nations, and He desires that His beloved will share intimate communion with Him during these appointed days. While these feasts were originally given to the Jewish people and are still their precious heritage, the Lord has opened the invitation to every individual and family that has been grafted into His natural olive tree. In Paul's teaching to the Roman church, he explains that the Gentile believers are like wild olive branches that have been grafted into a natural olive tree, whose roots support their faith. The eleventh chapter of Romans gives a fuller understanding of this mystery.

We are living in a highly prophetic season, in which the biblical calendar is being restored to the Body of Messiah. Even so, there is never disdain in the Lord's heart for those of His people who honor Him on the only dates they know and love Him sincerely. Nor should there ever be condescension in the hearts of Christians or Messianic Jews who honor the biblical calendar. All that we do and teach must be motivated by humility and love for our brothers and sisters, especially His young and tender ones. Without sincere affection for one another, even a good teaching is in vain and will not bear good fruit (see 1 Cor. 13).

Embracing these truths is voluntary, and the Lord respects the honest decisions of His children, for He is a humble and respectful Person. As His people begin to comprehend the Father's heart in this teaching, a desire will grow within many to learn how to observe these days and seasons, freely and voluntarily.

There is great reward for those who love and celebrate these appointed times voluntarily.

> *Yet when I preach the gospel, I cannot boast, for I am compelled to preach. Woe to me if I do not preach the gospel! If I preach voluntarily, I have a reward; if not voluntarily, I am simply discharging the trust committed to me (1 Corinthians 9:16-17).*

Paul was in big trouble if he didn't preach the Gospel, because this was his life's assignment and destiny from God. He was a humble servant, merely doing what was required of him. Others, who preached voluntarily, might have reaped great reward for doing so.

In a similar vein, I am required by God to love and observe these feasts. Not only am I a Messianic Jew, but my life's assignment and destiny is to teach, preach, and model the wonder and intimacy of the Lord's ancient paths and precepts, the beauty of His living Torah quickened by His Spirit. I cannot teach what I do not live out, and woe to me if I tell others to do things I myself do not wholeheartedly embrace in my private life. I am simply discharging my responsibility, and I do not believe I will reap any particular reward for keeping the appointed feasts of the Lord.

But to those of you from among the nations who are not required to keep them: in most cases, it is not your life's assignment and theme. It is an extra blessing, like gravy on the meal. Therefore, you will reap greater reward for celebrating them voluntarily, out of a joyful and obedient heart.

Some will gradually make lifestyle changes, while yet in the midst of nations who do not consider the Lord's timetable when planning their schedules. These matters must be embraced without legalism or a religious spirit. There is a world of difference between legalism and obedience. Since there is always a danger of observing these special seasons legalistically, let us now precisely draw the fine line between legalism and obedience.

LEGALISM VERSUS OBEDIENCE

Legalism could be described as trying to earn God's favor by performing a set of behaviors and abstaining from other behaviors. Another aspect of legalistic motivation involves earning the respect or admiration of others, hoping to be noticed for your holy or righteous acts. The Lord Yeshua used the expression, "to be seen... [and] honored by men" (see Matt. 6:1-18).

If we live a holy and upright life but don't care if anyone else notices us, then we are not doing these things to be seen by men. But in addition to this caution, let us make sure that our only desire is to please our Father's heart, rather than thinking that we have earned God's favor or glory.

The Lord once spoke to me the following word: *"You have not earned My glory, Jill. I do reward you according to the cleanness of your hands and the purity of your heart."*

At first, this word seemed contradictory to me. I knew that the second sentence was echoing the words of David in Psalm 18:20-24. There seems to be a distinction between earning His favor and receiving special rewards from Him. A parent might tell a child to clean up the playroom, without offering payment for this required chore. However, if the child does an outstanding job, the parent might surprise him with a special treat or reward. It is not a payment, but a reward. My best understanding is that we cannot earn His favor or His glory, for these are gifts His generous heart freely gives us. It is nevertheless a biblical reality that He rewards the upright, according to His appraisal of their deeds and the motives of their hearts.

In both of the biblical examples below, the attitudes of the heart make the critical difference between the Lord's acceptance of our righteousness and His rejection of it. These heart attitudes are deeper than any outward or ceremonial practice; in fact, they can only be seen and discerned by God Himself. While "justice, mercy, and faithfulness" might sometimes be observable in our outward actions, they are usually attitudes of the heart or secret acts of righteousness, seen only by God.

> *Woe to you, teachers of the law and Pharisees, you hypocrites! You give a tenth of your spices—mint, dill and cummin. But you have neglected the more important matters of the law—justice, mercy and faithfulness. You should have practiced the latter, without neglecting the former. You blind guides! You strain out a gnat but swallow a camel (Matthew 23:23-24).*

> *"Love the Lord your God with all your heart and with all your soul and with all your mind." This is the first and*

greatest commandment. And the second is like it: "Love your neighbor as yourself." All the Law and the Prophets hang on these two commandments (Matthew 22:37-40).

There is no amount of performance that can earn God's favor (the Hebrew word for favor is *chen*, which is also translated in some verses, "grace"). It is easy to understand that we cannot earn grace, since the word means "gift."

Legalism implies that we can act in strict adherence to biblical laws, or even to church laws, and thus be considered righteous by God. If meticulous observance could win His approval, surely the Pharisees of the first century would have won first prize for scrupulous attention to detail. But true obedience is about a heart in love! When we love God with all our heart, soul, and strength, we never wish to grieve Him or ignore something dear to His heart. A heart in love always tries to obey, motivated by affection and a desire to please.

It is easy to judge the Pharisees for their hypocrisy, but isn't the Church populated with Pharisees as well? I fear our hypocrisy will be more severely judged than theirs, because we are accountable for obeying all the words of the Lord Yeshua in our Bibles, as well as the other inspired New Testament instructions about fleeing from all hypocrisy and double-mindedness (see James 3:8-12; 1 Pet. 2:1; 1 Tim. 4:2). Christian legalism and hypocrisy should absolutely terrify us, for I believe it will send many professing Christians to hell (see Matt. 7:21-23).

Obedience is best described by the following heart attitude toward the Lord: "Father I love You, and I love Your Son, Yeshua. I want to be like Him, and to walk as He walked. If it would make You happy for me to walk in any of Your appointed times and seasons, please help me learn; I open my heart. Please show me how to do this; I don't want to be legalistic, but I want to make You feel welcome and loved in my celebrations. I know Your character has never changed since You wrote about these festivals, so help me to grow. If and when I take my first baby steps, please meet with me and let me feel Your pleasure in me, so that I know that this pleases You." Anyone who prays this sincerely will not be disappointed by Him who is quick to respond to His children's honest questions.

THE YEARLY FEASTS OF THE LORD

The Lord is saying, "Remember Me. Remember what I have done for you. Most of all, remember My love!" Since we tend to become distracted and to drift from intimate communion with the Lord, His Word is an anchor for our souls. His calendar is a compass to direct us to the "everlasting paths." They lead us to remembrance of the past and preparation for the future. And they are "now" fulfillments, as well.

There are seven feasts on His calendar. The climactic fall feasts occur in the seventh month, the holiest month on His schedule. The festivals can be divided into four spring feasts and three fall feasts. The first three form a unit, and the last three form a unit. Pentecost stands in the long, dry summer, as a bridge between the past and the future.[13] The best description of the biblical calendar, laid out in order, is found in Leviticus 23.

Before we study each holiday's significance, let's look at a brief overview of the calendar, as God defined it.

1. *Passover* remembers the Israelites' exodus from hundreds of years of slavery in Egypt, and the redemption of a newborn nation, a people belonging to the Lord. It was the blood of the Passover lamb that rescued the Israelites from the destroying angel, who struck down every firstborn in Egypt. It is the blood of Yeshua that covers our hearts, rescuing us from a hideous and eternal "living death."

2. *Unleavened Bread* is a seven-day period, beginning with Passover. During this week we eat no foods made with yeast. Leavened bread will spoil quickly, but unleavened bread will remain uncorrupted. Since the Lord's body did not undergo decay in the grave, His incorruptibility was a picture of pure and unleavened bread, without the yeast of sin in His life.

3.   *First Fruits* occurs on the third day after Passover and is an offering of the first barley that comes up in the early spring. It is like a Thanksgiving before the main crop has come in. By offering the Lord the first part of our crops, we are showing Him that we trust Him for a greater harvest in the weeks to come. The Lord Jesus was raised from the dead on First Fruits, the third day after Passover; this demonstrates that He went ahead of us, as the first one to be harvested from death. Since the Father raised Him to life, we can trust Him to resurrect an enormous harvest of the righteous dead.

4.   *Pentecost or the Feast of Weeks* occurs fifty days after the Sabbath of Passover (see Lev. 23:15-16). In Hebrew, *Shavuot* means "weeks," and in Greek, *Pentecost* means "fifty." We count off seven sevens, which is forty-nine days. Traditionally, the Israelites received the Law of Moses on this day, fifty days after coming out of Egypt. Also, on this same feast, fifty days after Yeshua's resurrection, the Holy Spirit was poured out on the Jewish disciples, who were waiting in Jerusalem for the gift and power of the Holy Spirit. So both Israel and the Church trace their birth to this season.

5.   *The Feast of Trumpets* is also called "Rosh HaShannah," which means "Head of the Year." Later in the book, you will also see me refer to this festival as "The Memorial of Blasting," because the Lord called it by this name in a word He gave me while writing Chapter 6, which is a literal translation of the Hebrew name. This holiday, along with Atonement and Tabernacles, occurs in the seventh month on the calendar. It is a solemn "wake-up" call to repentance,

commemorated by many blasts of the ram's horn, or *shofar*. It also prepares us for the Messiah's soon return, which will come with a startling trumpet blast and will produce instant repentance on the earth.

6. *The Day of Atonement or Yom Kippur* is the only 24-hour fast day commanded in the Bible. It is the most solemn of the feasts, in which the high priest would enter the Holy of Holies, only on this day, to offer blood for the sins of himself and the people of Israel. In the Book of Hebrews, we see that Yeshua was a greater high priest than those of Levitical lineage, and that He entered Heaven's tabernacle with His own blood to make atonement for all the sins ever committed before and after His sacrificial death.

7. *Tabernacles* is the last and most joyful feast, which lasts seven days. It remembers the Israelites living in tents during their long sojourn in the desert without permanent homes. We see that God has always desired to dwell or "tabernacle" with His people on earth, from the Garden in Genesis till the last words of Revelation, when "the dwelling of God is with man, and He shall live with them forever" (see Rev. 21:3). The earth is not our permanent home, and we live in mortal tents, looking forward to a permanent home whose builder and architect is our Father, God.

Chapter 2

THE FEAST OF PASSOVER

Take your son, your only son, Isaac, whom you love, and go to the region of Moriah. Sacrifice him there as a burnt offering on one of the mountains I will tell you about (Genesis 22:2).

Abraham took the wood for the burnt offering and placed it on his son Isaac. The beloved son struggled up the hill, carrying the wood of his own sacrifice on his back. He glanced up at his father, who was resolutely walking toward the mountain, without allowing his eyes to meet Isaac's questioning gaze. Surely his father had thought to provide an animal for the offering. But he only saw the sharpened knife and flaming torch in his father's hands. He would ask about the missing animal.

"Father, the fire and the wood are here, but where is the lamb?"

Although this question was unanswerable, Abraham spoke from a deep reservoir of trust, despite the pounding of his heart.

"God Himself will provide the lamb for the burnt offering, my son."

He built an altar, bound his son, and lifted up his knife to the trembling boy's throat. Seconds before slaughter at the hands of the one he loved and trusted, Isaac was rescued and redeemed from destruction.

The angel of the Lord called out, "Do not lay a hand on the boy. Now I know that you fear God, because you have not withheld from me your son, your only son."

Abraham looked up and there in the thicket he saw a ram caught by its horns. The ram was Isaac's substitute (see Gen. 22:1-14).

Later, another Son would stagger up the hill, with the wood of His sacrifice on His back. He looked up at His loving Father, but His Father would not meet His gaze. There would be no substitute for this Hebrew son, no last-minute rescue, because He *was* the substitute. They would nail Him to the wood He bore. He was the Lamb, who would redeem every death sentence ever to be handed down to sin-infested humanity. God did not spare His Son, but would use His blood to buy back the world from the merciless and fallen angel of eternal death.

REDEEMED FROM SLAVERY

We reap what we sow. Joseph was sold by his jealous brothers into slavery, and within several generations, their descendents were ruthlessly enslaved in the very nation where their innocent brother had suffered cruel injustice (see Exod. 1:6-10). The Israelites were afflicted with hard work in the fields, irrigating crops and building the treasure cities for Pharaoh's aggrandizement. The center of our Passover narrative is that "they made their lives bitter with hard labor and cruel bondage" (see Exod. 1:11-14).

Pharaoh also practiced genocide, by commanding that the baby Hebrew boys be killed at birth. He would later reap what he sowed, for God would exact from him the firstborns of Egypt. In fact, well before the ten plagues, the Lord warned Pharaoh, "Israel is My firstborn son" (Exod. 4:22-23). Pharaoh would pay with his own son's life for not allowing God's first-born son to go free.

Under Messiah's arms of love, the Father has many adopted sons and daughters from the nations, but Israel is His firstborn son. *Harming Israel is costly to the nations—more costly than they can bear.*

The first fourteen chapters of Exodus tell of the gripping, high-stakes confrontation between the meekest man on earth, possessing no political power or standing, and the most powerful and autocratic ruler in the known world. If there were not a powerful yet invisible King in Heaven, who causes "justice to roll on like a river" on the earth (Amos 5:24), Pharaoh would have been insane to let several million slaves go free, with all of their youth and livestock.

The backs and blood of slaves carry the economic prosperity of any nation heedless enough to enslave them. Our nation is no better than ancient Egypt, for we too were guilty of ruthlessly oppressing an innocent people for hundreds of years, unto death, poverty, degradation, and demoralization. May God, in His great mercy, take away the guilt of our bloodshed, and may we witness the full restoration of the African-American people to their God-appointed blessings, destiny, and nobility. Amen.

Can any nation prosper indefinitely on the exploitation of slaves if there is a God in Heaven? When the Hebrew cries reached the ears of the God of Heaven, He spoke to his servant Moses:

> *I have indeed seen the misery of My people in Egypt. I have heard them crying out because of their slave drivers, and I am concerned about their suffering* (Exodus 3:7).

Though the Lord seemed to wait for several generations before the weightiness of His response was felt, He was indeed concerned about His people and had formed a plan of redemption, though it would cost Him everything in the future.

On the tenth day of the first month, called *Nisan*, every Israelite family chose a perfect little lamb and took care of it until the fourteenth day. Then at twilight, the father of the household slaughtered it and put its blood on the doorframes of their house.

Though nine increasingly painful plagues came upon Egypt, due to Pharaoh's unrelenting pride and greed, the most devastating blow was yet to fall: the swift destruction of every firstborn of Egypt, from the king to the servants, even to the beasts of the field. It was precisely the blood over the Israelite doorways that would cause the destroying angel on assignment to pass over those covered ones, hidden under the brushstrokes of shed blood. The innocent always die for the guilty.

An animal died to cover Adam and Eve with its own skin when they violated God's command. The secret sin of Joseph's brothers was reaped in future oppression upon their generations, and innocent Hebrews suffered. The firstborn Egyptian children, babies, and animals died in one dark hour of wailing; surely, the little ones were innocent. The perfect lambs' blood was required to save millions of Hebrew lives.

And what can be said of the Righteous One, who was hanged on a tree, accursed on our behalf and wretched? He did this to remove the filth and deserved punishment of the twelve billion souls who have sinned upon the face of earth from the beginning until this very day.

One night I couldn't sleep, and I was singing a praise song to the Lord. Although this took place in the season of the fall feasts, the Lord showed me a vision of Yeshua on the Cross; I saw the word PASSOVER written across His torn body in huge letters that stretched from His left hand to His right hand. Yeshua is the Passover, and He was crucified on the very day, and He died at the very hour that the lambs were being slain for the Passover meal (see Exod. 12:6; Luke 23:44-46).

THE GOD OF DISTINCTIONS

Passover showed that the Lord made a distinction between His people and those who were not His people, by the application of the lamb's blood to their doors. The Lord also made a distinction between the firstborn and all the other offspring in a family. This separation extended to man and beast, even to the birth order of livestock and pets. We see the Lord's intelligence, personality, and purposefulness all through Scripture. He made supernatural distinctions between people again and again, proving that nothing happens in a random or uncalculated manner. A few examples of past, present, and future distinctions are as follows:

Those behind the bloodstained door were unharmed, while others died.

Gideon's fleece was soaked with dew, while the surrounding earth was dry. Then, at his request, the miraculous sign was reversed, just to prove to him that God had spoken.

Babylonian soldiers accidentally died in great licks of flame, as they pushed three Hebrew youths into the furnace; the intended victims of the king's wrath walked out without even the smell of smoke on their clothes.

Jesse of Bethlehem's virile sons cowered in hopelessness, lacking the courage to meet Goliath in the field, even wearing their armor. Their youngest brother, an unprotected and inconsequential shepherd, flung one stone into the giant's forehead and became the exalted king of Israel and a mighty man of valor.

The vainglorious prime minister of Persia erected a stake on which to execute a devout and powerless Jew; within twelve hours, the arrogant ruler was dragged away to be executed on his own stake, while the Jewish civil servant became the most powerful man in Persia, next to the king. It turns out his little Jewish cousin was the queen; *who knew?*

Two men will be standing in a field; one will be taken, while the other is left to face upheaval and wrath. One woman will be sealed on her forehead with the invisible mark of God's ownership; her co-worker or neighbor will make the expedient choice to be sealed with the idolatrous mark of the beastly system of human ownership and subjugation.[1]

When the New Covenant was established in the greatest Passover the world will ever know, the same ancient seal of distinction and of God's protection could be seen. We see a lamb, its blood and deliverance; we see death pass over the sealed ones. But the Lamb is a man: an innocent man; a perfect man; a humble and generous man; a Jewish man. He is filled with healing power and good deeds and utterly undeserving of a criminal's agonizing death. This man's blood covers the doorframes of our hearts with a mark only visible to the eyes of Heaven.

When the hour of judgment and separation comes, one population will be spared, and another group will not be spared. There will be no protection or provision, apart from the covering blood of the sinless One.

Then those who feared the Lord talked with each other,
and the Lord listened and heard. A scroll of remembrance

was written in His presence concerning those who feared the Lord and honored His name.

"They will be Mine," says the Lord Almighty, "in the day when I make up My treasured possession. I will spare them, just as in compassion a man spares his son who serves him. And you will again see the distinction between the righteous and the wicked, between those who serve God and those who do not" (Malachi 3:16-18).

THE BIRTH OF A NATION

This feast celebrates Israel's original redemption from slavery in Egypt and her birth as a freed people, a new nation under God's covenant. The miracles that accompanied the Exodus were so staggering that nothing like them has ever been seen on the earth. When has a dictator stumbled into a head-on collision with the supernatural reality of the living God? How did plagues of pestilence, vermin, hail, and darkness affect only the Egyptians, leaving the neighboring Hebrews unscathed? When have we seen the walls of the sea pushed back on both sides, so that a million straggling and escaping slaves, carts, and animals could walk down across a dry path between the gravity-defying waves? When did the greatest army in the world plunge recklessly after them, seeing an open path before them, only to have the towering heights of sea water collapse mercilessly upon them as soon as their presumption trapped them in their midst?

On the night of hiding under the blood, the slaves were purchased back by God from the cruelty of Pharaoh. They walked out of Egypt as a redeemed people. They were pursued as escaping slaves, but when Pharaoh's armies floated up onto the shores of the Red Sea, the Hebrew slaves were indeed a free people. Israel was as a newborn baby in the desert, covered in blood and with uncut umbilical cord, where no other nation would care for her or show her her pity (see Ezek. 16:4-5).

In the third month after her departure, in the Sinai desert, she received her legal constitution and marriage covenant with the God who had freed her. With the Law of Moses, she was now birthed as a new nation under

God, ready (or so it seemed) to sojourn into the land promised to her fathers, Abraham, Isaac, and Jacob. She was commanded to be light to the Gentile nations around her, displaying the holiness, provision, and supernatural protection of a people God has sealed with His own Name.

Since Yeshua told us that He came to fulfill the Law of Moses, rather than to abolish it (see Matt. 5:17), we know that His sacrifice was the culmination of the Passover commemoration. Those who wisely hide under His blood comprise a vast company of people, from every ethnicity—Jew and Gentile—gathered under the protective shadow of the Lord.

We were purchased back from enslavement to our own rebellious and sinful natures and are a family of beloved sons and daughters, commanded to display God's holiness, provision, and protection. As ancient Israel was destined to be a light to the nations, we are also to be a light to those still in darkness, those outside of this generous and undeserved covenant. The invitation to apply the Lamb's blood to the door of our hearts has been extended to all nations, until this very day. Passover is our own personal atonement and rebirth, through the Lord Yeshua's infinitely valuable sacrifice.

TELLING THE STORY

We celebrate the Passover every year in the spring, at sunset on the fourteenth day of Nisan, and we begin the Feast of Unleavened Bread for the next seven days, from the fifteenth to the twenty-first day. On our Roman calendars, this holiday falls on a different date each year, during late March or throughout April. As we learned in the first chapter, while the Christian date celebrating the Lord's resurrection *should* always coincide with the third day after Passover (or perhaps on the first Sunday after Passover), these two holidays have been artificially separated by the fourth-century church, as if they bear no connection to one another.

This schism between the biblical and the Christian calendar is one of the vital corrections the Lord is now addressing to His beloved Bride. This book is one of many voices echoing this needful adjustment and restoration to His children.

47

The Lord instructed Moses that this would be an everlasting ordinance for all generations (see Exod. 12:14). We will remember and retell the miraculous deliverances He displayed in Egypt, showing concern for His enslaved people and rescuing them in a dramatic confrontation with Pharaoh and the gods of Egypt. One of the verses we recite every year is:

> *And when your children ask you, "What does this ceremony mean to you?" then tell them, "It is the Passover sacrifice to the Lord, who passed over the houses of the Israelites in Egypt and spared our homes when He struck down the Egyptians."*
>
> *On that day, tell your son, "I do this because of what the Lord did for me when I came out of Egypt." This observance will be for you like a sign on your hand and a reminder on your forehead that the law of the Lord is to be on your lips. For the Lord brought you out of Egypt with His mighty hand* (Exodus 12:26-27; 13:8-9).

Notice that the common element in both of these Scriptures is, "You will tell your children what I did for you." The telling of the story is so much a part of Passover that, as we eat our ceremonial foods, we read from a special booklet that is only used on this holiday. This traditional booklet is called the *Haggadah*, which means, "the telling." It provides an orderly structure of psalms, recitations, and explanations of why we eat symbolic foods and observe other customs.

We call this ceremonial meal the *Seder*, which means "order." In addition to a fabulous meal, we eat special foods that symbolize various elements of the story.

Since one of the great themes of Passover is that God distinguishes between people and events, we have a recitation in the Seder called, "The Four Questions." The youngest child asks, "Why is this night different from all other nights?" He or she then proceeds to identify four distinctions that set this night apart from ordinary meals. These special foods and customs are not found in any other ordinary meal in our year. This night must always be set apart from all other nights.

Each of these foods not only has meaning in the original context of the Exodus, but also has a richer meaning in the context of the Lord Yeshua's final Passover meal, or "last supper." We will take a close look at some of these foods momentarily, but here is an overview of the main symbols:

1. *Matzah* is flat, unleavened bread; this represents the hasty departure of the Israelites when they escaped, which meant that they had no time to let their bread rise.

   The symbolism of the purity of unleavened bread will be expanded on in the next chapter, as we study the Feast of Unleavened Bread.

2. There are *four cups* of sweet wine or grape juice; each cup has a biblical meaning relating to the story of the Exodus.

3. *Parsley*, which represents the spongy hyssop plant, used to paint the doorframes with the blood of the lamb. We dip the parsley in a cup of salt water and eat it. The salt water represents the tears that our forebearers wept while in slavery. The green vegetable also represents the hope of springtime, which comes after the time of weeping.

4. The *shank bone* of a lamb is on the Seder plate, representing the slain lamb, which used to be eaten at the Passover meal. Many Jewish families no longer eat lamb at this dinner, for reasons we will cover in our detailed view.

5. *Horseradish* is the best approximation of the bitter herbs commanded by the Lord in the Exodus instructions. It symbolizes the bitterness of slavery.

6. *Charoset* is a sweet mixture of apples, nuts, wine, and cinnamon. It stands for the mortar used to make bricks for Pharaoh's structures, and also the sweetness of the promise of freedom.

7. The *afikomen* is a mysterious broken matzah. In addition to eating matzah with our meal, there are three special pieces of matzah that are wrapped in a cloth. During the ceremony, the middle piece is broken in two, and one half is hidden. Later in the service, the hidden piece is found, and becomes the *afikomen*. This symbol has no obvious connection to the Exodus, but it contains amazing New Covenant symbolism concerning the body of the Lord Jesus.

The Golden Chain of Continuity

The telling of this story is an unbroken chain stretching back to that dark night of wailing in 1446 B.C., when the Egyptian firstborns were struck down by the Angel of Death. It is hard for us to grasp that for 3,500 years, Jewish families have consistently told the story of Passover to the next generation, in an unbroken chain of remembrance. Each link in the chain is a family or a generation of families. It stretched across geography and history from Moses to David. It touched the exiles in Babylon and the priestly Maccabees resisting the brutal idolatry of Antiochus IV. The hope of Passover extended to Persian Jews, fasting in sackcloth to be delivered from Haman's genocidal scheme, and to the Jewish children of Europe, targeted by Hitler's genocidal scheme. This memorial chain reached Russian Jews, who suffered in Siberian prisons for attempting to learn Hebrew. The promise of Passover freedom still beckons impoverished Ethiopian Jews, waiting to be granted citizenship in Israel.

Despite my people's failings, which are painfully chronicled in the pages of the Bible, the Christian community owes a monumental debt to the Jewish people. We have carried God's Word, Name, and reputation to the nations, through three thousand years of our generations. *In times of living faith and heroic martyrdom, in times of dead traditions and hypocrisy, in times of national catastrophe and persecution, the very existence of the Jewish people testifies of God's faithfulness to His covenants.* Our scribes have laboriously copied the scrolls of the Law and the Prophets by hand, letter by letter, with no tolerance for error or variation. The Hebrew Scriptures have been preserved with unparalleled accuracy. The regathering of the Jews to the land of Israel after nineteen centuries of dispersion to the four corners of the earth, the resurrection of the Hebrew language after nearly 2,000 years, and the preservation of the Scriptures and the Lord's feasts all testify of His faithfulness. *The Lord's feasts and His calendar have been carried and deposited into almost every nation on earth by this resolute and covenant-bound people, even when their belief in God faltered.*

When believers in Messiah celebrate Passover, we tell the story of humanity's redemption. We remember Yeshua's death until He comes. We honor Him every time we honor the blood of the Lamb. Yeshua is the Passover; He was crucified on the very day, and He died at the very hour that the lambs were being slain for the Passover meal (see Exod. 12:6; Luke 23:44-46). Mark 15:25 tells us that He was lifted up on the Cross in the third hour, which would have been nine in the morning, according to the Jewish reckoning of time. Luke testifies that from about the sixth hour until the ninth hour, the sun was darkened. The Lord Yeshua died before the sun had set on that Passover, as our Lamb.[2]

The telling of the Passover is the perpetual chain. We will still be recounting it in Heaven (see Rev. 15:3-4). Even the Holocaust could not silence this undying witness of God's deliverance. Shall we keep silent, or will the true Church join in singing the song of Moses and the song of the Lamb?

THE VITAL ELEMENTS OF A SEDER

In ancient times, the Passover meal was simpler than it is today. The only biblically required elements were the lamb, the matzah, and the bitter herbs. Some of the other foods may have also been present by the time of the Lord Yeshua's final Passover on earth. Of course, the Jewish people have always participated in some version of the "telling," with psalms, hymns, prayers, recitations, and much praise for God's deliverance.

At the modern Seder table, there is a great deal of ceremonial activity and an elaborate meal. Some Seders will go on for two to four hours with a long ceremony before the meal, and a shorter section after dessert. However, many shorter and "easier" Haggadahs have been written for individuals, churches, or Messianic congregations who cannot devote hours to these readings but still wish to enjoy the Passover celebration. All of these praiseworthy resources are provided at the end of this chapter.

Some Orthodox Jews eat, discuss, sing, and pray all night long, in keeping with Exodus 12:42. This passage tells us that just as the Lord kept vigil that night, the Israelites are to keep vigil as well.

I must admit, I have never stayed up all night at a Seder, and I honestly have no desire to do so. Some would enjoy this intense fellowship into the late night hours, and if God's glory falls upon us, who would want to leave? But generally, I get restless and tired if it is very long, having spent days preparing the meal and the ceremonial foods, and leading more than one Seder each year.

The Lord will guide and direct each individual or church into the right length and type of ceremonial literature to use. One of the purposes for this book is to provide practical tips to help you choose the best one for your needs and desires.

There are a great variety of Haggadahs to choose from, for the use of your family, congregation, or church Seder. Let us break them down into two categories: those written by Jewish people who do not believe that Yeshua is the Messiah, and those written by believers in the Lord. The clear distinction is that the non-Messianic Haggadahs have all of the expected material about the Exodus from Egypt, but obviously do not contain any references to the Lord Yeshua's suffering, last supper, death, resurrection, or future return. The ones written by Messianic believers, whether of Jewish or non-Jewish origin, will glorify the Lord Yeshua and explain His fulfillment of the true and deepest meaning of Passover. All of the literature I will recommend to the reader is glorifying to the Lord Yeshua.

Without Yeshua woven through the service and readings, I personally would feel empty and cheated of my spiritual blessing. That does not mean that another believer might not be blessed to participate in a "traditional" Seder, without overt references to Yeshua.

I could never judge those who feel that way, or those Jewish believers who are required to do so out of respect for unbelieving family members. This is perfectly understandable. However, unless one has family obligations, I believe that the Lord Yeshua should not be set aside, but should feel honored at His own celebration.

The ceremony and traditions are very valuable, as these symbols portray glorious realities about our God. We can learn much about biblical history and Jewish values, as well as finally grasping the Hebraic identity of the Lord Yeshua and His ministry. The point of "the telling" is to bring us back to a place of awe, wonder, and gratitude at the way God showed Himself to be a powerful force against the gods of Egypt. However, the only truly needful element, far above every ritual or tradition, is communing with the Lord Himself as a beloved Person who is present in the room. As we recount what the Lord has done for Israel and for us, let us not neglect to remember the great love relationship and intimacy which He has personally purchased for us.

When we are too fixated on performing a ceremony correctly, it is hard to remember that the Lord is a personal and intimate God. If we put the ceremony ahead of the intimacy, I think it might hurt His heart. Our Father is joyful when His children, Jew and Gentile, celebrate this feast. He desires to bask in this time, as one would dine with a precious friend.

THE FOUR CUPS

Throughout the Passover, we drink four cups of wine. Each cup has a biblical message and carries into the Lord's Passover supper of the New Covenant. It is fine to substitute grape juice if you prefer. The four cups originate from the following passage:

> *Therefore, say to the Israelites: "I am the Lord, and I will bring you out from under the yoke of the Egyptians. I will*

*free you from being slaves to them, and I will redeem you
with an outstretched arm and with mighty acts of judgment.
I will take you as my own people, and I will be your God.
Then you will know that I am the Lord your God, who
brought you out from under the yoke of the Egyptians. And
I will bring you to the land I swore with uplifted hand to
give to Abraham, to Isaac and to Jacob"* (Exodus 6:6-8).

The Lord never wastes words, and this passage contains four or five separate promises, which at first glance might appear to be redundant. But they are distinctive phases of deliverance. Not only did Israel need to pass through each of these stages, but we as individuals must as well in our journey from slavery to the Promised Land.

"I will bring you out" involves the Lord physically or spiritually rescuing us from the cage, prison, or tormenting darkness we were trapped in when He found us.

"I will free you from being slaves" speaks of a change in legal status from slaves to freed people. The Israelites were still slaves when they escaped from Egypt, and we are not legally free at the moment the Lord pulls us out of our prison.

"I will redeem you with an outstretched arm" refers to the financial transaction that transfers our ownership from satan to God. He bought back the Israelites from slavery and death with the blood of the perfect lamb. He purchased every soul on the earth from the enemy with the blood of His beloved Son. He was the only one whose blood could purify the ocean of our accumulated filth, due to His perfect obedience, sinless life, and suffering.

"I will take you as my own people, and I will be your God, and I will bring you into the land of promise" is really a three-fold, final *"I will."* Once we are brought out, freed, purified, and legally purchased, God is able to take us into His Holy place, into His arms of love. We can rest in the permanent and irrevocable place of unending love and security. Having sealed us as His own, no onslaught or strategy of our cruel and merciless enemy can snatch us out of His hands. *In the wounds of His hands, our names and faces are deeply etched, engraved as permanent remembrances of the ones His soul loves and paid for.*

*There remains, then, a Sabbath rest for the people of God;
for anyone who enters God's rest also rests from his own
work, just as God did from His* (Hebrews 4:9-10).

*See, I have engraved you on the palms of my hands; your
walls are ever before me* (Isaiah 49:16).

Each of these four cups represents these four realities. The first cup is called the "Cup of Sanctification," in which we are set apart for the Lord. This cup introduces the consecrated atmosphere of Passover, separating this meal from all other ordinary meals, and setting our hearts apart for our Beloved.

The second cup is lifted up during the story of God's breaking of Pharaoh's stubborn pride with many afflictions. In fact, each plague against Egypt was God's assault on one of their many gods, such as the Nile River, the frog goddess, and the sun god.

Before we actually drink this second cup, we remember how much the Egyptian people suffered during the ten plagues, and we dip our fingers into our wine ten times, placing the wasted drops like blood on our napkins, as we recite and remember each miserable plague. The meaning is that some of our wine of joy is diminished, as we see the suffering of our enemies. How a nation suffers needlessly when its leaders come into collision with the God of Israel! This cup is sometimes called "The Cup of Freedom" or "The Cup of the Plagues."

The third cup comes after the meal and is called "The Cup of Redemption." This represents the slaughter of the innocent lamb, the costly price of redemption. A human life is infinitely valuable and cannot be purchased with money or gold. Only blood can purchase a living soul into whom God has breathed and imbued His own image.

*For the life of a creature is in the blood, and I have given
it to you to make atonement for yourselves on the altar; it
is the blood that makes atonement for one's life* (Leviticus
17:11).

This third cup is the one that Yeshua connected with our personal redemption in His blood, which was about to be offered to God. In the original Passover, this redemption cost all of Egypt its firstborn sons. In the greater covenant of eternal redemption, the cost was God's firstborn Son. *The price of a human soul is more costly than we could bear, so the Righteous One bore the cost in His flesh and upon His soul.*

> *In the same way, after the supper He took the cup, saying, "This cup is the new covenant in My blood, which is poured out for you"* (Luke 22:20).

Because Luke kindly adds this detail, that the Lord took this cup after the meal, we see that Yeshua was using the third cup, the cup of personal redemption, to represent His sacrifice. This greater act of redemption would seal the New Covenant. It would open the way into eternal life for anyone who chooses to partake in this blood covenant.

The fourth cup is called "The Cup of Praise." The Seder meal concludes with great joy as we sing psalms and spiritual songs about the wonder of our Father God.

Heartfelt praise that brings the Lord joy can only come out of the heart of a lovesick worshiper. Many can sing songs and recite passages full of words of praise. Man's lips can utter many true and biblical words about God. This is true of Jewish people as they conduct a holy ceremony, and it is true of professing Christians as they attend a worship service. There is outward behavior, and then there is inward motivation.

God is looking for relationship, not religion (see Isa. 29:13). He is an intimate God. He is neither a dispassionate school teacher nor a rigorous drill sergeant, strictly scrutinizing a perfectly executed recitation. *With grateful hearts, may our words of praise pulsate with the reality of a heart in love!*

Some scholars believe that the Lord Jesus never got to drink the fourth cup of praise on that final night. Perhaps the third cup of the New Covenant in His blood was the last wine He would taste until all would be fulfilled in the Kingdom of God. The Scriptures tell us that they sang a hymn (see Mark 14:26), so we know that He was praising His Father until

His last breath and last drop of blood. But we simply don't know from the scriptural accounts whether or not He drank the cup of praise. In my opinion, He probably drank the praise heartily, since He would soon drink the bitter cup about to be held out to His lips.

As believers, we have experienced all four cups of wine. The first is the cup of sanctification: we are set apart from this world and consecrated for Him.

Even as we drink the second cup of rejoicing over our escape from the prison of darkness, our joy is diminished as we weep over the poor souls who are daily being swept into eternity without the blood of the Lamb to provide a canopy of heavenly safety and rest.

The third cup has become our Salvation. His Name is Yeshua, which means "salvation" in Hebrew. Each time we drink this cup, whether at a Passover Seder or in a commemoration of "the Lord's Supper," we remember the price He paid to purchase us for God, to buy back a people for Himself. We will never understand the cost, not even when we reach Heaven.

And we have tasted the cup of praise. There is joy, glory, and praise to be experienced in this life as we live out the righteousness, peace, healings, intimacy, and freedom known only to citizens of the Kingdom of God.

But in another sense, we have not yet drunk the cup of praise. In the same way that our Bridegroom said that He would not drink it again until He drinks it with us anew in the Kingdom of Heaven, we too will not truly drink that fourth cup until He returns and takes us away from this sin-corrupted earth. On that day, we will sit down with Him in intimate fellowship at His banqueting table, and together we will drink it anew in the presence of our Father.

THE BITTER AND THE SWEET

I have eagerly desired to eat this Passover with you before I suffer. For I tell you, I will not eat it again until it finds fulfillment in the kingdom of God (Luke 22:15-16).

The Lord Yeshua sincerely desired to enjoy this final Passover with His disciples, despite the ordeal He would face in just a few short hours. If it had been me, I would not have looked forward to this last meal, to say the very least. Its pleasure would have surely been spoiled by the stomach pain that accompanies the torment of fear.

But the Lord knew the secret of peace and joy in the face of impending sorrow and pain. He was a humble servant who lived to bless, heal, and rescue others, never thinking of Himself or His personal preferences. *And so, even at that final dinner, He was not thinking about what His enemies were about to do to Him. He was thinking about how He could bless His friends during their last precious hours together.* Yeshua was determined to squeeze out every last drop of teaching, affection, warnings of what would come, and even the washing of their feet before the unthinkable would become reality.

As He staggered up the hill with His cross, He was still thinking of others and not of Himself. The women of Jerusalem mourned and wailed for Him, but He told them, "Daughters of Jerusalem, do not weep for me; weep for yourselves and for your children" (Luke 23:28-29). He was thinking about the city he loved, and what the merciless Romans would inflict upon it within one short generation.

His father Isaac had watched God provide a lamb at the last minute, which saved him from slaughter. *But now there was no last-minute rescue for this beloved Son of Abraham, no other lamb to take His place on the altar of love.* He was the Lamb, and there was no other way to make atonement in the Holy Place. Oh, Yeshua, how tempting it must have been for You to get out of it. If You had chosen to be rescued, what would Your Father have denied You? But You set Your face like a flint and became the Lamb, so that we could be Isaac, the rescued one.

During our Passover Seder, we eat both bitter herbs and sweet *charoset*, the walnut, apple, and cinnamon "mortar," which is usually everyone's favorite part of the meal. Most participants wisely take a tiny taste of the horseradish but a generous portion of the *charoset*.

Obviously, we would all prefer that this life would be a sweet and easy life; no one would ever ask for pain, loss, bitterness, or wailing. Suffering and sorrow were not a part of God's original plan. It is our sin and evil on this earth that create suffering, hunger, slavery, human trafficking, persecution, perversion, abortions, assaults, and murder.

Our journey in this realm contains both sweetness and bitterness. As the Son of Man who could identify with all of our temptations and trials, the Lord Jesus knew both the bitter and the sweet. As He showed us how to triumph in both, we must follow His example. When we are taken to be with Him, only sweetness will remain. But for now, we share in the fellowship of His sufferings (see Rom. 8:17).

When my family lived in Israel, there was a haunting song that was very beloved, written by Israeli songwriter Naomi Shemer. In Hebrew, the song is called "Al ha D'vash v'al ha Oketz," which means "The Honey and the Sting." Here is an approximate translation of the lyrics: "Oh God who is good, please watch over the honey and bee sting, the bitter and the sweet. Watch over our baby daughter. Do not uproot what has been planted in us, and do not take away our hope. Watch over the rushing waters and the blazing fire, and guard us. Keep watch over both the honey and the sting, both the bitter and the sweet, dear Lord, I pray."

It seems to me that this is a mature and wise perspective, as we now enter the time of both glory and suffering. *Before our eyes, the earth will be filled with the glory of the Lord as the waters cover the seas* (see Hab. 2:14), *but the same generation will see the greatest time of sorrow ever seen in this world, not to be equaled before or after this generation* (see Matt. 24:21).

May the Lord watch over His people, both Jewish and Gentile. May He keep Israel in the day of her trouble. May He help and protect all who call upon His Name, and may His people be kept through the days of sweetness and bitterness. We will remember Your love in that day, and we will testify: "We have tasted Your goodness; Your love is better than wine!" (see Ps. 34:8; Rom. 10:13; Song of Sol. 1:2).

THE AFIKOMEN

There is a remarkable and mysterious practice that has become an integral part of the traditional Seder, which is still not fully understood by non-Messianic Jewish worshipers. It is widely accepted that this practice did not exist at the time of Yeshua's ministry and that it arose at some point after His death; however, it is difficult to pinpoint the exact time frame of its origination. To believers in Yeshua the Messiah, the symbolism of this ceremony is so obvious that any other explanation seems like theological acrobatics.

Soon after the dipping of the green vegetable in salt water, the leader holds up a packet of three large pieces of matzah, wrapped together in a linen cloth. Each piece of matzah is separated by a layer of the cloth, and the leader pulls out the middle matzah and holds it up. He then breaks this middle piece in two and secretly hides it somewhere around the house, wrapped in the cloth. Later, after the meal, the children will search for this missing piece. The child who finds it will bring it back to the leader, who will then make sure it "fits" with its other broken half, and will give the child a "payment" for the piece. Thus, the two pieces become one whole again, and a price is paid to ransom back the missing piece.

The rabbis have several possible interpretations of the three pieces. One is that these pieces represent three tiers of the Jewish population: the priests, the Levites, and the general people of Israel. Another interpretation holds that the pieces stand for God, the mediating priest, and the people of Israel. Still others say that they represent Abraham, Isaac, and Jacob.

Obviously, believers in Yeshua assert that the middle piece represents the mediating priest. He is the only one who is willing and able to stand in the gap between God and the people. He stands between God and man in the place of intercession and in the place of sacrificial atonement.

> I looked for a man among them who would build up the wall and stand before me in the gap on behalf of the land so I would not have to destroy it, but I found none (Ezekiel 22:30).

He was broken as a sacrificed lamb; His body was wrapped in a linen cloth and hidden away. After some time, He was found and made whole again; He was raised to life. This broken one has ransomed back many from their brokenness, and we are also made whole along with Him (see Heb. 9:15).

What is even more interesting is the word itself, *afikomen*. It seems to be the only non-Hebraic word found in the Seder. It is a Greek word, which the rabbis have concluded means "dessert," since it is eaten after the meal. However, according to biblical scholars Kevin Howard and Marvin Rosenthal, this word is the second aorist form of the Greek verb *ikneomai*, and can best be translated, "I came."[3] Others have translated it, "the one who has come," or "that which comes after."

How did this clearly Messianic symbol come to be found in the traditional Seder? We have already seen that the apostles in Jerusalem informed Paul that myriads, or tens of thousands, of Jews had accepted Yeshua as the Messiah in Jerusalem alone (see Acts 21:20). Throughout the land of Israel, their numbers may have been as high as one million. This early believing Jewish community exerted no small influence on colleagues, friends, and family.

During the years that culminated in the Roman destruction of Jerusalem in A.D. 70, the Romans laid siege and finally broke through the northern wall of Jerusalem. The army had been pushed back several times by Jewish resistance, and on its third attempt, the enraged 10th Roman Legion, under General Titus, finally made a successful, hellish onslaught on Jerusalem.

They destroyed God's temple, and over a million Jews were murdered in a few years. So intense was their brutality and hatred for the Jews that five hundred Jews a day were seized and crucified around the walls of Jerusalem. This included women and young children who had ventured out to search for food, due to the starvation imposed by the siege.[4] The survivors were driven out of the land of Israel, which was largely desolated. The Jewish people were widely dispersed into many nations, which would have included large numbers of believers. These now carried their messianic influence far beyond the boundaries of Israel.

This national calamity created a number of upheavals in Jewish worship and practice. First, with the temple destroyed, there was no more opportunity to sacrifice a lamb for Passover. Now, they would need to find a symbolic replacement for the lamb. This destruction of the temple and the sacrifice system is the reason why most Jewish families no longer eat a lamb at the Passover meal; instead, we eat chicken or other non-sacrificial meats. Thus, the shank bone on the Seder plate became a reminder of the lamb that used to be sacrificed.

Second, Jewish believers in Yeshua were already using the unleavened bread as a symbol of His body, broken for them. When they celebrated Passover, they were breaking the matzah in remembrance of His death (see Luke 22:19). It is most probable that the believing community instituted the three symbolic matzahs wrapped in linen, with the middle piece representing their risen Lord Yeshua, the mediating priest. This practice probably began in Jerusalem, spread throughout the land of Israel, and finally influenced Jews who had been dispersed to almost every nation in the known world.

Even the non-Messianic Jewish community began using matzah as their substitute for the lamb, and that mysterious little Greek word, *afikomen*, was inserted into every Passover celebration throughout the nations and has continued until this very day.

The golden chain of His redemption story has been stretched out from the Roman Empire, through the Byzantine, Islamic, and Ottoman Empires, and from colonialism into this post-modern age. The Lord, always working behind the scenes to ensure that His Word is disseminated to every generation, made sure that His Jewish people both knowingly and unknowingly carried the story of Messiah's broken body to their children, and to their children's children. This perpetual chain is still unbroken; may His faithfulness be praised!

This morning, March 3, 2008, I was asking the Lord if I had found His heart in the writing of this Passover chapter, and I received several words from Him; this word concerns the *afikomen*:

> I AM the hidden treasure, buried in the folds of cloth and the layers of matzah. I AM hidden; though they eat My body, I AM hidden from their eyes. I AM the pearl, the treasure, the One broken and waiting to be discovered by the youngest child. This signifies that only one with the heart of a child can find Me and recognize Me, hidden in the room.
>
> It is a surprise party. Normally, the guest of honor is

surprised when the other guests jump out and greet him. I AM the guest of honor in the ceremony of the afikomen, and when I jump out, they will all be surprised. I was here all along, waiting, in their very Passover. It was always Me, broken, buried, raised to life, but waiting to be discovered by the leaders of My banquets, by the leaders of My Jewish people, even their Sanhedrin.

When they find the afikomen, they find Me. Then that which was broken will be made whole. They will hold up the whole piece with the missing half restored, restored and whole again. How can they find God without Me? I AM the missing piece, the broken piece, the hidden piece, the discovered piece, the redeemed-by-a-child piece, and the reconnected piece to the original piece from which I was broken off.

We will be made whole again, do not fear. This is My heart for the story of the afikomen. Tell My flock what I have told you.

THE HAND AND THE FOREHEAD

On that day, tell your son, "I do this because of what the Lord did for me when I came out of Egypt." This observance will be for you like a sign on your hand and a reminder on your forehead that the law of the Lord is to be on your lips (Exodus 13:8-9).

As we saw earlier, the Lord made four promises to the Hebrews, which tradition has associated with the four cups of wine served during the Seder.

I will bring you out from under the yoke of the Egyptians.

I will free you from being slaves to them.

A Prophetic Calendar: The Feasts of Israel

I will redeem you with an outstretched arm and with mighty acts of judgment.

*I will take you as my own people, and I will be your God
. . . and I will bring you to the land I swore with uplifted hand to give to Abraham, to Isaac, and to Jacob.*

The Lord promised to rescue Jacob's descendents, to free them, and to purchase them with the price of redemption. Finally, He promised to take them as His own people. The Lord bought and paid for their freedom, and now He would claim ownership of this newborn nation and people group.

When they were slaves, they were the property of Pharaoh and his taskmasters. Slaves are chattel; they are less than human in the eyes of their master. He can buy them, sell them, starve them, rape them, beat them, and work them to death if he has plenty more on hand. There is no Bill of Rights, no law under which they can hide or find refuge.

In many societies that have owned slaves, it was and is still common for the slave owner to place a brand or a mark upon their human property. It makes it easier for the slave to be identified as the property of a particular owner. The Nazis marked the Jewish prisoners with a number, which was tattooed into their flesh. Survivors still bear traces of this brutal mark.

As the Hebrews were fleeing through the wilderness, before they had even reached the "impossible" barrier of the Red Sea, God instituted His own mark of ownership upon His people, those who were called by His Name. However, His mark was not cruelly and involuntarily stamped or burned into human flesh, nor was it an implanted electronic chip or a laser imprint.

God's seal was an invisible mark of voluntary obedience, seen only by the eyes of Heaven. According to Exodus 13:9, this mark was the observance of the Passover, for all generations to come. "This observance will be for you like a sign on your hand and a reminder on your forehead that the law of the Lord is to be on your lips."

In my first book, I recorded a sacred experience I had after a three-day period of consecration to the Lord. In this visitation, the Lord expressed His appreciation that I had held nothing back from Him during those three days but had been wholly transparent to Him. The Lord stated that I had enjoyed His fellowship without expecting anything in return. The following is a brief excerpt from *Coffee Talks With Messiah*:

The Lord then granted me the following experience, which was a spiritual event, seen by the eyes of my spirit. The Lord took two of His fingers from His right hand and dipped them into the wound in His left hand, and His fingers had blood on them. He put this blood on my forehead (it was not physical blood), and He said, *"You are sealed forever. You are one of My own ones, and you will be with Me forever."*

I understand that all believers are bought with His blood and sealed with His Spirit (see 2 Cor. 1:22; Eph. 1:13). However, from the example given to Abraham, we can see that a believer's walk with God can include at least two stages of ownership by God, in which that believer is sealed by God into a greater promise. In fact, Abraham received four phases of the promises of his destiny, as we see in Genesis chapters 12, 15, 17, and 22.

By the time of Isaac's birth, Abraham had already displayed tremendous faith in God and had walked with Him for twenty-five years. Hebrews tells us he left his home to journey to an unknown land, he lived in tents, and he believed God for a son, although he was "as good as dead" (Heb. 11:8-12). Abraham said that he was a hundred years old when this promise came to him from God (see Gen. 17:17).

However, when told to sacrifice the son of the promise, Abraham displayed greater faith through the obedient action he took. The angel of the Lord then told him:

> *"Now I know that you fear God, because you have not withheld from me your son, your only son....I swear by myself,"* declares the Lord, *"that because you have done this and have not withheld your son, your only son, I will surely bless you and make your descendants as numerous as the stars in the sky and as the sand on the seashore"* (Genesis 22:12,16-17).

Even though Abraham had already demonstrated commendable faith, this incident shows that there can be a stage of obedience, self-sacrifice, and testing beyond the sealing moment of our salvation. James also cites Abraham's example, in which Abraham proved his faith through a difficult action of obedience, resulting in greater approval by the Lord.

> *Was not our ancestor Abraham considered righteous for what he did when he offered his son Isaac on the altar? You see that his faith and his actions were working together, and his faith was made complete by what he did* (James 2:21-22).

The four *"I wills"* represent four levels of belonging to the Lord. God showed Abraham these four "I wills." First, He brought him out of his idolatrous country. Then He made an unconditional covenant with him to grant him the land of Canaan. With the third promise, Abraham's children were marked with the blood covenant of circumcision. With the redemption of Isaac with a lamb came God's oath to multiply his seed over the whole earth, and to provide His only Son as the Lamb for all mankind. All the earth was blessed through Abraham's willingness to sacrifice his only son (see Gen. 12:3).

The fourth level is *"I will take you as My own, and I will be your God, and I will bring you into the land of promise."* I believe that when we love Him with all that is within us, He takes us as His own, and we are ready to move wholeheartedly into our destiny, no matter what the cost. He has placed His mark on our forehead, and there is no room for anyone else's mark of ownership or financial provision. I am not my own, but I am bought with a price (see 1 Cor. 6:19-20).

When God speaks of a mark on our hand or our forehead, He is symbolizing our deeds (the hand) and our thoughts (the forehead). Perhaps you have observed Orthodox Jews in prayer, whether in photographs taken at a synagogue, or at the Western Wall in Jerusalem, or during a long El-Al flight to Israel. (As you fly east into the sunrise, it is time for morning prayers, even if your body thinks it's the middle of the night!)

There are morning and evening times of prayer, which correspond to the hours of the morning and evening sacrifice in ancient times. During the morning prayers, highly observant Jews wear little black boxes that are strapped across their foreheads and wrapped around one arm (if you are right-handed, it would be placed on your left arm). These little boxes contain verses from the Torah, which is comprised of the first five books of Moses in our Bibles. The verses contained in these boxes are Exodus 13:1-10; 13:11-16; Deuteronomy 6:4-9; and 11:13-21.[5] The verses from Exodus are placed on the arm, since the Lord brought us out of Egypt with an outstretched arm. The Deuteronomy passages are placed on the forehead, since they speak of the focus of our hearts and minds. This custom, which has continued for well over 2,000 years, was derived from these passages.

> *These commandments that I give you today are to be upon your hearts. Impress them on your children. Talk about them when you sit at home and when you walk along the road, when you lie down and when you get up. Tie them as symbols on your hands and bind them on your foreheads. Write them on the doorframes of your houses and on your gates (Deuteronomy 6:6-9).*

These boxes are held firmly onto the head and arm by long leather straps. This practice of putting them on and taking them off each day is called, "Laying *t'fillin*."

These same verses in Deuteronomy are also the origin of Jewish families nailing a *m'zuzah* to their doorframe, which you may have seen when you enter a Jewish home. It is a tiny, rectangular box containing this same passage.

Isn't this remarkable? The Jewish people believed that the Lord literally meant for us to tie His Word to our hands—to constrain our deeds to righteous deeds—and to bind His Word to our foreheads—to impress them on our minds when we are tempted by the evil one to indulge in sinful thoughts.

Sometimes, when the Lord says something in Scripture, most believers just assume He did not mean it literally, but that He was being poetic or figurative. This is certainly true in some passages, but I have a feeling that there are more places where He really meant what He said quite literally, and we should not assume they are figurative. Perhaps the wearing of these boxes is one of those cases. However, whether or not people wear them, the motivations of the heart are more important than even the outward obedience.

We see this practice in the New Testament, but instead of the Hebrew word *t'fillin*, our Bibles use a word taken from Greek, *phylacteries*, for these boxes. Jesus comments on this practice in Matthew 23:5. He does not at all condemn it, but He sharply criticizes those who ostentatiously wear larger boxes and longer tassels on their prayer garments in order to look more pious and important to others. Again, it is the heart that He was scrutinizing.

The Lord was faithful to keep His promise to the Hebrews as they fled from Egypt as escaping slaves. They would wander for forty years, due to hardness of heart and unbelief. However, for all those years, He never broke His promise to take them as His own, to be their God, and to bring them into their own land. The Lord spoke a second word to me today, concerning His mark of faithfulness to the Israelites in the desert:

> My Glory did not depart from the Israelites when I was angry and they were unfaithful and complaining, when they committed harlotry early with the golden calf, and late with the Midianite women and their gods. But still, My Presence and My Manifest Glory went with them.
>
> How could I leave My son in the desert, in the wilderness as prey for every beastly and barbaric tribal entity that would have picked them off and ravaged them with sword and captivity before they could even become a nation, dwelling safely in their own land?
>
> It would be like a child who grew up to maturity in a rented apartment that had no running water or bathroom facilities or electricity. He used an outhouse, pumped water, and lit fires to read and keep warm. He survived, but when he became a man and was ready to take a wife, he needed to make a proper home for her. He needed to

buy her a decent little house where they could build a life and settle down and raise up their children, better than the way he was raised.

He didn't want to scratch out a miserable existence as he raised his children, but to live in peace and security in his own house. The Bible says, "Under his own vine and his own fig tree," eating the delicious fruits of his labors and of his hand, with his precious wife and children around his table.

When I brought Israel into his own land, this is how I felt about My firstborn son. Even when I was angry, hurt, and deeply offended by their conduct and the way they dishonored Me, I couldn't withdraw My Manifest Presence from their midst. I couldn't leave them in that terrible wilderness, like sheep without a shepherd, waiting to be picked off by the bullies in their neighborhood. These stood, drooling and lurking nearby with mauls and clubs, spears and sharpened swords, and also the hordes of uncircumcised Philistines and Canaanites who would make a meal of My people.

How could I turn away from Ephraim, before he could build a house and settle down to raise children? Even when he provoked Me to anger, how could I hand him over to the beasts? How could I give up My firstborn son, whom I loved and redeemed back from Pharaoh's icy grip at great cost? This is My heart for the wandering in the desert.

THE CUP OF ELIJAH

There is a beloved tradition toward the end of the Seder called the "Cup of Elijah." Throughout the meal, a special cup filled with wine is set aside on the table, designated for the visitation of the prophet Elijah, should he come to our Seder this particular year. Near the closing of the ceremony, we recite biblical verses about Elijah's return to earth. We raise his cup as a reminder that he should come, and we sing a time-honored song to him, translated: "Elijah, the Prophet; Elijah, the Tishbite; Elijah, the Gileadite. Come quickly and in our day; come to us with Messiah, the Son of David." This custom is based on the messianic promise in Malachi 4:5-6.

> *See, I will send you the prophet Elijah before that great and dreadful day of the Lord comes. He will turn the hearts of the fathers to their children, and the hearts of the children to their fathers; or else I will come and strike the land with a curse* (Malachi 4:5-6).

Devout Jews believe that the prophet Elijah will literally return to earth before Messiah comes. He was one of two men in the Bible of whom it is recorded that he never died, but was taken up to Heaven alive (see 2 Kings 2:1-12). This prophecy of Malachi, which was written about four hundred years before the time of Yeshua, gave birth to an end-time doctrine, which states that we cannot expect to see Messiah's coming until we have first seen the Old Testament prophet Elijah reappear on the earth, who will prepare the people for Messiah's coming.

This doctrine was in the minds of the Jewish disciples as they were coming down from the mountain, where they had just seen the prophet Elijah with their own eyes. They asked Yeshua, "Why then do the teachers of the law say that Elijah must come first?" (see Matt. 17:10).

Before we examine the Lord's answer to this question, let us return briefly to the Jewish view of both the coming of Elijah and Messiah, so we can understand this full cup of wine that sits patiently on the Seder table every year, waiting for Elijah to come and drink it with us.

The three main branches of Judaism do not believe that Yeshua of Nazareth was the Jewish Messiah. In fact, most Jewish people in the Reform and Conservative branches do not believe in a literal coming of Messiah at all. They may be hoping or even praying for an age of peace and safety to come to our people on this earth, but they dare not hope for a literal Jewish savior to appear on the scene and rescue Israel from all who hate her. Not a few are agnostics, neither with living faith in God, nor with any messianic anticipation. I myself was raised this way.

In some Jewish hearts, especially those of survivors and their children, the decimation of Europe's Jews in Hitler's holocaust has dashed or killed all hope that the God of our forefathers is still actively loving and protecting the Jewish people. It is an understandable dilemma: "If You loved us, how could You let this happen? Why didn't You rescue us from slaughter if You are the God of Israel?" I will offer a partial response to this seemingly unanswerable question, but I will do so after we complete this discussion about the coming of Elijah.

A belief in the coming of a literal Messiah is primarily found among the Orthodox Jews, particularly some Hassidic groups. A small number of these believed that the Messiah already came in the form of an esteemed elderly rabbi in Brooklyn, and they put great hope in him. However, he died a number of years ago and was not resurrected, as they had hoped and believed. A few still staunchly maintain that this rabbi was the Messiah, but I would suspect that sheer common sense has convinced most that this man could not have been the promised Messiah of Israel. Therefore, most are still waiting for the real one to appear.

The main difference between the Orthodox and the Messianic believers, with respect to Messiah's coming, is that they are looking for his first coming, and we are awaiting the reappearance of a Jewish Messiah who came 2,000 years ago and who bears the scars to prove it. When Yeshua does appear, those waiting for His first coming will be grieved to realize that He is the One who was already here, rejected as Messiah by their Sanhedrin. The prophet Zechariah foresaw this day of grieving and repentance on the part of the Jewish people.

> *And I will pour out on the house of David and the inhabitants of Jerusalem a spirit of grace and supplication. They will look on Me, the one they have pierced, and they will mourn for Him as one mourns for an only child, and grieve bitterly for Him as one grieves for a firstborn son (Zechariah 12:10).*

And so, in remembrance of a mostly discarded messianic anticipation, my Jewish people have filled a cup of wine for Elijah at the Passover Seder, year after year. Precious few actually think that this prophet from 850 B.C. will be joining them at the table. But traditions are beloved, and this one, based on a wonderful verse in Malachi, lives on.

In addition to filling a glass for him, one of the children opens the door of the house, looking expectantly around outside. We sing a sweet song to welcome Elijah the prophet, raise his cup, and leave the door open for a while, just to make sure he can get in.

At the risk of diminishing the sweetness of this custom, I really don't think a closed door would stop Elijah when God sends him back from Heaven to announce the coming of the Lord. When he appears in Jerusalem, everyone will know it is Elijah, and no door in the world will be able to stop him. I respect the fact that many believers and traditional Jews might love this tradition. We've been doing it for decades in my own family, but I've never been truly comfortable with it.

Now, let us press on beyond traditions, and into the realities of Malachi 4:5-6. The disciples were taken up to a mountain and were shown Moses and Elijah, along with their Lord in His glorified radiance. They asked Him, if He was indeed the Messiah, "Why do the teachers of the law tell us that Elijah must come first?"

The Lord answered them, "To be sure, Elijah comes and will restore all things. But I tell you, Elijah has already come, and they did not recognize him, but have done to him everything they wished" (Matt. 17:11). Matthew then tells us that the disciples understood that Yeshua was referring to John the Baptist, or more accurately, the "Immerser."

By this answer, the Lord was pointing to two parallel fulfillments of the Malachi prophecy. First, He reaffirmed that Elijah is coming and will restore all things. So there is a future reality we can expect, in which Elijah does literally return to earth for the purpose of restoration. But the Lord Yeshua added another element, a more immediate fulfillment of this word. His relative, John, immersed multitudes of Israelites in the waters of heartfelt repentance. John preached that sincere repentance was needed in Israel's heart to prepare the way for the Kingdom of God. This preparatory work had to be accomplished in Israel before the Lamb of God could appear and atone for her sins through His sacrifice.

Before John was even conceived, an angel of the Lord prophesied to his father, Zechariah, the "Elijah anointing" that would rest on his son. [More in-depth teaching on the following passage will be given in the final chapter.]

> ...he will be filled with the Holy Spirit even from birth. Many of the people of Israel will he bring back to the Lord their God. And he will go on before the Lord, in the spirit and power of Elijah, to turn the hearts of the fathers to their children and the disobedient to the wisdom of the righteous—to make ready a people prepared for the Lord (Luke 1:15-17).

John was not Elijah himself, and he plainly testified that he was not Elijah (see John 1:19-21). Even so, when the Lord Jesus was teaching about John's ministry, He referred to this same anointing that resided in John.

> For all the Prophets and the Law prophesied until John. And if you are willing to accept it, he is the Elijah who was to come. He who has ears, let him hear (Matthew 11:13-15).

When the Lord used a phrase like, "If you are willing to accept it," or, "He who has ears, let him hear," He was letting us know that this teaching is not obvious, simple, or clear-cut. He was saying that there are parallel layers of prophetic fulfillment; there is a "now" fulfillment, but there is also a "not yet" fulfillment still to come. In other words, He was telling us that John was like Elijah, because Elijah's powerful mantle rested upon him, to prepare the way for the Lord's coming. In some sense, "Elijah" had already come to prepare Israel with repentance for the first appearance of her king on the earth.

On the other hand, the Lord was telling us, "To be sure, Elijah is coming, and will restore all things (still in the future), but in some sense,

Elijah has already come in the person of John the Immerser" (see Matt. 17:11).

So, Elijah has come, and yet he is still coming in the future to prepare Israel for the return of the Lord Yeshua. Is he one of the two witnesses spoken about in Revelation 11? Yes, I very much believe that he is, but this would require another universe of teaching which is, sadly, not the purpose of this book.

The ceremony of Elijah's cup is a good reminder that the prophet Elijah will return to earth, just as Malachi prophesied. The Scripture will be fulfilled, and it is commendable that we carry this affirmation of God's Word into the Passover Seder, and across our generations. I personally do not think that he will walk into our house, sit down, and have a pleasant cup of wine with us.

I do believe he will appear in the temple courts of Jerusalem with electrifying and fiery preaching, and the zeal of the Lord will consume him and his enemies (see Rev. 11:1-14). As we recite during the ceremony of Elijah's cup in the Seder, "May He come quickly, and in our day, preparing the way for Messiah, the Son of David." May Yeshua's Kingdom come, and may His throne be established! Amen.

I must end this section with a third word that the Lord gave me this very day, after I had written this section, to insert into the teaching on Elijah's cup:

> How I wish it were My cup they would set out on the table! For one greater than Elijah is standing in their midst! The very Host and Living Sacrifice stands before them, dressed in My robes of celebration, robes of ceremonial honor, and they act as if I'm not even in the room. Instead, they look for Elijah, who is not waiting to drink the cup with his people, Israel. He is waiting to come in the zeal of the Lord of Hosts, to burn like a firebrand the message of repentance into the hearts of a stubborn and hardened people.
>
> Surely, Elijah will burn in the hearts of the remnant of

Israel, the survivors of the nations where they were scattered. But I have already come! They do not need to open the door of their houses and look for Me. I am standing in their midst in this celebration, which is Mine, and it is the door of their hearts I AM knocking on. This is the door Israel must open. The door of their hearts they must open to Me, the Host of the Seder and the Lamb they have eaten without understanding. This is My heart for Elijah's cup!

THE HOLOCAUST

Now, with a hope-filled heart, I will briefly address the agonizing question or controversy within the Jewish heart: "How could You let this happen, if You are a living, loving God? Why did You not rescue us from this torturous death trap of anti-Semitic persecution?"

There is much that can be shared, taught, and speculated about the severe tribulation of the Jews which arose out of "Christian" Germany, under Hitler's Third Reich. I will limit my comments to a stunning revelation of the Lord's love for His perishing people in the Holocaust.

My longtime friend, Lonnie Lane, is a Jewish believer who has written many outstanding articles for Messianic Vision's Web site on a number of Jewish issues.[6] One of these articles contains the following testimony from the gas chambers of the concentration camps, and is quoted *verbatim* below, with the author's permission.[7]

At one time I was working in the office of one of the Messianic organizations while writing articles for their magazine. I had access to the archives of the magazine which were kept in a vault. Deep in the vault were copies of this magazine from the 1930-1940s. Shortly after WWII several articles were written by Jewish believers who had been in the death camps but were liberated before it was "their turn." Without going into detail as to how they were able to observe this phenomenon, one person reported that a man in white robes was seen on several occasions walking among and interacting with the people in the "showers" just before the gas was turned on. He would have been the only person wearing clothing and as such would stand out from the others as unique among them. It could only be Yeshua! He came to them in their final hour.

Another article Lonnie Lane found at that time reported that, according to their estimate, approximately 10 percent of the Jews in the camps became believers in Yeshua: "That means thousands. Hundreds of thousands. That means God was faithful to rescue eternally those who wanted to follow Him. Our wonderful God. Our gracious Yeshua. Our merciful Savior."

I had never read anything like this stunning testimony, and I was deeply affected by it for many weeks. I shared it with my friend, David Michael, and was even more astonished to learn that he had heard a prophetic testimony many years ago that confirmed this eyewitness account. The following is a summary of what he heard.

David Michael was one of the speakers at a prayer summit hosted by the late Ray Bringham in 1984, which was held at a Christian retreat center outside of Manassas, Virginia. Sid Roth was also speaking at this conference, as was another highly prophetic brother from London, Vaughan Jarrold. Vaughan had been a missionary in a number of other nations over the years. When it was time for him to speak at the conference, Vaughan shared this account of a visit he had made to the Auschwitz camp, as remembered and told to me by David:

"I went to Auschwitz, and I was weeping and just sick inside. And I said to the Lord, 'I don't understand, Lord...Your people were in here, crying out to You, praying to You, pleading for You to help them, and You turned Your ear away. How could You not have answered them?'"

At this point in his testimony, Vaughan became heartsick and sobbed like a child in pain and disappointment.

He then continued, "How could you, Lord?" His voice became choked with emotion, as his normally deep and booming delivery lowered to an intense whisper, as he uttered these words in a penetrating, rasping, pathetic, horrified, and incredulous tone:

"How could You? How COULD You, Lord? How COULD YOU? I can't understand it, Lord."

Vaughan continued, "The Lord spoke to me and said, *'SON! When the three Hebrew men were thrown in the fiery furnace, who was it that stood there with them?'*"

"And I said, 'It was You, Lord.'"

"And He said, *'Yes, and even so, when those doors were locked, I came and stood with My perishing people, and revealed Myself to them; and you will see many of them in heaven, before the throne of God.'*"

Now, at long last, I have received two witnesses that the Lord Yeshua came to His perishing people in the gas chambers, in the place of death, misery, and annihilation. There may be more confirmations that will surface as these testimonies continue to be shared. It must be known and understood that the God of Israel and His Messiah did not abandon His Jewish people during the holocaust.

As I pondered this staggering revelation, I wondered if all who saw Him received Him, or if it was possible to encounter the Lord Yeshua at that terrible moment and yet not be willing to accept Him.

While I was thinking about this question, the Lord told me, *"There were two thieves on the cross."* I then remembered that these two men, crucified on either side of Yeshua, responded differently to their impending doom. One of them demanded that the Lord rescue him from the physical agony of death, saying, "Aren't You the Christ? Save Yourself and us!" (Luke 23:39).

I tried to imagine how I would feel at that terrifying moment. Knowing my own fear of death, I could picture myself thinking, "Surely if you are who you seem to be, if you have any compassion, you would get me out of this death camp. Don't talk about eternity; just get me out of here. Rescue me, and I will believe in you!" I would want to be rescued more than anything else, especially if I had never thought about eternity before.

But the other thief, knowing that physical survival was not his only problem, humbly asked, "Jesus, remember me when You come into Your kingdom" (Luke 23:42). He didn't demand or even ask for physical rescue. He knew that a death sentence was upon all mankind. Even if he had come down from his cross that day, he would have faced death another day in the near future. He was happy to receive a trustworthy assurance of eternal life in Paradise that very day, despite the agony tormenting his body.

That is why so many of my Jewish people gratefully received His offer of eternal life, which did not include physical rescue. A great cloud of evil had arisen over Europe, and millions of precious lives were devoured by this evil. The Church should have cried out with tears of intercession, with fasting and pleading, as Esther did. Perhaps the plans of the destroyer would have been significantly thwarted, or the time of tribulation shortened. Biblically, God has shown Himself to be responsive to the tears of His people; thus, the Church must rise up in this generation to plead with Him on behalf of the Jewish people and the nation of Israel, as Esther did.

So much innocent blood has been shed on the earth, and it cries out from the ground until the day when the Righteous Judge will make all things right again. Unborn babies are dying every day in their mother's wombs. Their blood is also crying out for justice. The Son was not physically rescued either, although His Father loved Him with a great and undying love.

But Yeshua is now glorified, and seated at the right hand of the Most High. Death could not hold Him, nor will it hold us who follow Him. This is the only consolation to our grieving souls in moments of bewilderment, disappointment, or martyrdom. A verse that now has very real and practical application to me is "Though He slay me, yet will I hope in Him" (Job 13:15).

We cannot know what would have been the outcome of God's plan for the salvation of the Jewish people, or for the birth of the nation of Israel, if the Lord had granted physical rescue to all of the victims in that terrifying seven-year tribulation of my people.

We don't even know if all who would have received immediate physical rescue would have walked with the Lord Yeshua after the nightmare was over. *Survival without salvation is a short-lived gift, and though immensely precious, it is without eternal benefit.*

Sometimes, He will not physically rescue us, but He has promised to take us to Himself in Heaven at the moment that our spirits leave our bodies (see Luke 23:43; 2 Cor. 5:8). As hard as it is to bear, this eternal promise must be sufficient for us, as it was for the humble thief on the cross. The Lord spoke this word to me two years ago as I was weeping bitterly over the cruelty and lawlessness of wicked men against His people. The full account of this revelation is recorded in my first book.

Sometimes I do protect My own ones. Sometimes I allow My servants to suffer. I do not love them any less because I allow them to suffer at the hands of evil men. The protected ones are not loved any more than the victims. Do I love My martyrs less than the ones I keep alive until the Rapture? Surely you do not believe that![8]

The holocaust was the culmination of a great and unspeakable evil that arose in Europe in the aftermath of WWI. The silence of the European church during that era of systematic genocide and demonic hatred was deafening. For an in-depth history of the church's anti-Semitic attitudes and actions, including its blindness during this savage persecution of the Jews, read *Our Hands Are Stained With Blood,* by Dr. Michael L. Brown.[9]

Here, I offer you the fourth word the Lord spoke to me today, concerning the protection only He can provide for His hunted and hated people:

Why would you die, O Israel? Why would you perish at the hands of the wicked, when I will cover you, hide you, and save you? Even now, a greater holocaust is being thought, felt, planned, conspired, and even now, publicly declared by your brutal and bloodthirsty enemies! Why would you die in your thousands, in your millions? Why would you again allow yourselves to be sheep to the slaughter, waiting in blind silence for the ruthless ones who hate you without a cause, hate you with a hatred energized by My enemy, the destroyer?

Come under My wings of refuge, Israel. Hide under My arms, My son, Ephraim. Come into My bosom, Judah, My heritage. Seek My protection, O Jerusalem, city where My Name longs to dwell and My feet long to rest. Only in Me is there deliverance from death. Only in Me is there **Yeshua** [salvation]. No man will help you on that day; do not look for it. Cry out to Me, and I will come to you quickly. Acknowledge Me in your feasts and celebrations, and you will be protected and hidden in the secret place of the Most High, even when they rise up to annihilate you. You will be safe if you hide in Me and do not cover yourself with lies, legends, false promises, and false peace negotiations. They are all lies!

Flee to Me now, before the next holocaust arises from the pits of hell and the fires of hatred. Why would you die, O Israel? This is My heart for the holocaust section.

Surely, Elijah is coming and will restore all things. He will prepare the way for the coming of Israel's King, the Lord Yeshua the Messiah. On that day, the justice of God will be established upon the earth. His justice will roll like a river from the very throne of God. Your Kingdom come, Your will be done, Your justice reign. Amen!

The kingdom of the world has become the kingdom of our Lord and of his Christ, and he will reign for ever and ever (Revelation 11:15).

But let justice roll on like a river, righteousness like a never-failing stream! (Amos 5:24)

PRACTICAL PASSOVER RESOURCES

For Christian and Messianic Jewish families, or for churches who wish to conduct a Passover Seder, the primary resource you will need is a Haggadah for each participant. In the spring of 2008, the Lord prompted me to write an original Passover Haggadah, which is included here in the Appendix of this book, and may be photocopied for the purpose of conducting a Seder with your church or family. It is called, "I AM the Broken Piece!"

My Haggadah contains the traditional elements, but also includes prophetic material that the Lord gave to me while writing this Passover chapter. The ceremonial aspects are somewhat compressed, in order to make room for more in-depth teaching on the centrality of the Lord Yeshua's redemptive work in the Passover.

In the beginning of the Haggadah, you will find a list of items needed to conduct a Seder. You may wish to purchase these special items from one of the resources listed below to give your Seder a lovely and ceremonial appearance. However, if you are on a tight budget, you can use regular plates, cups, candlesticks, and napkins for most of the ceremonial aspects of the Seder. The Haggadah also tells you special foods to buy, which are explained in this chapter.

The Holy Spirit will help and lead you as you gladden His heart with a sincere desire to grow into this celebration. He will not get upset if you don't do it "perfectly." He loves you and will be pleased that you are honoring His feast and His sacrifice.

One source where you can purchase ceremonial items is Messianic Jewish Resources International; another online store can be found at Jews for Jesus.[10]

Read the lists and helpful, practical tips at the beginning of the Haggadah before deciding if you wish to purchase Seder items—or use those you may already own.

Be blessed as you enjoy this rich and precious treasure in the Presence of the Lord!

Chapter 3

THE FEAST OF
UNLEAVENED BREAD

This seven-day feast is actually an extension of the Passover. In some ways, they are the same feast, because the most difficult part of preparing for Passover is the systematic removal of all forms of leavening from our homes.

Let us look at the connection between fleeing Egypt and eating unleavened bread:

> *With the dough they had brought from Egypt, they baked cakes of unleavened bread. The dough was without yeast because they had been driven out of Egypt and did not have time to prepare food for themselves* (Exodus 12:39).

When we recite the Passover story, we recount the fact that we fled in haste and had no time to let the dough rise. This was a real and practical problem. However, it is interesting to note that the Lord had actually commanded the Israelites to keep the seven days of Unleavened Bread *before* the slaying of Egypt's firstborn, before they fled from Pharaoh. The following passage appears earlier in Exodus 12, before their departure.

The Lord had this festival in His heart before it was connected to the realities of baking bread "on the run." It was to be observed for all generations, as a lasting ordinance. In Hebrew, the word is actually *olam*, meaning "everlasting, unending."

> *This is a day you are to commemorate; for the generations to come you shall celebrate it as a festival to the Lord—a lasting ordinance. For seven days you are to eat bread made without yeast. On the first day remove the yeast from your houses, for whoever eats anything with yeast in it from the first day through the seventh must be cut off from Israel.*
>
> *Celebrate the Feast of Unleavened Bread, because it was on this very day that I brought your divisions out of Egypt* (Exodus 12:14-15,17).

There are many spiritual blessings and hidden truths contained in this commandment and seven-day observance. The second half of this chapter will be devoted to spiritual teaching about leaven, sin, and incorruptibility. But before we look at the deeper meanings, let us first examine the practical realities of keeping this feast in our present culture. Before we find the spiritual layer in a commandment given by the Lord, we should first look at its natural and original meaning.

Many of the Lord's commands in the Bible concern our bodily functions and physical activities, such as eating, hygiene, bathing, cleansing the homes of leaven, sexual boundaries, childbirth and the monthly cycle, infectious diseases, and the days on which He does not want us to do ordinary work.

Hebraic thought is holistic, integrating the goodness with which God created man as body, soul, and spirit. All that He made was good in His eyes, and because of this, many of His precepts and instructions were about the physical aspects of life and holiness. The Lord was interested in our daily and yearly habits, as well as our lifestyle choices. He promoted cleanliness, holiness, health and hygiene, feasting, and once-a-year fasting; in addition, the Lord never forbade His priesthood from marrying and raising a family. The "virtues" of priestly celibacy (with the exception of those called to remain single) and poverty were not contained in His approach as to how His holy people should conduct themselves.

As we have seen, Greek thought is very different from Hebraic thought in several ways. *God's commandments and appointed times were very practical, physical, and experiential.* Greek thought was very idealistic, philosophical, and allegorical. The prominent Greek philosophies that affected Christian thought were Stoicism, which is indifference to pain or pleasure, joy or grief, taken from the philosopher Zeno; Neoplatonism, which is a philosophy of high-minded and visionary idealism, from Plato; and the practice of asceticism, which is living a rigorous life of self-denial. These mindsets were very influential in the early Gentile church and in the development of non-Hebraic theologies.

This type of thinking separated spirit from body, elevating the spirit and denigrating the body. The proper religious treatment of the body was therefore celibacy, poverty, and even harming one's own body to purify and free the spirit. This led to the infamous "self-flagellation" and "hair shirts" of the monastic life.

Because of this persistent Greek influence, it is hard for western Christians to understand the zeal with which observant Jews attend to meticulous details of foods, washings, and guarding the Sabbath. It might seem to be overly focused on outward lifestyle choices. It is true that God was more concerned about the motives of His people's hearts, but He was also interested in outward obedience. We see the Lord Jesus affirming this point in Luke 11:42. He commented on the Pharisees' practice of tithing, yet neglecting justice and mercy; He concluded by saying that they should have continued their practice of careful tithing, but without neglecting the weightier matters of justice and mercy.

Gentile believers are not required to practice the majority of the ceremonial laws given to Moses, including the eating of unleavened bread; the apostles only instructed them to keep four pivotal Mosaic laws, which are specified in Acts 15:19-21. However, all are welcome to voluntarily participate in the feasts to whatever degree they desire.

A Prophetic Calendar: The Feasts of Israel

In the next two sections, I will be sharing with you some very down-to-earth teachings about foods and the practical application of Mosaic Passover regulations to normal family life, whether Jewish or non-Jewish. So many of God's commandments are practical and down-to-earth. We should not always "spiritualize" them away.

This book is not about what is required of you. It is a library of scriptural knowledge that may be relevant and helpful to your intimate walk with the Lord Yeshua at this accelerated moment in your journey toward knowing His heart. Since each section is separate and clearly titled, any material that is not helpful to you can easily be "passed over," and you can freely move on to the more spiritual teachings in the sections that follow the food discussions.

However, if the Lord is drawing His beloved sons and daughters from the nations to His ancient celebrations, and is stirring a desire in you to learn how to incorporate these feasts into your lives, then this chapter might be of great encouragement and practical help to you. I pray His Spirit of confirmation will accompany my words.

As Messianic Jews, our family has observed Unleavened Bread for thirty years. I have run into many complications, which can be discouraging. As with all counter-culture decisions we make, it can be an uphill battle, unless you keep things very, very simple. Let us begin with the matter of leavened products and leavening agents.

What Is Leavening?

You might think this is a simple question with a very simple answer. Of course, it is a vast and complex subject, which has sparked much rabbinic discussion and analysis over the centuries. Many people ask me questions about what foods are permissible during this Passover week, and it would seem that the definition of leavening is still a mystery to Jew and Gentile alike! Since you have waited patiently for 3,500 years for a clear answer, I will now attempt to make this practical and simple for those readers who might try to incorporate this practice into their yearly calendar.

The Simple Answer: The obvious meaning of "leaven" in our cultural understanding is totally accurate. Those products that cause dough to rise are called leavening agents. The ones we are most familiar with are yeast, baking powder, and baking soda. If you would appreciate the basic bottom line, I would say: "Avoid all foods made with yeast, baking soda, or baking powder during this seven-day festival." This would be absolutely correct, and perfectly pleasing to our loving Father.

The First Complication: Although this sounds easy, it becomes hard when you start reading the ingredient labels on a thousand household foods. It is amazing how many foods contain yeast, which you would never suspect needed to be made with yeast. A few examples are salad dressings (most, but not all); almost all canned soups; many breakfast cereals; all sorts of dried soup mixes, gravies, taco seasonings, and many other "instant" products; many types of protein and snack bars; and almost all frozen lunches and dinners.

With a good magnifying glass in the grocery store, you can find a few precious exceptions, after reading through about fifty unpronounceable chemical ingredients. I suspect that in the eyes of our Creator, all of these added chemicals are "unkosher," meaning unhealthy and unnatural. Still, we eat them because of convenience. During these seven days, I take a break from virtually all processed food, eliminating the yearly reading of microscopic ingredient labels.

Another large group of products do not contain yeast, but contain other leavening agents. These would include cookies, crackers, many kinds of chips and snack foods, cakes, pies, pretzels, and cereals. Clearly, our choice of foods during this week is becoming quite limited. As for bought pies, the crusts are usually made with lard, which is the fat of pigs. Even if you don't choose to avoid these all year round, you might wish to do so during this set-apart season.

The Second Complication: There are many products that contain fermented or malted grains that are not labeled "yeast" on the package. The process of "malting" means steeping barley or another grain in water until it swells and germinates. Barley is usually malted for its flavor and is used in certain alcoholic drinks, such as beer.

However, it is surprising to see how many normal foods contain "malted barley" in their ingredients. Just to make us more confused, some foods say "malt extract" and others say "malto-dextrin." I'm not sure what these are, and I will not turn this wonderful holiday into a stressful crash course in food chemistry. When I am confused by a label, I tend not to eat that product, but there are times when I have set aside my confusion and eaten it.

By now, some readers might be thinking, "Why don't I just fast for a week and avoid this whole process?" The answer is that the Lord called it the "*Feast* of Unleavened Bread." It is indeed a feast, and He does not want us to fast during this week. It really is a good week, and I will share what my family and I eat at our Passover dinners and during these seven days, after I have laid out the final complication.

The Third Complication: In Hebrew, the word for leavening is *chametz,* which means "soured," or those agents which cause other foods to sour. Bacteria, yeast, or enzymes can ferment grain, dough, or flour, causing them to "sour" or swell with tiny pockets of gas. This is why bread dough rises and becomes lighter and less dense. In God's design for man's daily sustenance, the normal leavening of bread dough is a wonderful thing. The baker's yeast we use is nourishing to our bodies, and the light, risen bread is not only delicious but also very easy to digest.

However, during this unleavened week, we use special precautions. We put aside our normal intake of leavened bread and eat only matzah. The complication arises because there are strains of bacteria and infected wild yeast spores in the air. Therefore, we know that dough can begin to ferment or corrupt if moistened, even without deliberately adding baker's yeast. There is much spiritual wisdom to be learned from this occurrence in nature, which will be explored after the discussion of foods.

The rabbis were profoundly concerned about the moist, warm conditions that promote inadvertent fermentation in flour or dough that has not been kept cool and dry. This has produced a vast body of Jewish literature that explains the care we must take with the flour we use to bake our matzah, or unleavened bread.

For those who are interested in these details, the Jewish sages have provided us with much practical instruction about the guarding of flour—keeping it cool and dry—as well as baking our bread immediately after the water is added to the flour. It is imperative that the dough not be permitted to sit out in warm or moist air for more than a few minutes.[1] However, in our privileged generation, we can just go to the grocery store and buy a box of matzah that has been baked quickly from guarded flour.

It is not the purpose of this book to delve deeply into these elaborate safeguards. The Lord has made it clear to me that He desires to make these holidays enjoyable and not overly difficult for His beloved Bride from all nations, who are voluntarily celebrating His appointed seasons. How can we do this easily?

WHAT DO WE EAT FOR SEVEN DAYS?

There are special Passover foods displayed at some grocery stores in areas where there is a Jewish population. If you ask your local store manager if they could stock Passover foods, they might accommodate your request. These displays usually appear about three or four weeks before Passover. There are some pros and cons to these "approved" foods. I will share both sides of the matter, as one who buys a great deal of them every year, both for my family, and for the many church Seders my husband and I have led.

The advantage to these products is that they are all "Kosher for Passover," and we can theoretically enjoy them with abandon during the seven days of Unleavened Bread. They include the following items, in a well-stocked store:

- Passover cake mixes and coconut-based macaroon "cookies"

- Grape juice from Israel (which is not all that different from other grape juice)

- Matzah and these matzah-based products (you will notice that all these foods are matzah in disguise)

- Finely ground matzah, called "matzah meal," which is used as a flour substitute in some recipes. The cake mixes mentioned above use matzah meal instead of flour.

- Breakfast cereals that are made of matzah meal instead of the normal wheat, corn, and oat flour in regular cereal

- Special pasta and noodles made from matzah meal, rather than semolina flour

- Boxes of sweetened Passover noodle pudding mix, called *kugel*

- Boxes of seasoned matzah meal, created to make the beloved Jewish delicacy, "matzah-balls" which would float (if my mother made them), or sink (if you are not my mother), in your homemade chicken soup. To alleviate all guilt, let me clearly state that I use canned chicken broth and my matzah balls mainly do the back float.

My grandmother lived in an apartment building populated with so many other Jewish grandmothers that when my mother, brother, and I would get off the elevator and start down the hall toward her apartment, the whole building smelled like chicken soup. All year round!

- There is one more food that is mercifully uncon- nected to matzah, although I think there is some matzah meal hidden in the recipe, to replace the needed breadcrumbs: it is called "Gefilte Fish," which means "filled fish." It is made from ground carp with some eggs and seasoning, which is formed into balls, baked with carrots, and then canned in its own gelled broth. I realize that this sounds horrible. It is like a "fish meatball," and the more I describe it, the worse it sounds! The fish is served cold as an appetizer with a little horseradish, and believe it or not, it is not at all fishy and tastes wonderful. This is truly a delicious dish, and it is such a relief to be eating something other than matzah.

Now, here are some of the disadvantages of these special foods:

1. They are very expensive, for the quantity provided. The cake mixes in particular yield the world's tiniest cake, and you need to buy a lot more boxes of mix to obtain a decent quantity of cake for guests.

2. Virtually all of these foods are derived from matzah, which is a very low-fiber type of bread. It is made from guarded wheat flour, but the flour is white flour, without the bran found in whole grain breads. It is hard to find "whole wheat" matzah, though I saw it once. Therefore, if you eat nothing but matzah, and all of these matzah-based carbohydrates, you could have a problem. We need fiber in our diets to help our digestive tracts. In a moment, I will share a summary of what foods have worked very well for me and my family, to help with this fiber issue.

3. The third issue is not so much a disadvantage, but rather a point of confusion, and I'm not sure how to cope with this issue. The cake mixes, which are Kosher for Passover and completely approved by the strictest rabbis, rise beautifully in the oven. Many years ago, after enjoying these cakes for a long time, I wondered why they rose so well without leavening. I read the ingredients, and one of them is "sodium bicarbonate."

91

This is the chemical name for baking soda. These cakes contain baking soda, and yet are approved by the Orthodox guardians of Passover foods. However, the mixes do not contain regular wheat flour, but rather are made from matzah meal, which is ground from already-baked matzah. Therefore, the baking soda cannot ferment the grain, since it has already been baked into matzah.

This raises the question of whether baking soda is really leavening in God's eyes and whether or not the rabbis were righteous to approve this form of leavening for the sake of a marvelous cake mix. It is possible that the rabbis studied this matter and concluded that baking soda used with matzah meal is outside of the Lord's intended meaning of "souring" or fermenting.

I realize that many readers will not particularly care if certain foods are approved or not approved, and each one is free to make his or her lifestyle choices before the Lord. But because I receive so many questions about this matter, it is good to lay it out here for those who do care.

I love these cake mixes at Passover and have not ruled them out at all. It might be a rabbinic legal "loophole," but I haven't received a restriction from the Lord about this. I *think* it is fine, and have served these cakes at church Seders for many years. His Presence and blessing are always with us at these love feasts, and I have never felt convicted about these cakes. I just find the issue of baking soda a bit confusing.

To close out this food discussion, the following is a summary of the foods we eat during this week. It is important to state that all of my choices would not necessarily be approved by an Orthodox rabbi. Some Messianic Jewish believers, such as my husband, feel constrained to honor rabbinic injunctions about Passover foods, and some do not. I honor rabbinic scholarship but believe I am free before the Lord to examine the Scriptures for myself and to make choices according to His biblical commandments on this matter, as the Holy Spirit directs my understanding.

For fiber, I eat oat bran and also a health cereal called GoLean Crunch, made by Kashi. The ingredients in this wonderful cereal are all whole and unfermented grains and do not contain any malt, yeast, or baking soda. It is high fiber and totally kosher in my estimation.

We also eat eggs, cheese, beef, chicken, fish, potatoes in any form, vegetables, salads (but watch out for yeast in the dressing), fruits and dried fruits, macaroons, matzah and many derivative foods, such as matzah stuffing, "pizza" laid out on matzah instead of crust, French toast made with matzah instead of bread (you must soak the matzah in water first), and nuts. If a recipe requires something to be dipped in bread crumbs, we would use matzah meal.

There is also a way to bake a sponge cake with matzah cake flour and about eight egg whites, which are whipped into great stiffness. The air bubbles in the whipped egg whites cause the batter to rise in a Bundt pan in the oven, as long as the sides are not greased. There are recipes for Passover sponge cakes in Jewish cookbooks, and they are probably available online as well. I hope this amount of practical detail has been enjoyable for the reader. There is much more I could say about food and recipes, but I've provided enough so that anyone who wishes can now pursue more information.

REMOVING THE LEAVEN

For Jewish families around the world, there is a tremendous amount of activity and preparation before Passover. Cleaning the house, and more particularly the kitchen, is part of the physical purification and consecration of the home for this set-apart season. One of the biggest challenges is the biblical commandment to remove all leaven from your homes, so that none of it will be found within your houses for seven days (see Exod. 12:15-19).

In the more observant families, even normally kosher foods are set aside and are replaced with special foods assigned only for the week of Passover and Unleavened Bread. Special sets of dishes are brought out, and the dietary issues of separation are even more stringent during this week.

The mother and father spend many days going through cabinets and refrigerator, removing all leavened products or those that cause leavening.

In some cases, they will throw out the unwanted food. In other cases, they will symbolically "sell" the forbidden bag of food to a Gentile friend or neighbor who is willing to assume legal ownership of these leavened foods until the week is over. Then the family will "buy" back their bag of food from this helpful neighbor. It is a legal technicality that allows the Jewish family to say, "We don't own any *chametz*, nor is any found within our borders."

On the night before the Seder, the mother takes a few last bits of bread and deliberately "hides" them on a shelf or window ledge. Father and the children search the house for the stray leaven. When it is discovered, the father sweeps it clean with a feather and places it in a bag, which is burned publicly the next morning.[2] As the community burns their final bread crumbs, a sense of purity and cleansing settles into hearts and homes. They are ready to conduct their Seder, as well as the next seven days, with a pure home, a clear conscience, and, theoretically, a heart prepared to commune with the Lord their God.

LEAVEN AS A SYMBOL

There are several references to yeast in the New Testament. Two were spoken by the Lord Yeshua, and two were cited by the apostle Paul in his letters to the Galatian and Corinthian churches. Paul's references compare yeast to false teaching, malice, and wickedness (see Gal. 5:9; 1 Cor. 5:7-8). We will examine these in a moment.

The Lord's teachings about yeast include both a positive and a negative metaphor. First, let us look at the beneficial aspect of yeast:

> *The kingdom of heaven is like yeast that a woman took and mixed into a large amount of flour until it worked all through the dough* (Matthew 13:33).

This analogy demonstrates that yeast is a living organism. It grows, multiplies, and reproduces itself. In comparing yeast to the Kingdom of Heaven, the Lord Yeshua is showing us that the Good News of His

Kingdom is living reality which produces growth, restoration, and transformation.

The Gospel of His Kingdom has a life of its own. Where it is inserted, even in small measure, into a community or a human heart, it penetrates all areas into it has been introduced. The truth has a way of spreading out as a contagious joy. The Kingdom of God is revolutionary. Formerly dense and heavy lumps of dough are lightened and brightened, lifted up with the breath of the Holy Spirit, and given a delicious reason to live.

Likewise, when a seed of light and truth is introduced into a dark and corrupted human life, the transforming reality of the living Savior advances outward, cleansing and sweeping, bleaching and purifying, exposing and renewing every hidden corridor of the soul. The destiny and purposes of that individual become fresh and fragrant, like a newly baked loaf of bread. These changed ones become food and nourishment to others who encounter the germination of change in their lives. A tiny seed becomes a whole loaf of fresh bread, giving eternal life to all who eat it. Fermentation is a wonderful and God-given process.

The other picture the Lord Yeshua paints with the yeast metaphor is hypocrisy, particularly in those who say they are looking for a sign. In Matthew 16:1, the Pharisees and Sadducees came to the Lord and tested Him by asking Him to show them a sign from Heaven.

His reply was a rebuke: "You know how to interpret the appearance of the sky, but you cannot interpret the signs of the times." The Lord then privately told His disciples, "Be careful...Be on your guard against the yeast of the Pharisees and Sadducees" (Matt. 16:3,6).

To this account, the Gospel of Mark adds, "Watch out for the yeast of the Pharisees and that of Herod" (Mark 8:15). We learn later that the cunning and hypocritical Herod Antipas, who was normally stationed in Tiberius, had come to Jerusalem and was looking forward to questioning Jesus and seeing Him perform some miracle (see Luke 23:8). Although He was frequently found in the other cities around the Sea of Galilee, Yeshua never visited Tiberius.

The Pharisees, Sadducees, and secular Herod were all looking for a sign. Yeshua was not a performer, doing spectacular tricks for an awestruck crowd. The Lord knew that if He were to give them a sign, these men would neither love Him nor see the Father reflected and revealed in His ministry. In fact, the Lord had already performed many miracles, some of which the Pharisees and Sadducees had seen, others they had heard about from reliable sources. They were hypocrites. Yeshua would not display ostentatious signs on demand. A manipulative and unbelieving heart is not awakened to love and will neither recognize it nor cling to it when it comes.

To this "yeast warning" the Gospel of Luke adds one final detail: "Be on your guard against the yeast of the Pharisees, which is hypocrisy" (Luke 12:1). Some hearts are leavened with insincerity and evil intent. An honest question is never offensive to our patient and generous God, even when in our frailty, we express doubts to Him. But a question whose motivation is to entrap or accuse will be treated by the Lord with the contempt it deserves.

In Paul's grief-filled rebuke to the Corinthian church, he decries the sexual immorality and even incest found here (see 1 Cor. 5:1). He then adds a Jewish warning to this morally lax Gentile church:

> *Don't you know that a little yeast works through the whole batch of dough? Get rid of the old yeast that you may be a new batch without yeast—as you really are. For Christ, our Passover lamb, has been sacrificed. Therefore, let us keep the Festival, not with the old yeast, the yeast of malice and wickedness, but with bread without yeast, the bread of sincerity and truth* (1 Corinthians 5:6-8).

Although they had permitted gross immorality, the Corinthians were proud and boastful, when they should have felt shame (see 1 Cor. 5:2,6). In this passage, Paul pointedly refers to the Feast of Unleavened Bread, when all leaven is purged and removed from our homes. He explains that a small amount of yeast spreads insidiously throughout the whole congregation, which he likens to a batch of dough. The Lord's people should be pure and holy, an unleavened entity that is neither corrupted nor soured.

Paul warns them that by opening the door to sexual immorality, sin will proliferate and spread its poison through the Body of Messiah. A little leaven leavens the whole lump.

He then exhorts the Corinthians to keep the Feast of Unleavened Bread, a reminder of Yeshua the Messiah's sacrifice as the Passover Lamb. He compares the removal of yeast from their homes to the expunging of malice, wickedness, and sexual immorality from the midst of the congregation. Purity is urgently commanded, both outwardly in the body and inwardly from sincere and genuine hearts.

As Passover represents our personal salvation through Yeshua's sacrifice, the seven days of Unleavened Bread represent a period of cleansing and purification from our old lifestyles and ways. After we have made the faith decision to ask the Lord Jesus to forgive us our sins and to purify us through His blood, He frees us from satan's merciless enslavement and transfers our souls into His Kingdom of light.

We are not only redeemed slaves, but the Lord takes us to be His own people and seals us with His own Spirit. At this point, we can begin the process of removing the leaven of corruption and malice from our lives. It is our responsibility to cleanse our hands and purify our hearts, although His Spirit nudges us, supports us, and empowers us to do so continually (see James 4:8).

As we are reminded of the unusual and limited foods we can choose to eat this week, we are also mindful that all sexual immorality, idolatry, unholy entertainment, impure language, and addictions must be removed from our actions, words, and even our thoughts. It is a physical object lesson in holiness.

> *Be holy because I, the Lord your God, am holy* (Leviticus 19:2).

THE BREAD OF AFFLICTION

This unusual creative word below was given to me by the Holy Spirit as a "journal entry" from the desert.

> For seven days after leaving Egypt, the Hebrews ate unleavened bread. You see, the taste of Passover was still in their mouths.

When we left Egypt, we were like dreamers, like one awakened from a four-hundred-year nightmare. We stumbled out into the night air, where the screams and wailing of mourning parents still resonated like a siren in the atmosphere.

We had eaten a hasty meal, as those on the run will do. Now we sojourned for seven days, even through the dry sea beds of the Red Sea, even dancing in joyful unbelief as we saw the chariots sinking and the bodies of horses and drivers floating onto the opposite shore like bits of refuse.

Our meals were unleavened as we turned our backs on those shores of death, setting out on our adventure and leaving our pursuers to the birds of prey and the scavengers.

We were like dreamers, but the continual flavor of unleavened bread in our mouths reminded us that the precise and permanent end of our slavery was reality. It was our last taste of the bread of affliction, our last taste of the bread of haste.

Soon, we would run out of bread, and we would panic. The dream was becoming a nightmare of being stranded without supplies in a dreadful and vast wilderness! Surely, Egypt would be a better fate than slow starvation and thirst in the scorching sun, withering our tongues and cracking our lips.

The bread of haste was gone. Now we had all the time in the world, all the freedom one could dream about. But what good is time, and of what benefit is freedom when you wander in a waterless and cheerless desert? We are not desert owls! What are we doing here, and how can we get through it, into a real land with trees and water, food and shelter?

We would ask Moses. He would know what to do. But he didn't know, and we felt betrayed that he had brought us out here without a plan to find food and water. We reviled him, and he looked heartsick. What could we know of his secret intimacy and continual communication with the God-force that opened the walls of the sea to us? How could we know that he was getting his instructions moment by moment and had no human plan?

As he struck his staff upon a huge rock, it split open, and torrents of waterfalls gushed and poured out onto the desert floor! There was a fountain of living water flowing in the middle of a rock, in the middle of the desert! We drank and drank for hours, hundreds of thousands of us, and it never ran dry. We splashed and refreshed ourselves in this miraculous source of living water.

Soon, we were waking up to find white frost lining the desert floor, as far as the eye could see. What in the world...? "Mahn hu...? What is this?" Let's call it, "What in the world?" since we have no idea what it is. It tastes like wafers and honey. It is like bread, satisfying and substantial, yet sweet and delicate. Since when does a layer of bread cover the desert floor? Who has ever heard of such a thing?

We had eaten our bread of affliction. We would bake it every year at this time and eat it for seven days. We would remember our escape in haste. But from now on, until we reached the Promised Land, we would eat the bread that came down from Heaven!

THE CORRUPTIBLE AND THE INCORRUPTIBLE

Leavened bread spoils quickly when left for several days, unless artificial preservatives have been added. It is interesting that matzah never seems to spoil. We have kept boxes of matzah for many years (along with those prunes from the Nixon administration), and it has never grown moldy. It seems to be truly incorruptible bread.

As we have seen, both Yeshua and Paul compare leavening to malice, wickedness, and hypocrisy. Our bodies are earthly, and the consequences of sin have been passed down to us from Adam and Eve, our original parents (see Ps. 51:5; 1 Cor. 15:48-49). It is our own sin that causes our flesh to corrupt when our spirits depart from the body in death. All humans have sinned, except for Yeshua of Nazareth. Adam and Eve began to die slowly on the very day they sinned, and their bodies were corrupted with eventual death and decay from that moment on (see Gen. 2:17; 3:19; Rom. 3:23; 1 John 1:8). James tells us that the evil we speak with our tongues corrupts our whole body and sets our course on fire with the very flames of hell (see James 3:6).

Is it possible to be a son of Adam and yet be without sin? The title by which the Lord most frequently referred to Himself in the Gospels is "the Son of Man." We have also seen this title in the Old Testament, particularly when God spoke to the prophet Ezekiel, repeatedly calling him "son of man." In modern Hebrew, this is a frequently used expression, which means "human being." But the actual Hebrew phrase is *ben adam*, literally, a "son of Adam," or a "son of man."

Our Lord Yeshua was a sinless Son of Adam. His tongue was perfectly righteous with every word He spoke; His heart was purely upright and without malice, guile, or evil intent. He never entertained a sinful temptation, which the evil one continually threw at Him (see Heb. 4:15; Luke 4:2). He resisted sin perfectly, and because He was without sin, His flesh was not corrupted, nor could it spoil. Though for our sakes He was killed, His flesh was "unleavened" and could not undergo the normal process of decay and dissolution into the dust of earth. He would not return to the dust as do Adam's other children, but He would return to Heaven from where He originated.

In proving the Lordship of Yeshua to the Jewish crowds in Jerusalem, Peter cited the words of David, words David spoke prophetically about the incorruptible Son of David who was to come:

> *Therefore my heart is glad and my tongue rejoices; my body also will live in hope, because you will not abandon me to the grave, nor will you let your Holy One see decay* (Acts 2:26-27; Psalm 16:9-10).

Peter explained that our father David died and was buried. His body experienced the natural process of decay, yet he wrote these astonishing words that one of his descendents would be raised from the dead, incorruptible! We will look more at the resurrection in the next chapter.

Is it any wonder that the Lord Yeshua used Unleavened Bread to represent His own body? He associated Himself with the bread of affliction, the pure, unleavened bread of the Passover, the incorruptible flesh that could never spoil or be consumed by decomposition in the grave (see Deut. 16:3).

The unleavened bread is an amazing picture of the Lord's body. When we examine a sheet of matzah, we notice several unusual features. It is pierced with many holes. The Jewish authorities realized that when dough is punctured, it cannot inadvertently rise while baking. It also has a bruised and striped appearance, due to rows of dark brown, burnt areas on the surface of a flatbread baked hastily and at high temperatures. Isaiah speaks of the One who would be pierced, bruised, and scourged for our sakes. These words were written more than seven hundred years before Messiah was born.

> *Surely He took up our infirmities and carried our sorrows, yet we considered Him stricken by God, smitten by Him, and afflicted.*
>
> *But He was pierced for our transgressions, He was crushed for our iniquities; the punishment that brought us peace was upon Him, and by His wounds we are healed* (Isaiah 53:4-5).

And through the mysterious and marvelous ceremony of the afikomen, the unleavened bread is broken, buried, and hidden from our eyes. It will indeed be restored to its original piece, and all that is broken and cut off will be made whole again. Eat of *this* unleavened bread, and you will live forever!

When our Father rained down manna from Heaven to nourish the Israelites, He was preparing their hearts to recognize the true and living bread from Heaven. He was the One who would come to His hungry people Israel, their own Yeshua.

I am the bread of life. Your forefathers ate the manna in the desert, yet they died. But here is the bread that comes down from heaven, which a man may eat and not die. I am the living bread that came down from heaven. If anyone eats of this bread, he will live forever. This bread is My flesh, which I will give for the life of the world....he who feeds on this bread will live forever (John 6:48-51,58).

Chapter 4

THE FEAST OF FIRST FRUITS

The celebration of First Fruits is the first agricultural feast of the biblical calendar, and it consists mainly of a grain offering and sacrifices to the Lord. It occurs on the day after the Sabbath of the Passover week (see Lev. 23:11).

All biblical holidays begin at sunset and continue through the following day till the next sunset. Therefore, the Passover Seder takes place on the evening of the fourteenth of Nisan, the culmination of the Day of Preparation. Nisan is the name of the biblical month that corresponds to March or April on our calendars. Biblical holidays can fall on a different western date each year.

During that busiest of all days, we prepare not only for the Seder, but also for the whole week of unleavened bread that begins at the same time. The actual day of Passover falls on the fifteenth of Nisan, and First Fruits occurs on the day following the Sabbath.

There are two possible interpretations of the timing of First Fruits, because the Scripture uses the words, "the day after the Sabbath," which can mean 1) the seventh day, but it can also mean 2) the special "Sabbath" that is Passover itself, on which we also do no regular work. If we used the second interpretation, then First Fruits would always come the day after Passover. If we used the first interpretation, it would always fall on a Sunday, the day after the Sabbath that comes after Passover.

I believe the first interpretation, which defines "Sabbath" as the seventh day of the week, following Passover.

Therefore, First Fruits would always fall on the first day of the week ("Sunday") following Passover. As we will see in the next chapter, the Feast of Pentecost, which is another kind of "first fruits," also falls on the first day of the week. This is because we begin counting forty-nine days (seven weeks) from the First Fruits until Pentecost.

Since Unleavened Bread lasts for seven days, and Passover and First Fruits occur during this week, we see that these three holidays coincide and overlap. Obviously, in the Lord's mind, they are totally connected to each other.

FIRST THINGS FIRST

The first amazing thing about this festival is this: when the Lord instructed the Israelites to observe the yearly cycle of feasts, they were still in the desert, a people without homes or fields. They had no means of attaining self-sufficiency or providing for themselves or their families. This was a nation of sojourners, utterly dependent on the mercy of the Lord to satisfy their burning thirst and the hunger of their little ones and flocks.

There were neither ripe sheaves of grain nor vineyards dripping new wine. They had neither olive oil nor figs, neither wheat nor barley. The Creator led them to springs of water, or created them spontaneously out of rocks. He appointed a supernatural food for over a million people, a food that fell from the sky every morning, six days a week, for forty years. Oddly, it never fell from the sky on the seventh day. This food had never been seen or known since the foundations of the earth, but it nourished them inexhaustibly.

The Lord lovingly laid out the entire calendar year of festivals for Israel, knowing that after the desert, they would enter a rich and fertile land. Despite the present circumstances, the children of Jacob would once again farm their own fields, tend their vines and orchards, and graze their flocks in pasturelands by flowing streams. Then they would be required to present these agricultural and sacrificial offerings to Him, the One who had brought them out of Egypt into their own fertile land.

> *The Lord said to Moses, "Speak to the Israelites and say to them: 'When you enter the land I am going to give you and you reap its harvest, bring to the priest a sheaf of the first grain you harvest.*
>
> *"'He is to wave the sheaf before the Lord so it will be accepted on your behalf; the priest is to wave it on the day after the Sabbath. On the day you wave the sheaf, you must sacrifice as a burnt offering to the Lord a lamb a year old without defect, together with its grain offering...*
>
> *"'You must not eat any bread, or roasted or new grain, until the very day you bring this offering to your God. This is to be a lasting ordinance for the generations to come, wherever you live'"* (Leviticus 23:9-12,14).

The Lord of the Harvest was requiring that the first sheaves of ripe barley be offered to Him before the Israelites ate any of the new crops. In an agricultural society, a successful crop is a matter of life and death.

The Philistines worshiped Dagon, the god of grain, as well as a number of other Canaanite gods and goddesses, purportedly able to grant fertility to the land. The very heart of Canaanite idolatry was bound up in the appeasement of the gods for a productive yield and fertility in the flocks and herds (see Judg. 16:23; 1 Sam. 5:2).

The true and living God was extremely concerned about the hearts of His people, that they would remain devoted to Him despite the massive cults of pagan worship that would surround and entice them as they settled into the land of Canaan.

Just before they entered their land, the Israelite men were seduced by Midianite women and enticed to sacrifice to the Baal of Peor. This resulted in severe judgments from the Lord at the very gate of Canaan. In reality, the Lord was the only God who could actually bless the produce of the fields, the fruit of the vines, and the breeding of livestock.

A Prophetic Calendar: The Feasts of Israel

Since the apostle Paul tells us that the pagan gods are, in actuality, demons, it is unclear to me whether or not their limited "powers" might have affected a region's agriculture among those who worshiped them (see 1 Cor. 10:18-22).

In establishing the Festival of First Fruits, the Lord was instituting an offering that could be likened to an early Thanksgiving in advance of the harvest. By offering the Lord these first sheaves of barley, the individual and the nation were showing the Lord that they trusted Him for the entire season of harvest still to come.

In Israel, the barley is the earliest crop to ripen, although the almond tree buds one month earlier. The ground would be plowed in the fall months, after the final ingathering of the harvest.

As we will explore later when we concentrate on the fall feasts, the Jewish people would begin to pray for the autumn rains to come at the culmination of Tabernacles. This is also called the Feast of Ingathering, because the late-ripening crops and fruits are gathered into the barn for winter storage. As such, it is the last agricultural feast in the biblical calendar.

The seed would then be sown during the winter, about two months before the optimum time of germination. The newly planted seeds required the soil to be steeped in early rainfall in order to ripen in time for Passover in the first month.

In obedience to the Lord's command concerning first fruits, Israel's designated authorities would sow a part of the barley seed in a separate section of a field, located in the Ashes Valley, nestled in the slopes of the Mount of Olives.[1]

In the first month, as Passover approached, they would diligently check the ripeness of this special barley crop. When they determined that it was ripe, they would select some sheaves of grain and tie them with a ribbon to ensure that no one would inadvertently rob the Lord of His first fruits offering.

Then the little bundle was reaped and brought before the Lord in the wave offering and accompanying sacrifices described in the above passage from Leviticus 23. A detailed view of the first fruits grain offering can be seen in the following passage:

If you bring a grain offering of firstfruits to the Lord, offer crushed heads of new grain roasted in the fire. Put oil and incense on it; it is a grain offering. The priest shall burn the memorial portion of the crushed grain and the oil, together with all the incense, as an offering made to the Lord by fire (Leviticus 2:14-16).

HE WILL MULTIPLY WHAT WE GIVE AWAY

We have already seen that the Lord Yeshua became the Passover Lamb and placed the seal of His blood over the doorframes of our hearts. In addition, He has chosen the symbol of unleavened bread to represent His purity, brokenness, and incorruptibility. Both the Passover and Unleavened Bread have now been infused with the reality of Yeshua's life and death. Now we turn our attention to His fulfillment of First Fruits.

It was a few days before Passover, and a huge crowd had gathered on the northeast shore of the Sea of Galilee. The Lord Jesus asked Philip where they could buy some bread to feed these people, and Philip replied that eight months wages would not buy enough bread. But the Lord already knew that they would not be buying any bread that day. Andrew pointed out a boy who had five small barley loaves and two small fish. Would the child give away all that he had brought to feed his little brothers and sisters as they camped on the shore and listened to the Teacher?

Barley bread was the less nutritious alternative to wheat bread, the bread of the poor. Yeshua gave thanks in advance. He was ready to give away a small first offering of barley bread, knowing that a great harvest of multiplication was about to be granted by the Father of miracles, the Father of manna. Just as the heavenly manna was never exhausted, although more than a million people received three meals a day, six days a week, for forty years, so this earthly bread was not about to be exhausted until every soul was satisfied.

When they had eaten, the disciples gathered up twelve baskets full of bread fragments. As Pastor Curt Malizzi preached this very morning, "There were twelve disciples. That was one basket for each doubting disciple! As each one carried back his own basket of bread, he could reflect on the staggering miracle he had just witnessed with five small barley loaves and two small fish."[2]

Giving away first fruits is an exercise in childlike faith in the Father's willingness to multiply that which is blessed and given away. After this extended meal of continually breaking bread and finding yet more to break, five thousand men were fed, in addition to the women and children (see John 6:1-13; Matt. 14:21).

The next morning, the Lord Yeshua used the object lesson of the multiplied bread as a divine set-up for the most astonishing and controversial teaching He could ever have said to a Jewish audience!

The Lord told them that the bread they had eaten was temporary and would spoil; it was not worthy to be sought after. Rather, He admonished them to seek the food that endures to eternal life, which the Son of Man would give to them. The people reminded Yeshua that their forefathers had eaten the miraculous manna from Heaven that Moses had given them in the desert. Apparently, they felt the manna was a more spectacular sign than what they had just witnessed the day before. In response, the Lord told them,

> *I tell you the truth, it is not Moses who has given you the bread from heaven, but it is My Father who gives you the true bread from heaven. For the bread of God is He who comes down from heaven and gives life to the world....*
>
> *I am the bread of life. He who comes to Me will never go hungry, and he who believes in Me will never be thirsty.*
>
> *I am the bread that came down from heaven. I am the bread of life. Your forefathers ate the manna in the desert, yet they died. But here is the bread that comes down from heaven, which a man may eat and not die. I am the living bread that came down from heaven.*
>
> *If anyone eats of this bread, he will live forever. This bread is My flesh, which I will give for the life of the world* (John 6:32-33,35,41;48-51).

Passover was near. Unleavened Bread was near. First Fruits was near. The Exodus was on Israel's mind, as was the manna that fell from Heaven into a barren wilderness. They were mindful of the Father's heavenly provision of bread, which needed to be gathered fresh each day, bread that could sustain human life apart from any normal means of sustenance.

Moses was on Israel's mind, as was the first fruits offering of the barley harvest. They were hoping for a good crop this spring and a ripe little bundle of grain to bring before the Lord as a pleasing offering, guaranteeing an enormous harvest of bread from the earth. "Blessed art Thou, O Lord Our God, who brings forth bread from the earth!"[3]

Thus, the Lord taught the lesson of the Living Bread, using a miraculous multiplication of bread as the backdrop for this difficult teaching. As He fed His people with barley bread, how much more will He freely give Himself to us?

HARVESTED FROM THE GRAVE

Yeshua the Messiah was crucified on the Day of Preparation (see John 19:31). He died at the very hour that the Passover lambs were being offered. His body remained in the tomb for three days and three nights, though it did not corrupt, for He was Unleavened Bread. On the third day, on the Feast of First Fruits, He was physically raised up from the dead and appeared in the flesh to many.

Just as the first offering of barley was brought before the Lord as a pleasing offering on the day of First Fruits, so the perfect Lamb was harvested out from the grip of earth's decay, the first fruits of the dead.

We have previously noted the apostle Paul's teaching to the Corinthian church that Yeshua was the Passover Lamb.

> *For Christ, our Passover lamb, has been sacrificed* (1 Corinthians 5:7).

Later in this epistle, Paul expands their understanding of the biblical calendar by likening Messiah's resurrection to the Jewish and biblical feast of First Fruits, repeating the name of the festival twice.

But Christ has indeed been raised from the dead, the first-fruits of those who have fallen asleep....

For as in Adam all die, so in Christ all will be made alive. But each in his own turn: Christ, the firstfruits; then, when he comes, those who belong to him (1 Corinthians 15:20,22-23).

The resurrection of Jesus was the guarantee of an enormous harvest of the dead who will be raised on the latter day. In ancient Israel, if God was pleased with the first fruits offering, He would bless and multiply the crop to come. So it will be with us. Because our High Priest's offering was so totally pleasing to the Father, we will gain the bodily resurrection of the dead.

May His faithfulness be praised, for He has gone ahead of us. Yeshua was the perfect, ripe sheaf of barley, cut down in His prime, offered before the Lord, and freed from the agony of death forever for our sakes!

HOW SHOULD WE APPLY FIRST FRUITS?

Because of the nature of this festival, most believers would not know how to celebrate it or apply it to their lives. It is also common and partially accurate to suppose that giving our tithes to the Lord is the modern-day equivalent of this feast.

There is a difference between the commemoration of first fruits and tithing, and it is important for His people to distinguish between these two acts so that His blessings can be opened up to us as individuals and communities. You have noticed that there are many different types of offerings in the Old Testament, each one having a different meaning and function. The burnt offering is not the same as the sin offering or the thank offering. One is pure worship. One is restitution for wrongdoing. One is giving back in gratitude. In the same way, there are differing types of offerings still in God's heart within the New Covenant community. I will explain the different functions of these two offerings, and we will see a bit more about this in the next chapter on the later First Fruits celebration, Pentecost.

Tithing is a regular, continual practice of offering 10 percent of our increase, which is usually a paycheck in this society. The Lord does not suggest, but requires, that we tithe. Some believers say it is optional to tithe, but it is not optional. If you do not tithe, the Lord concludes that you love money more than you love Him, and that you do not trust Him to provide for you when you give away the first 10 percent.

> *"Bring the whole tithe into the storehouse, that there may be food in my house. Test me in this," says the Lord Almighty, "and see if I will not throw open the floodgates of heaven and pour out so much blessing that you will not have room enough for it"* (Malachi 3:10).

In a sense, tithing is a type of first fruit offering, because we are taking off the first 10 percent we earn or receive, and giving it to Him for His Kingdom purposes. But while tithing is a type of first fruits, there is also a separate first fruits offering that is neither a regular offering, nor a percentage of our income. The true first fruits offering came only once a year in the Bible and was related to the first appearance of the barley crop in the spring. It was a whole offering, the first part of the harvest completely given to the Lord.

Since many of us do not live in a strictly agricultural society, our first fruits will usually not involve crops. However, it can involve our farms or gardens, as well as our monetary reaping. To make this very simple, I believe I should share with you several precise ways that I have applied first fruits to my life. I will give two examples that might help you, and then I will share a word that the Lord gave me this morning to insert His heart into this chapter.

There have been years when I planted vegetables in a small garden in our yard. I am a poor gardener, and most years I don't have time to do this. But one year, I had worked hard and planted a nice plot of vegetables. The zucchinis were the first ones to ripen, and I picked the first three beauties with great pride and joy, since I have no gardening ability.

Although I had never thought about this, the image of first fruits popped into my mind as I beheld these first three zucchinis, and I knew the

Lord wanted me to give them away. However, I immediately sensed that just giving away three raw zucchinis was not honoring to Him. We had a Muslim family living next door to us, and I knew that He wanted me to turn these zucchinis into muffins and give them to my neighbors. They were very shocked and delighted when I brought over these warm muffins, full of cinnamon and moist with squash and raisins. Having four children, my neighbors loved them, and I got to tell them about the biblical concept of offering first fruits to the Lord by sharing my first produce with them. I believe this object lesson remained in their memories. They knew we were Jewish believers in Jesus, and this gift pointed them to the Lord.

The second example involves money, not vegetables. When I wrote my first book, I was required to start a business in order to keep very separate and strict accounting of expenses and income. I had never wanted to be in business, and this was a huge and difficult step for me.

At a speaking engagement that took place a few weeks before my new book and worship CD were to be released, a number of people wished to order my materials in advance. I was honored that they were giving me orders several weeks before I would have the books and CDs available to send to them.

When I got home that day and calculated the advance purchases, I was stunned by the amount they had given me, although in the worldly appraisal of doing business, it was a very small amount. I was excited because I had invested a great deal in the production of these materials and looked forward to recouping some of my losses. I said to the Lord, "Thank you! This is like the first fruits of my new little business!"

His answer came immediately: "What do you do with first fruits?"

My joy was short-lived. Being a good student of the Bible, I knew the answer to His question.

I replied, "You give it all away."

Neither He nor I said any more about it. I immediately gave the entire sum to the recipient His Spirit placed upon my heart at that moment. To be honest, it was a little painful to give away that whole first amount. It felt costly to me, but I knew that He saw everything I did, and trusted that He would cause others in the future to buy my books and CDs. Needless to say, since that offering, the Lord has been faithful to honor His part of the covenant, as I was faithful to give it away.

Now that I've shared a few practical examples, I'd like to offer the word that the Lord gave me this morning, when I asked Him if I had found His heart in the writing of this feast.

> My people perish for lack of knowledge. If My people would bring Me all of their first fruits offering, wholly and with joyful and voluntary hearts, they would experience a greater abundance than they can even dream about.
>
> I wildly bless and extravagantly pour out on those who bring their first fruits sacrificially to Me. It seems wasteful, after investing so much in a business or a crop. It seems like just when you are starting to pull ahead, see some increase, receive back a little of what you put in, then I ask you to give it all away. To go back to "zero" after the numbers were just beginning to show a yield and an increase.
>
> Oh, how I love to see the first fruits offering! Many of My people tithe, and this is good and right. The tithe is a partial and continual type of first fruits; it is a regular lifestyle contribution.
>
> But the Feast of First Fruits is once a year. In the life of an individual or community of faith, it could arise more than once a year because it will not always be tied to the agricultural cycle. It might be tied to business, art, even sports investments. In some cases, it can be related to historic celebrations, such as celebrating the civil rights movement with a special offering to Me from the African-American community, whom I have redeemed from slavery at such cost and have raised up into high positions of influence in the land.
>
> I have not yet received My first fruits offering from My believing African-American communities for the new

businesses, new elevations and appointments, new successes, new educational ventures, new investments, new ministry doors, new books, authors, artists, playwrights, scientists, and athletes.

Both individuals and communities should bring Me the first fruits offering when a new venture takes off. You know how restaurant owners will put the first dollar bill they earned up on the wall, near the cash register? Well, that is a secular counterpart to My heart for first fruits. They should give the first hundred dollars to Me right away, after asking Me where I would like them to give it. I will bless any new restaurant owner who does this, even if they went into debt to open the restaurant. If they bring Me the first fruits instead of hanging it on the wall, I will multiply their business and lift them out of debt.

The secret of debt removal is the first fruits offering. Tell My flock how to do it, so it will be practical and easy for them.

HEAVEN'S BREAD

Yeshua the Messiah is Heaven's bread. He distributed earthly bread, which was vastly multiplied as He gave it away. His Father had given their forefathers heavenly bread, which was vastly multiplied for forty years.

He then gave away His own flesh and blood, of more value than all the grain fields and breadbaskets of the entire earth. When He gave away Heaven's bread, the Lord Yeshua was giving away Himself. First, He gave Himself away to twelve Jewish disciples. Then they gave Him away to the towns of Judah and the cities of Israel.

The Jewish apostles subsequently gave Him away to all the nations of the earth, freely distributing His living bread and the power of His Holy Spirit. As they gave their lives to bring Yeshua to the nations, all who received Him were granted new life in their spirits, souls, and on the last day, in their corrupted physical bodies as well.

As He gave Heaven's bread to us, we will give Him out to Israel and to the nations. Our bread will never be exhausted, nor will our oil jars run dry. We will be filled daily, waiting in His Presence in intimate communion, receiving our manna daily from Him and then giving it away.

He was the First Fruits from the dead, redeemed from the earth. As God the Father accepted His Son's first fruits offering, so we too will be harvested from the earth and will sit down with the Lord Yeshua the Messiah at the banqueting table of His love. Amen.

Chapter 5

THE FEAST OF WEEKS (PENTECOST)

The fourth spring feast is an extravagant culmination of the harvesting season of grain. It is also the final and climactic fulfillment of the Lord Yeshua's first coming to earth, even as the first three spring feasts were also completions of His redemptive assignments from the Father.

Each spring feast was designed by God to enact a living parable of Messiah's future entrance into history. They were pictures that would prepare Israel's heart to recognize the perfect embodiment of these feasts in Yeshua's life; the feasts were imprinted in Israel's collective memory. He came as the Teacher, the Breathing Torah, the Passover Lamb, the pure and guileless Unleavened Bread. He was the first Sheaf of Barley to be harvested from the earth.

Each festival showed a part of the Lord's heart. First, we saw a God who was concerned for the enslavement of His people, and who stretched out His mighty arm against the gods of Pharaoh, to bring them out. We remembered what He had done to free and redeem us, by eating the Passover Lamb and the bread of affliction.

We trusted in the Lord for a coming harvest by offering Him the first little bundle of perfect barley sheaves, reaped before all the others that would come. The Lord Yeshua burst forth from the sealed tomb, as did a

117

number of other Old Testament saints who were reaped from death in the train of His resurrection. He was the First Fruits from the dead, the early harvest. Now we can trust Him for the massive harvest of the righteous dead, when the earth can no longer bear to hold us.

WHEN YOU HAVE EATEN, REMEMBER ME!

The unleavened barley bread was humble fare, and it was not difficult to remember our neediness and vulnerability in a barren landscape.

He took us from the dependency of a helpless, squalling child in the desert, to a favored and thriving nation in a fertile land. But lest we think that our own strength had brought forth bread from the earth, He commanded us to bring Him the first fruits of our earliest crop, the barley.

It would be easy to forget to appreciate Him when our farms and orchards prospered and our appetites were well-satisfied. A generous husband loves to pamper His sweet wife, but it is profoundly hurtful when she grows aloof and complacent, unaware of His kindness or provision. If she were to use Him for His benefits, but not cherish and appreciate Him as a person, it would cause His noble heart much pain. If she were to take credit for her prosperity, or attribute it to others, it would provoke Him to jealousy.

If the Lord provided bountifully for His people, it was for fellowship, thanksgiving, intimacy, and responsive sacrificial devotion. The grain was to be enjoyed in His presence, in His very house. The first fruits of the later and greater wheat harvest provided the backdrop for the lavish celebration of thankfulness that closes out the season of the harvest.

SEVEN WEEKS AND COUNTING

From the day that the set-apart barley sheaves were waved before the Lord, the Israelites were to count off seven weeks. The counting of these forty-nine days brought them to the wheat harvest, the more nourishing and valued grain. Wheat bread was the bread of prosperity, its flour producing the choicest baked goods.

The Feast of Weeks (Pentecost)

This festival was called by several names in the Bible: the Feast of Weeks, the Feast of Harvest, and the Feast of First Fruits. It was a second type of first fruits, with greater joy, celebration, and costly sacrificial offerings.

Most importantly, the Lord's final word on this feast was always concerning the poor, the widows, orphans, and foreigners. Because there are a number of biblical passages on this celebration, I have combined them into one passage below, to convey the most information without repetition.

> *From the day after the Sabbath, the day you brought the sheaf of the wave offering, count off seven full weeks. Count off fifty days up to the day after the seventh Sabbath, and then present an offering of new grain to the Lord. From wherever you live, bring two loaves made with two-tenths of an ephah of fine flour, baked with yeast, as a wave offering of firstfruits to the Lord...*
>
> *Celebrate the Feast of Weeks with the firstfruits of the wheat harvest....[and] by giving a freewill offering in proportion to the blessings the Lord your God has given you. And rejoice before the Lord your God at the place He will choose as a dwelling for His Name—you, your sons and daughters, your menservants and your maidservants, the Levites in your towns, and the aliens, the fatherless and the widows living among you. Remember that you were slaves in Egypt, and follow carefully these decrees...*
>
> *When you reap the harvest of your land, do not reap to the very edges of your field, or gather the gleanings of your harvest. Leave them for the poor and the alien. I am the Lord your God* (Leviticus 23:15-17; Exodus 34:22; Deuteronomy 16:10-12; Leviticus 23:22).

We notice that God instructed us to celebrate this festival fifty days after the earlier first fruits offering; no absolute date was given for Pentecost because it depended on the timing of the barley offering. The Israelites were to count off seven weeks from the waving of the barley, and on the fiftieth day Israel would offer the second first fruits to the Lord; this time, it would be the wheat harvest. The Greek word for this festival is *Pentecost*, meaning "fiftieth" (see Acts 2:1-2). The Hebrew word for "Weeks" is *Shavuot*, and this is how most Jewish people, and certainly all Israelis, will refer to it.

To the best of my understanding of the biblical texts, it would always fall on the first day of the week (Sunday), due to both festivals of first fruits occurring on the day after a Sabbath day. As I explained earlier, scholars are not agreed on which "Sabbath" the Bible is referring to, but I am fairly convinced that the Lord meant the regular, seventh-day Sabbath, rather than the "special Sabbath" of Passover.

A BANQUET IN JERUSALEM

As the Lord showed the Israelites the timing of this feast, He also instructed them on the place. Israel was commanded to rejoice "in the place where He would choose for His Name to dwell." It was not clear at the time which place He was referring to, although the descendants of Jacob were aware that Abraham had journeyed to Mount Moriah. This was the mountain chosen by God, where Abraham was to sacrifice his son Isaac.

When the Lord commanded this, He was referring to Jerusalem, although the wandering Israelites had not yet entered the land of Israel. The mountains of Jerusalem were still a Jebusite stronghold, not to be conquered for roughly another three hundred years by King David. Our loving Lord spoke prophetically to Israel, before they could enact these feasts in their own land. Once the city became Israel's capital and center of worship, the Feast of Weeks was one of the three major feasts in which all Israelite men were required to come up to Jerusalem for the celebration and the sacrifices.

> *Three times a year all your men must appear before the Lord your God at the place He will choose: at the Feast of Unleavened Bread, the Feast of Weeks and the Feast of Tabernacles. No man should appear before the Lord empty-handed* (Deuteronomy 16:16).

The Feast of Weeks (Pentecost)

It was very important to the Lord's heart that His people gather in His house for His appointed banquet of choice meats and breads baked with fine flour. Much of the tithe He had commanded to be set aside was to be used for feasting and rejoicing in His mountainous banqueting hall, Jerusalem, the City of the Great King.

> Be sure to set aside a tenth of all that your fields produce each year. Eat the tithe of your grain, new wine and oil, and the firstborn of your herds and flocks in the presence of the Lord your God in the place He will choose as a dwelling for His name, so that you may learn to revere the Lord your God always.
>
> Then you and your household shall eat there in the presence of the Lord your God and rejoice. And do not neglect the Levites living in your towns, for they have no allotment or inheritance of their own (Deuteronomy 14:22-23;26b-27).

The King was giving a party three times a year, and it was to be a sweet time of intimate fellowship with Him, which the Lord greatly looked forward to. He wanted His children to enjoy these "date days" with Him as well. *Throughout the Bible, God makes it clear that these days were not reserved for Israel alone!*

There are a number of passages that show us that it was always His desire for all the nations to come up to Jerusalem to meet with the King of the whole earth. Ultimately, this will be fulfilled during the Millennial reign, but as with all future promises, there is a "now" fulfillment for those with ears to hear. The loving Lord has invited His people from all the nations to come into His banqueting hall. As it is written:

> And foreigners who bind themselves to the Lord to serve Him, to love the name of the Lord, and to worship Him, all who keep the Sabbath without desecrating it and who hold fast to My covenant—these I will bring to My holy

mountain and give them joy in My house of prayer... for My house will be called a house of prayer for all nations (Isaiah 56:6-7).

On this mountain the Lord Almighty will prepare a feast of rich food for all peoples, a banquet of aged wine—the best of meats and the finest of wines. On this mountain He will destroy the shroud that enfolds all peoples, the sheet that covers all nations; He will swallow up death forever (Isaiah 25:6-8a).

Of course, we do not have to physically travel to Jerusalem to celebrate these times of fellowship with the Lord. There may be a special time when He provides for you to visit the land of Israel. Even so, the Lord is with us wherever we dwell, and He knocks on the door of our hearts through these appointed times. If we open the door, the Lord Yeshua Himself will come in and eat with us, and we with Him. Wherever He is pleased to dwell, this place becomes His holy mountain, where we can rejoice in His Presence.

THE FREEWILL OFFERING

As we saw in the first section of Scriptures, the Feast of Harvest includes a "freewill" offering in addition to the required sacrifices. The Lord specified that the people should give in proportion to the blessings the Lord had given to each one. It would be contradictory to say that the Lord *required* a freewill offering. If He required it, it wouldn't be voluntary, would it?

Until recently, I never understood the freewill offering. There were so many sacrifices in the Old Testament, and it was hard to grasp why each type was necessary to perform. The one thing that most had in common was that the Lord required them.

If you look carefully at Deuteronomy16:10, the Lord does not actually use the word "require" when speaking about the freewill offering. He simply says, "Celebrate and rejoice by giving a freewill offering." It is as if He is suggesting that if we bring this offering as a thankful response, our joy and celebration will be enhanced. That would certainly be in keeping with His gracious and respectful character.

During my "three days" (covered in my first book), the Lord finally explained to me that the freewill offering was completely voluntary. I had been asking Him over the years about giving, and how much to give to certain ministries. I was hoping to get a clearly stated directive from Him, so it would be easy to know what to do. It surprised me very much when He told me, *"It is completely your decision. That's why they call it a 'freewill offering.'"* It sounds quite obvious now, but for some reason, this was confusing to me for many years.

You may recall that in the first chapter, we looked at Paul's comment that he was compelled to preach the Gospel. It was not optional for him. He added that if others preached voluntarily, they might receive a reward, but if he didn't preach, "Woe is me" (see 1 Cor. 9:16).

This helps us understand that the required sacrifices were necessary; the Lord did not consider them mere suggestions. Israel and her priesthood were not rewarded for offering the mandatory sacrifices. To not do so was a matter of life and death ("Woe is me if I don't!").

We each know in our hearts how much the Lord has blessed us in a given year. He knows that we know. He leaves it up to us to decide what is proportionate to the blessings we have received, and what offering would be appropriate. This is one way the Lord examines our hearts to see what choices we make, when He gives us complete freedom to choose what to give. The Feast of the Harvest is a joyful time of abandon, with intense thankfulness.

In many churches, pastors and teachers will make a distinction between the tithe and the offering. I believe that this is accurate and in keeping with the Lord's heart in the Old Testament sacrifice system. These special offerings only take place several times a year and are clearly in addition to our normal tithing. So, tithes and offerings are not the same, and it is helpful to know how the Lord feels about this matter. In the last chapter, we looked at the difference between regular tithing and the yearly "first fruits offering." Here, we are highlighting the "freewill offering," which seems to be a voluntary gift at the time of the three major feasts (Unleavened Bread, Pentecost, and Tabernacles) in proportion to His special blessings to us.

Our giving is extremely important to Him. This is not because He needs our money, but because the way our hearts feel about our money affects our love relationship with Him. As it is written, "You cannot love both God and money."

Two Leavened Loaves

During the first fruits of the barley, we saw that the grain offering was unleavened, and part of it was mixed with oil and incense and burned before the Lord. In the later first fruits of the wheat harvest, the offering consisted of two leavened loaves of wheat bread, which were waved before the Lord but not burned. They were to be eaten by the priests as part of their special meal, along with the meat of sacrificed lambs. The Lord had previously commanded that no grain offering made with yeast or honey could be burned (see Lev. 2:11).

Many have wondered why this grain offering was leavened, while all other festal grain offerings were unleavened, and then burned. Some scholars have concluded that the two loaves represent a future partnership of two people groups. This mystery would not be unveiled until the New Covenant was established and the Holy Spirit had been poured out (on Pentecost!). Paul refers to this new entity as "One New Man," or as Messianic teacher and prophetic evangelist Sid Roth aptly translates it, "One New Humanity."

The New Covenant has joined together those who were formerly separated by a wall of mutual distrust and distaste: Jew and Gentile have become one family in Messiah Yeshua. We are still leavened loaves, because we are still earthly and imperfect; we have not yet received our eternal and incorruptible bodies, which will be unleavened and without the contamination of sin. But for now, we resist the old nature, and we crucify our will and our rights daily.

A second understanding of the two leavened loaves is simply that God wanted His people to enjoy the delicious, light bread of celebration at this feast, rather than the austere and unleavened barley bread of the Passover. The Feast of Weeks did not call for the Bread of Affliction, but rather for a lavish banquet of the best foods for the whole house of Israel.

As we noted earlier, yeast is a living organism that the Lord created to raise up a lump of dough into a nourishing staple of a festive meal. It is the airborne strains of bacteria and yeast that contaminate and spoil dough, but the good yeast is a part of our Creator's design for His people's nutrition and enjoyment.

THE GIVING OF THE LAW

Exodus 19:1 tells us that in the third month after leaving Egypt—"on the very day"—the Israelites came to the desert of Sinai. It was here, at Mount Sinai, that they received the laws that had been directly revealed to Moses by God.

There are several different Hebrew words used throughout the first five books of Moses that are usually translated "laws," "judgments," or "statutes." One of these Hebrew words is *torah* (see Deut. 1:5), which means "instruction."

As Judaism has developed over many centuries, *Torah* is now the most commonly used term for the compilation of all the laws and governing principles given by God to Israel in the Scriptures.

According to Jewish tradition, the Feast of Weeks has come to be called, "The Time of the Giving of Our Torah" by observant Jews. This tradition is based on this passage from Exodus 19:1.

The biblical passages on this feast do not directly connect it to the receiving of the Law on Mount Sinai. Even so, the arrival at the Sinai Desert "in the third month" could place the giving of the Law very close to fifty days after crossing the Red Sea. The only problem with this theory is that after arriving in the Sinai Desert, Moses was up on the mountain for forty days with the Lord before coming down with the tablets. After the terrible idolatry with the golden calf, Moses returned to the top of Mount Sinai and remained for another forty days before bringing down the new tablets of the Law.

Then again, Moses did receive the revelation from the Lord during that first forty-day period, and so it could be argued that the Law was already given, despite the delay in the people receiving it. (See the section entitled, "From Death to Life," for a detailed view of the consequences of the golden calf incident.)

Despite this difficulty in timing, the Jewish people consider Shavuot, the Feast of Weeks, to be the anniversary of the giving of the Law of Moses. This commemoration of the giving of Torah has largely replaced the earlier agricultural aspect of this holiday, due to the dispersion of the Jews from the land of Israel.

When the Jewish people were driven from their land by the Romans, their temple and worship system were demolished, and it was no longer possible to bring their offerings of crops and animals up to Jerusalem to present before the Lord. In the countries where they had been scattered, they developed alternative customs that allowed them to celebrate the Feasts of the Lord without the sacrifices and temple ceremonies.

Israel traces its birth as a nation to Mount Sinai, and the late spring celebration of the Feast of Weeks is considered to be the anniversary of Israel's origination. When Israel left Egypt, they were not yet truly free. A nation without God's law is not a free nation. In the absence of righteous standards, lawlessness will inevitably abound, breeding violence and mob rule.

THE GIVING OF THE HOLY SPIRIT

Just as an earthly nation cannot function properly without God's laws, so a "holy nation" of His New Covenant representatives on earth cannot function without His power living in them.

When the Lord Yeshua, risen in the flesh, appeared to His disciples, they were overjoyed. The thought of never seeing Him again was too depressing and grievous to bear, since they had set all their hopes in Him. After three days of mourning, the unthinkable occurred (though the Lord had told them it would), and He came and ate with them again. They were wild with joy and incredulity; Yeshua had died, but now, He was very much alive and back in their midst!

He was now in a glorified body, and after a number of intermittent appearances over a forty-day period, witnessed by hundreds, the Lord was taken up into Heaven from the Mount of Olives. The disciples craned their necks in astonishment, gaping at the unprecedented sight of the Son of Man ascending into a cloud.

He had been raised from the dead on First Fruits and had visited them, alive, for forty days. Yeshua had ascended into Heaven, and it was now about ten days before the Feast of Weeks, the joyful festival of provision and harvest.

Luke reports that they "returned to Jerusalem with great joy, and stayed continually at the temple, praising God" (see Luke 24:53). Their number was about one hundred and twenty male and female disciples, and they remained in constant prayer until the Feast of Weeks, also called Pentecost, arrived. On the very day it came, they were gathered together in prayer (see Acts 1:14-15; 2:1).

> *Suddenly a sound like the blowing of a violent wind came from heaven and filled the whole house where they were sitting. They saw what seemed to be tongues of fire that separated and came to rest on each of them. All of them were filled with the Holy Spirit and began to speak in other tongues as the Spirit enabled them (Acts 2:2-4).*

Acts records at least fifteen different languages that were spoken that morning by these Israeli disciples. As we know, all devout Jews made pilgrimage to Jerusalem three times a year, not only from various regions of Israel, but also from every nation where they had been taken during the Assyrian and Babylonian invasions (722 B.C. and 586 B.C., respectively).

> *Now there were staying in Jerusalem God-fearing Jews from every nation under heaven. When they heard this sound, a crowd came together in bewilderment, because each one heard them speaking in his own language. Utterly amazed, they asked, "Are not all these men speaking Galileans?" (Acts 2:5-7)*

A Prophetic Calendar: The Feasts of Israel

The Lord orchestrated the pouring out of His Spirit on the day when all godly Jewish men would be in the temple courts, worshiping at the Feast of Harvest. As they wondered at this great sign, Peter stood and addressed them.

> *"This is what was spoken by the prophet Joel:*
> *'In the last days,' God says, 'I will pour out My Spirit on all people. Your sons and daughters will prophesy, your young men will see visions, your old men will dream dreams. Even on My servants, both men and women, I will pour out My Spirit in those days, and they will prophesy'"* (Acts 2:16-18).

Peter preached the message of the righteous Messiah, who was rejected by the leaders of Israel and crucified "with the help of wicked men." He assured his Jewish brothers that death was not able to keep the Lord Yeshua, as King David had prophesied in Psalm 16. Now, He was exalted at the right hand of God and had poured out the Holy Spirit on His people this very day, in fulfillment of Joel's prophecy. He was indeed both Lord and Messiah.

The godly worshipers were cut to the heart and cried out in mourning, "Brothers, tell us what we must do!"

Peter did not condemn them, but offered them peace from God upon their guilty consciences: "Repent, and be immersed [in water] in the Name of Yeshua the Messiah for the forgiveness of your sins. And you will receive the gift of the Holy Spirit" (see Acts 5:38-39).

On that awesome Feast of Weeks, three thousand Jewish souls were saved and became followers of the Lord Yeshua. When they returned to their own countries after the feast, they led thousands of Jewish friends and family to salvation.

Israel still awaits her Messiah, just as many believers in Jesus still await an outpouring of the Holy Spirit in power, to bring in the bountiful and final harvest of the earth's population. However, Messiah has come, and the Holy Spirit has been poured out!

The Feast of Weeks (Pentecost)

FROM DEATH TO LIFE

As we consider the account in Exodus 32, we cringe at the shameful memory of the golden calf. Moses had been up on the mountain with God for forty days, and the people could not make sense of his disappearance. They demanded that Aaron give them a tangible object to worship, because the human heart was designed to worship *something*. Even agnostics have placed their devotion somewhere, although perhaps they would not recognize this attachment as "worship."

As the man of God was descending with their tablets, inscribed by the very finger of God, he heard a riotous orgy echoing through the desert air. Joshua thought it was a war cry, but Moses corrected him: this was not a sound of victory or of weakness. It was just noise, a wild and senseless "Woodstock" of idolatry.

Although Moses had just pleaded with the Lord to spare Israel from His wrath over this betrayal of covenant, he too was now burning with anger, and he smashed the sacred tablets to the rocks. He burned the detestable calf, ground it into powder, and made the Israelites drink it. Then he commanded the Levites to go out among the revelers and strike down their brothers with the sword. In addition to the sword, the Lord struck the people with plague, as a further punishment for this great sin (see Exod. 32:27-28,35).

On that day, which should have been a holy and awesome day of receiving the Law of God, three thousand Israelites were slaughtered by their own relatives. It was the wages of harlotry and a sobering lesson.

The Jewish people celebrate the Giving of the Torah on this day, but no one would wish to recall the punishment that befell them as a result of idolatry so soon after leaving Egypt.

On a future Feast of Weeks, some fourteen hundred years later, the Holy Spirit would be poured out from Heaven on the Lord's Jewish apostles and a great crowd in Jerusalem. As the good news of the Kingdom of God was preached that day with power, and in many languages, three thousand Jewish souls were saved! *Although the giving of the Law was marred by the painful memory of three thousand deaths, the giving of the Spirit resulted in three thousand lives being redeemed from wrath, unto eternal life!*

By the Lord Yeshua's death and resurrection, we have been transferred from death to life! By the power of His Holy Spirit, we are transformed into the righteous and holy servants we so desperately wish to be but cannot attain merely by trying to be "good."

THE LORD'S HEART FOR THE HUNGRY

As I was nearly finished writing this chapter, the Lord spoke to me of His heart for this feast. In each chapter, I have asked Him to help me find His heart to impart to the reader. This was the word I received:

> My heart in all of these feasts has always been for the poor. Do you see the golden grain fields of Israel, brimming with harvesters and foremen? How eager is the landowner to see and receive the fruits of his labor, his months of diligently plowing, fertilizing, and sowing good seed into the rich soil! How he needs My early autumn rains to come and prepare his soil, after a long and withering summer. How he rejoices to see the latter spring rains come in and help the barley to grow and the new wheat to germinate.
>
> Do you see My hungry disciples walking through someone else's grain field, gladly and gratefully pulling heads of grain to eat? It didn't take many kernels to satisfy them, and yet they had to endure criticism and accusation of harvesting on the Sabbath!
>
> Did not My Torah say that the gleaners who were poor could come and eat grain from the field of the landowner, as long as they did not put the sickle to the grain? What a man can carry in his hands to satisfy his own hunger is not harvesting. It is the provision of My Torah for the poor.
>
> Do you see Ruth, following the servant girls of Boaz, behind the harvesters, picking up the kernels that the servant girls missed? She did not feel worthy to eat the

crumbs that fell from Boaz's table, and even his dogs ate the crumbs. She followed behind, not even for her own hunger; but she was thinking about Naomi's hunger, and how important it was for her to eat a nutritious meal and keep up her strength and spirit.

When I granted a bountiful crop to My Israeli landowners, I expected My first fruits of the barley and then the wheat. I expected them to leave much behind for the poor, the gleaners, the foreigners, the widows and their children, the orphans and their little brothers and sisters, those without money to buy food.

A field full of ripe grain is like a banqueting table. I have spread out a table for the nations, a ripe field for all the peoples. The poor and the disenfranchised need to be welcomed at My table and to eat of My fields. That is why I added the verse about the poor at the end of Shavuot. Seven sevens are yours, but the fiftieth part is for the poor, after you have given Me My first fruit.

My priests eat it and are glad, for they have no portion. If My people withhold their first bread, My priests have no provision, for I have provided their portion from the obedience of My landowners, whose crops I have blessed. It is not just for their sake that I have blessed their fields, but for the priests and the Levites and the poor and the foreigner who doesn't know how to fit in and make a living in society.

Shavuot is for gratitude, for reaping abundantly with joy at My generosity, and Shavuot is for the poor. My people will raise up the poor Moabitess, and spread the corner and the wing of My prayer shawl over her, and bless her to rise up to surpass them. She will become greater and wealthier than they who gave her of their crumbs and their gleanings. She will become a bountiful Mother of Israel, blessing her people in return.

As Israel showed kindness and mercy to Ruth, so now My Bride from the Gentile nations will become a mother to hungry and hapless Israel, and she will cover My people as they have covered her when she was still a nobody. This is My heart for Shavuot.

Celebrating the Feast Now

For believers who attend a Spirit-filled church, there should already be a special commemoration of the Day of Pentecost each year. However, I have noticed that many churches do not seem to recognize this day on which the Holy Spirit was poured out on His New Covenant people and the inhabitants of Jerusalem.

This holiday does not appear on most calendars; the dates for Pentecost 2009-2012 are 5/29/09, 5/19/10, 6/8/11, and 5/27/12.[1] Remember that the feast will actually begin the *evening before* these dates. These days will not necessarily fall on a Sunday because they were chosen as the fiftieth day after Passover, rather than after the Sabbath of Passover week. Church calendar planners will choose the Sunday just before or after these dates for Pentecost. Check a church calendar to see which Sunday they have chosen, though it will be very close to the Jewish dates above.

Even if a church celebrates Pentecost, many do not fully understand the biblical connection to the Feast of Weeks, the very feast on which the Lord chose to grant miracle-working power to His followers.

The phrase, "Behold the Lamb of God" has little meaning, apart from an understanding of Passover; in the same way, the Day of Pentecost has its context and meaning in the Feast of Weeks. It is through the biblical calendar that we gain wisdom about God's appointed times and seasons.

I will offer here a few wonderful suggestions for celebrating this feast, whether in a church service or in a small gathering of kindred spirits who love to fellowship with the Lord and each other at His holy rehearsals.

1. Play anointed worship music. Sing, dance, and worship the Lord with much abandon and heartfelt

exuberance. Read Scriptures aloud to each other; there are many possible Scriptures, but here are a few of my favorites:

2. The Book of Ruth is closely associated with this feast, due to the commandment about the gleanings of the field coming in the same biblical passage as the Feast of Weeks. This historical romance is set in the days of the Judges, during the barley and wheat harvests. Ruth's testimony is rich with intimacy and has staggering implications for the Church-Israel relationship. Much more about Ruth and Boaz is revealed in the closing chapter of this book. It is very appropriate and rewarding to read it on this feast.

3. Any or all psalms are always appropriate. But in particular, read from the fifteen "Songs of Ascent," Psalms 120-134. These are festive songs that celebrate the joy of the worshipers as they ascend to Jerusalem's holy hill to worship the God of Israel.

4. The Ten Commandments, found in Deuteronomy 5:6-21, are extremely important standards to live by and to store in our hearts. In addition, reading them is a way of honoring the giving of the Torah to His covenant people. Also, Deuteronomy 6:4-9 is the pivotal biblical call to worship the one true God, recited by observant Jews every day of their lives. It also includes the verse that the Lord Jesus said was the most important command in the entire Bible, and therefore, it deserves the Church's full attention (see Matt. 22:37).

5. If you are hosting Jewish people or families, try to serve dairy products, such as cheesecake, or cheese-filled

raviolis and other related foods that do not contain any meat. It is a Jewish tradition to eat dairy foods on this holiday. Why do we eat dairy foods? We eat dairy because the sages liken the Torah to "milk and honey." Now, will you please eat some dairy?

6   Read the passages from Acts about the pouring out of the Holy Spirit, and any other verses the Lord will show you from His Word that concern the wondrous and energizing manifestations of the loving and powerful Holy Spirit of God.

7.   Give a special offering to any ministry the Lord will show you. Give in proportion to how the Lord has blessed you during the past year. Since receiving the prophetic word from Him concerning the poor, which I recorded in the previous section, I believe it will especially please Him if we give an offering to the poor at this season. You can choose any ministry that honors the Lord by helping the poor, whom He considers His friends. If you want to bless the poor in Israel, consider giving to "Vision for Israel," headed by Barry and Batya Segal (www.visionforisrael.com).

This chapter concludes the teachings on the spring feasts. *Amen!*

PART II

THE
FALL FEASTS
OF THE LORD

Chapter 6

THE MEMORIAL OF
BLASTING (TRUMPETS)

THE THREE FALL FEASTS

The four spring feasts formed a composite picture of the Lord Yeshua's first coming, including His sacrifice, resurrection, and His gift of the Holy Spirit. In the same manner, the three fall feasts create a stunning, three-fold revelation of Yeshua's return. His second coming will not be as a sin offering, but as the Dread Champion, the Righteous Judge, the Captain of the Armies of Heaven (in most translations, "the Lord of Hosts"), and the Reigning Sovereign of the Universe.

We have seen that one of the Hebrew words used of the feasts is *mikrah,* which could be translated, "rehearsal." These festivals, particularly those in the spring, recount God's past mighty acts in human history.

The Lord was never a passive or unconcerned God; rather, He was always actively intervening, even invading the affairs of men. *His incarnation as one of us is the most spectacular example of the Lord's lovesick and purposeful involvement in the earthly realm.*

In the spring, as we rehearse past memories, we are also encountering the person of the Lord in a very present reality. It is a far cry from a "stroll down memory lane." He is eternal and very much alive in the celebrations

137

of these appointed times. The Lord meets us as we meet with Him, and He does not intend for these ceremonies to be dry or religious in the slightest. They are intended to be intimate, experiential, intense, and if I dare to say it, even passionate. The heart begins to beat faster.

As the spring feasts symbolize past fulfillments, so the fall feasts could be better described as rehearsals of a future event. In fact, they are preparations for a series of events that comprise the Lord Yeshua's return.

The finality and irrevocability of His appearance in the skies cannot be over-emphasized. It will be too late to rehearse for this play when opening night is upon us. It will be too late to get ready and to make our robes white with the blood of the Lamb. It will be too late to trim our lamps and buy extra oil, which will light our way in that dark and terrible night. When the blast of the trumpet shatters the universe and penetrates our earthly atmosphere, it will be too late to clean up our lives.

The fall feasts are all about preparation for His Bride and the full restoration of His covenant people, Israel. We will look intently into the preparation needed for this cataclysmic day in the final chapter.

The Lord has given us these feasts so that we will be prepared when these things come upon us. He has provided holy and needful rehearsals, so that not one of His precious children will hear those bone-chilling and soul-shattering words, *"It is too late!"*

The three-fold panorama of the return of the Lord Jesus is comprised of the Feast of Trumpets, the Day of Atonement, and the Feast of Tabernacles. I intended to refer to this first fall feast as "The Feast of Trumpets" when I began writing this chapter. However, the Lord gave me a prophetic word in which He called it by a different name, one that is actually a more precise rendering of the Hebrew title. This word is recorded at the end of this chapter, but from now on, I will refer to this first fall feast as "The Memorial of Blasting," because the Lord corrected me on this point.

THE SEVENTH MONTH IS HOLY

The three fall feasts all take place in a fifteen-day period in the seventh biblical month of Tishri; on our calendar, this would be

September or early October. Students of the Bible have noticed that seven is a holy number to the Lord. From Genesis to Revelation, we see numerous references to the number seven, beginning with Creation and ending with the final judgments of the world. If we were to note every prophetic usage of the number seven, it would fill many chapters of this book. Let us look at a few examples that underscore the holiness of the seventh month on God's calendar.

The Lord God created the heavens and the earth in six days, but He set aside the seventh day as holy, and He ceased from His creative work. From this original design, the Lord designated the seventh day as special, a command that is reasserted throughout the Mosaic Law (see Lev. 23:3) and frequently referenced in the Gospels and Acts.

The Lord also reserved every seventh year as a "sabbatical" year; this meant that no plowing or sowing of the fields was to take place in the seventh year. The land was to enjoy its "Sabbath rest," and the Lord promised to give Israel enough food during the sixth year to sustain them until the next permissible planting and reaping (see Lev. 25:1-7).

This agricultural Sabbath year was so important to the Lord that He warned Israel of the punishment for future disobedience before they had even entered their land. If Israel ignored this law, they would be exiled from their land, and it would enjoy its time of rest without them (see Lev. 26:43). Later, when this tragic seventy-year exile occurred, the Lord again brought up the issue of the sabbatical year. It was not His desire to exile His people from the land He loved, but their stubborn refusal to let the land rest forced Him to give it one year of rest for every seventh year they had exploited it (see 2 Chron. 36:20-21).

In the Book of Revelation, the Lord Yeshua spoke of seven lamps, seven angels, and seven stars. He is described as a Lamb before the throne of God, having seven horns and seven eyes. The Lord tells us on four occasions that there are seven Spirits of God (see Rev. 1:5; 3:1; 4:5; 5:6). The scroll of the coming judgments is sealed with seven seals, and its contents reveal seven trumpets of punishment and seven bowls of unmitigated wrath.

In this holiest of months, the seventh month, all three of these connected feasts occur, all within an intense fifteen-day period.

A Prophetic Calendar: The Feasts of Israel

The Memorial of Blasting

Say to the Israelites: "On the first day of the seventh month you are to have a day of rest, a sacred assembly commemorated with trumpet blasts. Do no regular work, but present an offering made to the Lord by fire" (Leviticus 23:23-25).

The Memorial of Blasting is the only festival that falls on the first day of a month, at the sighting of the new moon. This is the darkest night in the lunar cycle, when only a tiny sliver of moon appears.

In ancient Israel, the exact night on which the new moon would appear was uncertain, due to an irregular number of days in the lunar cycle. While we estimate it to be twenty-eight days, the true number averages a bit over twenty-nine days. Therefore, designated Jewish authorities would keep watch for the sighting of the moon and would sound the trumpet to notify the people that the new month had begun.

In the case of this feast, it was critical that Israel was prepared for that moment when the ram's horn, or *shofar*, would blast through the Judean countryside, and signal fires would be lit from hill to hill. Its long, penetrating sound created godly fear and awe, shaking us out of complacency, and bringing the same response we feel when we hear the siren of an ambulance shattering the quiet night.

The *shofar* is sounded on the opening evening of this special day; in addition, the Jewish people have incorporated three specific types of blasts throughout the twenty-four hour observance.

The ram's horn produces two tones: a lower and a higher tone. One blast hits the low note quickly, and then holds the high tone as a long, steady note. The second type of blast consists of three shorter repetitions of both notes. The third kind of blast has a staccato repetition of the higher note, which could be likened to the hammering of a woodpecker, echoing through the woods. It is easier for you to simply hear these blasts than it is for me to describe them in words. Still, I try.

It is interesting that, at this particular holiday, we are not recounting any victory or event from Israel's history. In fact, the Lord does not really explain the meaning of this feast. He simply says that we are to hold a sacred assembly, marked by the blasts of the ram's horn, and do no regular work. This feast falls in September or early October, as do the other two connected feasts.

There were two types of trumpets cited in the Bible. One was the ram's horn (*shofar*), reminiscent of the ram caught in the thicket by its horns, who became the substitute for Isaac on the altar of sacrifice. The other type was a pair of trumpets, hammered in silver, which the Lord described to Moses in Numbers 10. Both types are sacred and have ceremonial functions in the Lord's feasts, as well as other uses.

Since the biblical passage on the Memorial of Blasting does not specify which kind of trumpet is to be used, we cannot be certain. However, it is likely the silver trumpets, which are specifically connected to New Moon celebrations and the feasts in Numbers 10; this holiday is both a New Moon celebration and a feast. Alternatively, it could be referring to the ram's horn, due to a reference to the *shofar* used at the Day of Atonement, only ten days later. Even if God's original intent was the silver trumpets, it is acceptable to blow the *shofar* on this feast, since these instruments are more accessible than silver trumpets and have been blown for thousands of years by observant Jews. You can order a *shofar* from Eagles' Wings at www.eagleswings.to.

First, let us look at the biblical functions of blowing either the ram's horn or the silver trumpets described in Numbers. The following scriptural examples were compiled by Kevin Howard and Marvin Rosenthal.[1] One purpose was to assemble the tribes for breaking camp and setting out (see Num. 10:1-7). A second function was for rejoicing at His sacred assemblies, feasts, and New Moon celebrations (see Lev. 23:24; Num. 10:10). A third use was to gain victory in a military battle, muster the army for war, or sound an alarm for battle (see Num. 10:9; Judg. 3:27; 7:22; Neh. 4:20; Ezek. 33:3). The fourth occasion was to install a new king (see 1 Kings 1:34; 2 Kings 11:14).

All four of these functions of the trumpet remind us of the Lord's return:

1. We will break camp on this earth and set out for our destination in His Kingdom;

2. We will rejoice at the largest sacred assembly ever called, meeting Him in the air;

3. We will sound the imminent battle cry to the nations, as the Dread Champion finally appears to wage war against His enemies;

4. We will coronate the returning and reigning King of Israel, as Lord over all the earth.

The kingdom of the world has become the kingdom of our Lord and of His Christ, and He will reign for ever and ever (Revelation 11:15).

"ROSH HASHANNAH"

Most people believe that this holiday is called *Rosh HaShannah*, which literally means, "the head of the year." In Jewish tradition, since the destruction of the Temple and the sacrifice system, it has become the Jewish New Year celebration. It is not illogical to call this feast "the New Year," because the fall months do mark the beginning of the civil year, just as in our culture, the school year begins in September.

Almost all Jewish families observe this holiday as the New Year. It is a very loving and supportive gesture to wish our Jewish friends and colleagues a good and healthy year when this season rolls around. I certainly greet people this way.

Even so, to be biblically precise, the Lord stated that the spring month of Nisan, the month of Passover, was to be considered the first month in the Hebraic year. And so, we have more than one type of New Year to contend with. If we add the Roman New Year in early January to our menu, we would be starting our year three times a year! That is really a bit much, don't you think?

It is not at all wrong to call this feast "Rosh HaShannah," because it is widely known by this name. However, I think the Lord is also pleased when we call it by the name many Bibles use, which is the "Feast of Trumpets." Finally, since the Lord showed me that it is literally called "The Memorial of Blasting" *(Zich'ron T'ruah)* in Leviticus 23:23-25, that is a good name as well. However, if you do call it the Memorial of Blasting, no one else will know what you mean; you will have to tell them to read my book!

It is traditional on this holiday to eat apples dipped in honey, which symbolizes wishing each other a sweet year to come. Our family usually eats our apples and honey before I serve the holiday meal on the evening that begins the feast. Always remember that all biblical holidays begin *the evening before* the day that is noted on normal calendars.

We welcome this feast as the sun sets, with the sweetness of apples and honey, which reminds us of how precious and sweet is our Lord's love and provision to us, and our prayers for His blessings on the coming year.

In case anyone is interested, I usually cook a brisket in burgundy, water, tomato paste, and dried onion soup mix (this makes awesome gravy), with potatoes, several vegetables, and some kind of death-by-chocolate dessert. I just thought you'd like to know! I also serve a similar meal on the eve of Yom Kippur, before we fast, and also on Passover, except for a few changes in the menu to accommodate the food limitations discussed in chapter three.

HE IS LORD OF THE FEASTS

As has become obvious throughout this book, I have a high accountability to the Lord for my private obedience with regard to these biblical feasts. I am very aware that He sees every decision I make concerning these days, whether or not anyone else is aware of what I do. I try to be obedient to the scriptural commandments to "do no regular work" on these days. This would include laundry, shopping, work, banking or business, and most forms of entertainment.

However, there have been many times in my walk with God when I was really not sure how to apply His biblical instructions to my practical life as a mother of young children. After coming back to the States from Israel when the children were little, I needed to determine how to instruct them about keeping these feasts.

They would often ask me, "*Ima*, are we allowed to do this or that?" *Ima* is the Hebrew name for "Mommy." We had to make many decisions over those years, hoping they were acceptable to God. One was to let them watch the only two movies we owned that were of Jewish content. These consisted of a battered old video of "Fiddler on the Roof," and "Yentl," a particularly beautiful Barbra Streisand film, set in late 19th-century eastern Europe in a Jewish Bible school for boys, called a *yeshiva*. Perhaps not all Christians would appreciate this movie, but it is among my favorites. This is just one example of my trying to honor the biblical command, while making practical decisions about how we would spend these "days off."

Now, to the point I was actually trying to make. Since 2005, I have been consistently attending a series of intense repentance conferences with other intercessors, sponsored by World for Jesus Ministries, led by Nita Johnson. Through these difficult meetings, the Lord has called for His church to weep and deeply repent on behalf of our nation, for the shedding of innocent blood on American soil.[2]

These conferences tend to be scheduled on biblical holidays, due to the spiritual significance of meeting for intense prayer at these appointed times. In the fall of 2005, the Gathering was scheduled to begin on the day after the Memorial of Blasting. As I began to make the travel arrangements for myself and others, I realized that the only day we could travel to the conference was on this holiday. I was grieved and deeply conflicted as I realized this. The way I felt about this high holy day would make it impossible to engage in all of the activity and commercial transactions involved in this trip. These included the flights, car rental, hotel and restaurant arrangements, as well as being away from my family, when I have always been at home with them on these feasts.

I remembered how Peter felt when he had the vision of a sheet being let down from Heaven, full of crawling and creeping things, to which the Lord said, *"Arise, Peter, kill and eat."*

Peter replied, "By no means, Lord, I have never eaten anything unclean." The Lord answered, *"Do not call anything impure that God has made clean."* He was showing Peter that this vision pertained to his ministry to the Gentiles, and was not actually about food. After the spiritual meaning was shown to him, the sheet was taken back into Heaven, and he was not required to eat these creatures (see Acts 10:9-16).

As Peter had felt, I also felt conflicted, because I had never done such a thing on a biblical feast. I said to the Lord, "You know I do not transact business on Your feast days. I can't travel on 'Rosh HaShannah,' doing all that work, paying money, carrying heavy baggage, and transacting all manners of business." I decided I absolutely could not do this, for it would violate my life's testimony of obedience. I would skip the conference, but I wasn't sure if this was what the Lord would want me to do.

After praying about it for about a week, I received a prophetic word. The Lord asked me, *"How would you honor Me on this day if you stayed home?"*

I told Him I would stay at home with my family, worship, rest, and read my Bible, as I have done for many years. The intercessors, with whom I would normally be meeting for prayer on this festival, would be away at the conference; I would simply meet with God in my home.

He continued, *"How would you honor Me if you traveled on that day?"*

I answered that while spending the whole day traveling, I would think about the purposes for this trip, help my friends with all the travel arrangements, and spend three days weeping for the salvation of this nation.

His simple answer set me free from my mental anguish.

"Then go, and honor Me."

The Spirit of the Lord is able to cut through all of my fears and normal prohibitions, concerning the "right" and "wrong" way to honor these feast days.

As Yeshua said, "The Son of Man is Lord of the Sabbath" (Luke 6:5).

In the same way, the Son of Man is Lord of His own feast days. I honored Him by going to that gathering, and much good fruit was brought forth for me personally, and for our beloved America.

While we all worship the same Lord, we do not have the same assignments and destinies in our lives. Whether or not you decide to incorporate any of these feasts into your lifestyle, you are dearly beloved, and the Lord will guide you into your perfect destiny as you earnestly seek Him for wisdom.

The Terrible Day of the Lord

In ancient Israel, the prophesied "Day of the Lord" must have seemed like a wonderful, future day of deliverance and peace from the ruthless domination of outsiders.

The Israelites had been oppressed in an almost unending series of conquests, captivities, sieges, and wars. First, they were slaves in Egypt and were then intermittently under the tyranny of Canaanites during the days of the Judges. With periods of peace and independence, Israel endured the cruelty of the following successive Gentile superpowers: Assyria, Babylon, Medo-Persia, Greece, and Rome (see Dan. 2:31-43; 7:2-7).

Despite Israel's idealistic longings, the Lord warned them not to look forward to "that day," but rather, to dread it.

> *Woe to you who long for the day of the Lord! Why do you long for the day of the Lord? That day will be darkness, not light.*
>
> *It will be as though a man fled from a lion only to meet a bear, as though he entered his house and rested his hand on the wall only to have a snake bite him.*
>
> *Will not the day of the Lord be darkness, not light— pitch dark, without a ray of brightness?* (Amos 5:18-20).

> *That day will be a day of wrath, a day of distress and anguish, a day of trouble and ruin, a day of darkness and gloom, a day of clouds and blackness, a day of trumpet and battle cry against the fortified cities and against the corner towers* (Zephaniah 1:15-16).

The prophet Joel also warned that the Day of the Blast of the Trumpet is a terrible day, a siren-like wail of warning, and a wakeful battle cry to shake us out of our complacency:

> Blow the trumpet in Zion, sound the alarm on My holy hill. Let all who live in the land tremble, for the day of the Lord is coming, it is close at hand—a day of darkness and gloom, of clouds and blackness (Joel 2:1-2).

Not only did ancient Israel look forward to that day, but also charismatic Christians and Messianic Jews tend to dance joyfully to songs about the day when the trumpet will sound; the Church is eagerly anticipating the Day of the Lord. This is not completely wrong, and I am able to dance joyfully to these songs, as well. Even so, my spirit is aware that we may be misunderstanding the terror and severity of that day of reckoning, on which the Lord Himself sounds the *shofar*.

In the New Covenant, Peter also warns believers that this day will be terrifying and destructive. It will not only be dreadful for the unprepared, but I believe it will also be a dark and frightening day for the righteous. The point is that this will not be a day of happiness and celebration.

Imagine how Noah and his family felt when the door of the ark was closed, and they had to see hundreds of their neighbors and relatives left outside the ark of safety, as the terrible storm descended. Genesis 7:16 says that "the Lord shut him in." This means that the door could only be shut from the outside, because the Lord knew that if Noah was able to open the door from the inside, he would have been moved by the pleading of his neighbors to do so.[3]

> The day of the Lord will come like a thief. The heavens will disappear with a roar; the elements will be destroyed by fire, and the earth and everything in it will be laid bare . . . that day will bring about the destruction of the heavens by fire, and the elements will melt in the heat.

If it is hard for the righteous to be saved, what will become of the ungodly and the sinner? (2 Peter 3:10,12; 1 Peter 4:18).

Even so, Joel added comfort to his warning, and Paul confirmed that "all who call of the name of the Lord will be saved" (Joel 2:32; Rom. 10:13).

HAS THE BRIDE MADE HERSELF READY?

The *shofar* blast was intended to bring trembling and self-reflection, to dissipate complacency and self-contained independence. The Lord is uncontrollable, uncontainable, and unpredictable. He makes us uncomfortable. His Day of Trumpets is a wake-up call after a long, dry summer.

The trumpet blast is symbolic of the return of the Lord. The Lord told us that He will come on a day we do not expect it; He will surprise us. It is too late to get ready when the midnight cry rings out. *Our clothing must be clean and ready for the appointed day when the trumpet sounds, the Bridegroom is announced, and the door to the wedding banquet is shut.*

> *At that time, the sign of the Son of Man will appear in the sky, and all the nations of the earth will mourn. They will see the Son of Man coming on the clouds of the sky with power and great glory. And He will send his angels with a loud* **trumpet call,** *and they will gather His elect from the four winds, from one end of the heavens to the other...*
>
> *If the owner of the house had known at what time the thief was coming, he would have kept watch and would not have let his house be broken into. So you also must be ready, because the Son of Man will come at an hour when you do not expect Him...*
>
> *At midnight the cry rang out: "Here's the bridegroom! Come out to meet him!" Then all the virgins woke up and trimmed their lamps. The foolish ones said to the wise, "Give us some of your oil; our lamps are going out."*

> *"No," they replied. "There may not be enough for*
> *both us and you... go... and buy some for yourselves."*
> *But while they were on their way to buy the oil, the bride-*
> *groom arrived. The virgins who were ready went in with*
> *him to the wedding banquet. And the door was shut.*
> *For the wedding of the Lamb has come, and His bride*
> *has made herself ready* (Matthew 24:30-31;43-44;
> 25:6-10; Revelation 19:7b).

Surely, the Memorial of Blasting is a rehearsal for the return of the Lord Jesus. He has warned us to prepare our hearts for that day, that we would be found doing the Master's will in the season of His coming.

HONORING THE MEMORIAL OF BLASTING TODAY

Although this day is truly a solemn assembly, it is hard for Spirit-filled believers to stay solemn. The Lord has given us joy as we celebrate, although there is a special dignity and seriousness that accompanies the Memorial of Blasting and the Day of Atonement. The culmination of our joy does not occur until the Feast of Tabernacles.

If you feel a desire to observe this special day but aren't sure how to go about it, there are a couple of options. One option is to visit a traditional synagogue and to try to enter into the worship service. However, this could be either enjoyable or frustrating, depending on your personality, knowledge base, and spiritual inclinations.

Some believers might feel "lost" in such a service, which moves through a large number of liturgical prayers and readings that are almost exclusively in Hebrew. Apart from passages that are translated, the visitor will have no idea what he or she is praying and will not be able to keep up with the flow. Some high holiday prayer books contain a good amount of English translation, and this is always beneficial to outsiders who are not well-versed in the Hebrew language.

Even so, many Christians would prefer a ceremony that is not only understandable in English, but that also speaks of the Messiah; some prefer a less formal service, with more personal and spontaneous prayers. Many will not feel completely free to relax and worship the Lord in the formal synagogue service, although some in the Messianic movement both enjoy and benefit from this path.

Because of my relationship with the Lord and personal preferences, I am more comfortable in an environment of creative worship, Spirit-driven prayer, Scripture reading, prophetic acts, and anointed music. While each one is free to seek the Lord about what would honor Him on this day, I will share a sample of how our small prayer group has celebrated this feast in our meetings.

There is probably more material listed below than you might need, but the reader can select any of these suggestions to build a custom-made special prayer and worship service for those motivated to honor the Lord in this way. As you will see, the reading of the Scriptures, worshipful songs, and intercessory prayer are the key elements.

By the way, you can also use this sample service as a model on which to build a worship service for the Feast of Weeks, Day of Atonement, Tabernacles, Purim, or Hanukah. Of course, the Scripture readings and songs might be modified to fit the theme of each holiday.

As with all Jewish holidays, this feast will fall on a different date each year. However, our normal calendars have this holiday marked as "Rosh HaShannah," and ten days later, the Day of Atonement is called "Yom Kippur" on most regular calendars.

To make it easier to plan your service, let me begin by recommending some of the best worship CDs that we have used countless times to usher us into the Presence of God. Certain songs will be perfect to insert between these passages of Scripture. In this way, the participants do not become tired. It is healthy to break up any service with anointed songs, which give you a chance to sing, raise your hands, dance, or just enjoy soaking in the goodness of the Lord.

Below, I have not listed every CD these artists have produced. I am listing the ones that pertain to this sample worship service. Each list is not meant to be exhaustive of what is available, and you can find their other CDs on their Web sites.

The first group of songs I will recommend can be found at www.galilee-ofthenations.com which is a division of www.integritymusic.com.

- Ted Pearce's *Zealous Over Zion*
- *The Road to Jerusalem*, which is a Messianic compilation CD produced by Yochanan Ben Yehuda, and sung by a variety of artists.
- Barry and Batya Segal's *Sh'ma Yisrael* and *Go Through the Gates*
- *Adonai,* a compilation of Messianic artists

The second group is from Messianic worship leader, Paul Wilbur. He has produced some of the most excellent music available for worship. His Web site is www.wilburministries.org.

- *Jerusalem Arise!*
- *The Watchman*

Our beloved brother, Marty Goetz, has given us some of the sweetest and deepest ballads of worship ever to be recorded. His Web site is www.martygoetz.com.

- *The Love of God*

THE MEMORIAL OF BLASTING: A JOEL 2 SOLEMN ASSEMBLY

Blow the Shofar, if there is a participant who can blow it. If not, you can use either the first song listed below, or the last song listed, as a substitute for a live blast. Both of these recordings contain the sound of the shofar and can replace a live performance. Below, the CD titles are italicized, while the song titles are not.

Songs: "Aaronic Benediction" from *Adonai,* track 1 (includes shofar blast)

"Praise Adonai" from *Jerusalem Arise!* track 6, also found on *The Road to Jerusalem*, track 12.

Readings:

Leviticus 23:23-25

Numbers 10:9

Psalm 92 (read in unison)

Psalm 98 (verse 6 is about the Feast of Trumpets)

Songs: "Lord God of Abraham" from *The Watchman*, track 1. Optionally, if you want more worship music, continue to track 2 on *The Watchman*, which is a highly energetic and lengthy rendition of "Adonai" (the song, not connected to the CD by that same title.)

Readings:

Psalm 84 (read in unison)

Psalm 27:4-6

Psalm 19:7-11

Psalm 105:8-11

Songs: "Go Through the Gates" from the CD *Go Through the Gates*, track 3, and/or, "O Shout for Joy" from *The Watchman*, track 3

Readings:

Psalm 102:13-18

Psalm 24:7-10

Ephesians 2:11-13

Isaiah 56:6-7

Songs: For an energetic song, play "Zealous Over Zion" from *The Road to Jerusalem*, track 6. (this same song is also track 1 on the CD *Zealous Over Zion*), and/or, for a slower, softer song, play "For Zion's Sake" from *The Love of God*, track 8 (although the back cover says "track 9," it is really on track 8.)

Readings:

Isaiah 62:1,6-7;10-11

Romans 11:25-27

Songs: "Sh'ma Yisrael" from *The Road to Jerusalem*, track 1 (includes shofar blast). This track spills smoothly into track 2, a short, spoken declaration from Esther. As this concludes, fade volume quickly before track 3 begins.

Silence before the Lord for about a minute

Blow the shofar, if one is available.

Have a time of prayer, if desired:

Pray for Israel, using any or all of the Scriptures included in this service. The verses can serve as a springboard for further prayer.

Songs that can be played softly in the background, or in addition to the prayer segments: "Let the Weight of Your Glory Fall" and next two tracks, "For Your Name is Holy" and "Kadosh" from *Jerusalem Arise!* (tracks 11, 12, and 13.) Other gentle, worshipful music can be used at any time during the service.

Readings:

Psalm 102:13-18

Isaiah 62:1,6-7; 10-11

Romans 9:1-5

Romans 11:1,11-12; 17-18; 24-27

Pray for America (play any songs and read any Scriptures that promote intercession and repentance.)

2 Chronicles 7:14

Daniel 9:4-19

Psalm 33:10-11

If desired, pray for your region and the Church. Close the service with a song or the blast of the shofar once more. *(If you do this service on the Day of Atonement, do not serve food or coffee after the meeting, unless your meeting ends at, or after sunset, the end of the 24-hour fast.)*

I hope that these ideas are of practical help to the reader. We will now close this chapter with the Lord's own heart for the Feast of Trumpets.

THE LORD'S HEART FOR THIS FEAST

As I was completing this chapter, I asked the Lord to show me His heart for this feast and waited to see if He would give me a special word to submit to the reader. Before He spoke His Word to me, the Lord first told me to read Numbers, chapter 10, and He called my attention to verse 9.

> *When you go into battle in your land against an enemy who is oppressing you, sound a blast of the trumpets. Then*

you will be remembered by the Lord your God and rescued from your enemies (Numbers 10:9).

After reading this verse, He reminded me of a terrible attack I had undergone two nights before, somewhat similar to the "Terror Test" I recorded in Chapter Four of *Coffee Talks With Messiah*.[4]

In this current incident, I had just returned from a long day of ministry, and while sleeping, experienced overwhelming and paralyzing terror from the enemy; I am not to share the details of this oppression, because the enemy is not worth the paper, nor does he deserve any recognition.

As I was warring in my mind against this fearful evil, I found myself unable to dispel it. After what seemed like a long, losing battle, I didn't know what more I could do, and was tempted to give up. I then felt the Holy Spirit show me to just worship Adonai (the Lord), rather than continue to fight.

As I worshiped Him in my mind, ignoring the force of fear still upon me, I heard my daughter Keren's voice call out to me, a welcomed interruption in the midst of severe oppression. As I heard her sweet voice, I knew that she was still awake, and if I called out to her, she would come in and pray for me, and this crushing dread would leave. I forced myself to cry out her name as loud as I could, and suddenly I was awake, and the evil presence was gone.

Looking at the clock, I realized it was almost midnight, and no one was at home besides Keren and me. I walked to her room, to tell her what had just happened to me and how hearing her voice had helped me. However, she had been asleep for quite a while and had not actually called out to me, despite what my ears heard. It was the Lord, sending me her voice of comfort so that I could rally my strength and escape from the onslaught.

As I recalled this event, the Lord showed me the words of Moses, which he spoke whenever the ark would set out on the journey: "Rise up, O Lord! May Your enemies be scattered; may Your foes flee before You" (Num. 10:35).

He then asked me, *"What does Keren's name mean?"*

I was stunned as I realized the other meaning of her Hebrew name, *Keren Chen.* We had named her a "Ray of Grace." *Keren* means a ray of the sun, but its primary meaning in Hebrew is *horn*. Perhaps the sun's rays were so named because of their shape, flaring out at the ends, like a horn. When King David used the phrase "the horn of my salvation," the Hebrew reads, *"keren yishi"* (Ps. 18:2).

And so, through this unsettling incident, the Lord showed me that by crying out Keren's name, I was raising a desperate cry to Him, sounding the alarm. In the passage above, God had promised to *remember us* and to save us from our enemies when He heard the sound of the trumpet in a fierce battle. It was in this context that He spoke the following word to me this morning, in response to my request to show me His heart for this feast:

> The battle cry has gone out and **must** be sounded. My people do not understand the concept of a memorial blast before the Lord, being heard by My ears and causing Me to remember them in their hour of adversity.
>
> When you sound the horn, the keren yishi [horn of my salvation], you are raising a piercing and penetrating cry for help, which I cannot help but respond to. My heart is deeply moved when I hear the sound of My people who love Me and fear Me and are called according to My Name. When I hear them raise the battle sound, that desperate alarm, **"Help me, Adonai,"** that is how I hear it with My ears.
>
> I remember them and come and save them from My enemies. And when they sound the blast of remembrance on My feasts and new moons, it is a sound of joy and gladness, it is the voice of the Bridegroom and the voice of the Bride, mingled together in a cry of love, in a shout of passion!
>
> Get ready, for your Bridegroom comes! Sound the horn and blow the trumpet; say to the cities of Judah, "Behold Your God." Say to My Bride, "Behold your Bridegroom."
>
> I will remember you when you blow the trumpet blast of remembrance. I will come to you when you cry out to Me to save you from your enemies; when I hear the sound of your cry, I will remember.

That is why this day is called the "Memorial of Blasting." It is true that you are remembering Me by obeying this command, but **your** memorial is rising up to Me! It causes Me to remember you.

That is why I do not explain this feast, as saying, "When you celebrate this feast, you are commemorating such-and-such, an event I have done for you." **No!** This holiday is a **fire drill!** You are practicing sounding the alarm so that I will remember **you** in the day of trouble. You are releasing the trust that will need to come when you are in the life-and-death battle with your enemy, and you will need to learn how to sound the battle cry and raise the alarm.

You will need to know, from past experiences that were not life and death, that I came to your rescue; I heard and responded to your battle cry. I came and remembered you because your memorial of blasting has come up before Me many times, and I will remember you in your final life-and-death battle.

My people need to sound the memorial blast and be silent before Me. Then they need to cry out to Me with their voices, to cry out and call upon Me to come and save them, to come and rescue them from the fangs of the fierce lion that is already waiting to devour My people.

A great slaughter is being prepared. Learn to blow the trumpet in Zion and teach each other to sound a literal alarm on My holy mountain. Thus you shall be saved from your enemies, and thus says your God. I AM the Lord your God.

I will close this chapter by blessing each reader with the Lord's fervent desire for each one He has created:

"May your name be inscribed and sealed in the Lamb's Book of Life!" Amen.

Chapter 7

THE DAY OF ATONEMENT

Passover was the day of our personal atonement, the day the perfect Lamb was sacrificed in our place. We are the ones who were rescued from death because a substitute lamb was found; we are like Isaac, freed from the altar of death. Yeshua's precious blood must be personally applied to the doorposts of our hearts, and this brings each individual to salvation in the New Covenant.

Now we will examine the original purposes, as well as the Messianic fulfillment, of the holiest day on the Jewish calendar: *Yom HaKippurim*, also called "Yom Kippur" or the "Day of Atonement." This day comes ten days after the Memorial of Blasting, and it is also a foreshadowing of the Lord's sacrifice, yet in a different way from Passover's fulfillment.

The Hebrew word *kippur* means covering or atonement. In the Old Testament sacrifice system, the sins of the high priest and the sins of the people were "covered" by the blood of bulls and goats. According to the precise instructions of the Lord to Moses and Aaron's descendants, this blood was carefully applied to the Atonement Cover, the altar of incense, the Tent of Meeting, and the altar of sacrifice. The Atonement Cover was behind the curtain in the Holy of Holies, while the altar of incense was in front of the curtain in the Holy Place.

This covering was effectual, yet temporary, in that it needed to be reapplied every year at this time. We also learn later, in the Book of Hebrews, that the conscience of the worshiper was not truly cleansed by this life-preserving ceremony (see Heb. 9:8-9). Even so, the Lord considered the people cleansed within the ordained framework of the sacrificial system, before Yeshua came to earth and offered Himself.

In Jewish tradition, the ten days between the Memorial of Blasting and the Day of Atonement are called "the Days of Awe." This is considered a consecrated period of time, when we reflect on our walk with God and the condition of our hearts. Observant Jews will use this time to repent of all known sins committed within the last year, so that on the soul-afflicting fast day, their legal records will be "cleared" of guilt by the Judge. The blessing they use to bless one another during these ten days and on the Day of Atonement is "May you be inscribed and sealed in the Book of Life."

It is very biblical to bless someone in this way. Moses referred to this Book, as did King David and the prophet Daniel (see Exod. 32:32-33; Ps. 69:28; Dan. 12:1). The Lord Yeshua spoke of it in Luke 10:20, and other New Covenant references include Philippians 4:3; Revelation 3:5; 20:15; and 21:27.

However, we know that since Messiah's sacrifice, there is only one way to have your name found in the Book of Life. Even though repentance and fasting are important elements, those who understand the cost of atonement realize that no amount of self-sacrifice can permanently remove sin. The shedding of innocent blood was always the method of atonement required by our holy God. Fasting simply does not replace the need for a blood atonement, as we will explore throughout this chapter.

For the life of a creature is in the blood, and I have given it to you to make atonement for yourselves on the altar; it is the blood that makes atonement for one's life. Therefore, I say to the Israelites, "None of you may eat blood, nor may an alien living among you eat blood" (Leviticus 17:11-12).

If anyone's name was not found written in the book of life, he was thrown into the lake of fire (Revelation 20:15).

Even so, the Lord sees every heart, and to the sincerely repentant, He will reveal Himself. To those observant Jews who seek Him, and ask Him to restore the temple sacrifice system to the Jewish people, He will reveal Himself as the perfect and final sacrifice for sin, and they will receive Him. This is the gracious character of the God we serve.

AFFLICT YOUR SOULS WITH POVERTY

The tenth day of this seventh month is the Day of Atonement. Hold a sacred assembly and deny yourselves, and present an offering made to the Lord by fire. Do no work on that day because it is the Day of Atonement, when atonement is made for you before the Lord your God... to cleanse you. Then, before the Lord, you will be clean from all your sins (Leviticus 23:26-28; 16:30).

In the days of the Tent of Meeting, as well as the first and second temple, this solemn day required a very precise service of sacrifices and the sprinkling of blood. Only the high priest could perform this exacting duty in the Holy of Holies, and he was not to enter this inner chamber on any other day of the year.

At the destruction of the second temple in A.D. 70, all of the daily and yearly sacrifices ceased, and the priestly descendants of Aaron could no longer perform the duties the Lord had laid out for them. They were now dispersed from Israel into foreign lands and had no access to Jerusalem or its temple.

Because the cleansing of their souls depended on performing these carefully applied blood sacrifices, the Jewish people were at a loss as to how to make atonement for their souls. I am speaking of Jewish people who did not yet realize that Yeshua of Nazareth had made atonement with His own blood for the world's sins, including those of His people Israel. We will examine the sacrificial requirements and how the Lord Yeshua fulfilled them in the next section. For the moment, let us focus on the command to fast.

In the absence of blood sacrifice, the only instruction that remained and could be obeyed by Jews in other nations was the command to "deny yourselves" (NIV). This phrase is rendered "afflict your souls" in the New King James Version. The verb used in Hebrew is *anitem et naf'shotechem,* which means "to make poor your souls." This has always been understood to mean fasting from all food and drink. And so, a rigorous fast has been observed for this twenty-four hour period since the giving of the Law some 3,400 years ago.

However, during periods of Israel's apostasy, there were a number of wicked Israelite kings who neither observed nor enforced this command; thus, while there was always a remnant who fasted on this holy day, many years were marked by a general, national disobedience. There are many today who choose not to fast on Yom Kippur, both in Israel and abroad; they have decided that this ritual is an antiquated relic without benefit.

The concept of "afflicting your souls with poverty" was echoed in one of the most well-known teachings in the Gospels. The Lord Jesus pronounced a series of blessings upon those who display godly attitudes in a teaching found in Matthew 5:3-10, often called the "Sermon on the Mount." The first blessing He spoke was *"Blessed are the poor in spirit, for theirs is the kingdom of heaven."* The word for "poor" is the Hebrew word *ani,* the same verb as the one used in Leviticus 23.

In another teaching, the Lord spoke of self-denial:

> *If anyone would come after Me, he must deny himself and take up his cross and follow Me* (Matthew 16:24).

While the Day of Atonement is the only commanded fast in the biblical calendar, the Lord was speaking here about a fasted lifestyle, although He was not only referring to food. He was warning us that to follow Him, whether we are Jew or Gentile, we must learn to deny ourselves, to become "poor in spirit," and to deny the urgent demands of our fleshly nature. This refers to denying pride and self-importance, and taking on a humble and servant-like attitude. It also includes some physical self-denial, although it is natural to desire food, comfort, shelter, sleep, and physical safety. It goes against our instincts to deny ourselves through fasting and self-sacrifice. However, this is the cost of discipleship.

This does not mean that we always live a punishing or ascetic life, but it does mean that our bellies are not our god, and our convenience is not God's highest concern. There are seasons for joy and celebration, for abundant feasting and blissful resting. The Hebrews knew how to feast and how to fast. They were acquainted with tambourines and dancing, as well as sackcloth and wailing in the streets. There is "a time to weep and a time to laugh, a time to mourn and a time to dance" (Eccles. 3:4).

As we learn to discipline ourselves, we might fast one meal a week or forty days a year. A long fast could be a partial fast, where one is still eating, but the intake is small, and the choices are limited. My daughters and I practice this method from time to time, and it is very manageable for a longer period of seeking the Lord. A fast from all food is difficult, but it is not as impossible as our fears would tell us. However, I always drink some water on a three-day fast, because I become too weak from dehydration after the first day. For an awesome book on the incredible breakthrough that comes through the fasted lifestyle, read *The Hidden Power of Prayer and Fasting* by Mahesh Chavda.[1]

Some might give up meat, sweets, television, sports, or other pleasures we forsake for a season to pursue the incomparable pleasure of His intimate friendship. The Lord will gently help each believer know what He would like us to do. He Himself modeled this lifestyle and embodied this teaching so that we could walk as He walked. The Lord Yeshua did not live for His own personal gratification, and neither should we.

Despite all this, we cannot help but be filled with unspeakable joy, because of how wonderful the Lord is, and how much He has done for us. Even on Yom Kippur, while we are fasting and our bodies are grumbling about it, we cannot repress our joy. Even on this solemn day, while in prayer and fasting and without my beloved coffee, my dear fellow-intercessors and I have still found ourselves dancing with joy.

The Day of Atonement speaks of sanctification, a lifestyle in which our flesh comes into alignment with our spirit, rather than the other way around. It calls the Bride to a life of discipline and purpose, in which we understand the seriousness of our sins and what they cost the Lord. We are required to love Him more than we love our own flesh and pleasures, our own bank accounts, and even our own family members. This is part of living the sanctified life and the crucified life, though it is an unpopular Gospel in our self-indulgent culture. Consider the most difficult words of the Lord Jesus:

> *Anyone who loves his father or mother more than Me is not worthy of Me; anyone who loves his son or daughter more than Me is not worthy of Me; and anyone who does not take up his cross and follow Me is not worthy of Me. Whoever finds his life will lose it, and whoever loses his life for My sake will find it* (Matthew 10:37-39).

Most of us have read these words, and we give mental agreement to them. But it seems that very few believers actually live as if the Lord was deadly serious about His standards of our worthiness. If He really meant what He said, and I think that He did, many of us have a lot to think about, including myself.

The sanctified life is a life dedicated to serving the Lord, not one filled with our own agendas, entertainment, and ambitions. To deny ourselves might even mean moving to another country and being martyred there. The higher the calling, the higher the price one must pay. At Passover, we learned to endure the bitter, while enjoying the sweet.

The cup the Lord drank was bitter, so that our cup could be sweet. Even so, we also must drink of the bitter cup at times, as we follow Him wherever He leads. When James and John asked Yeshua if they could be seated at His right and left hand in His glorious Kingdom, He asked them if they could drink His cup or be immersed in the immersion of suffering He would undergo. The phrase "drinking His cup" was a metaphor for sharing in His destiny of martyrdom. They answered that they could, and He replied:

> *You will drink the cup I drink and be baptized with the baptism I am baptized with, but to sit at My right or My left is not for Me to grant* (Mark 10:39-40).

Once when I was taking communion alone, the Lord granted me an amazing experience. After I had eaten the piece of matzah and was meditating on the cup of His suffering, I sensed His presence with me in the room. I could see with the eyes of my heart that the Lord was also holding a cup in His hand, and that He wanted to drink it with me.

I held out my cup of grape juice to Him. Just before drinking His cup, the Lord held it out toward me, and He spoke a traditional Jewish blessing: *"L'chaim!"* For those who have seen *Fiddler on the Roof,* you will remember that when drinking a toast to the bride and groom at a Jewish wedding, we declare, "L'chaim!" This means, "To life!" I noticed that the Lord had a bittersweet smile on His face as He pronounced this toast. The Lord was drinking the remembrance of His suffering, and I was drinking nothing but life.

I answered Him, *"L'chaim bi'shua,"* which means, "to life in Yeshua." Before drinking, I added, "It's death to You, but it's life to me."

I sensed that the Lord didn't want me to watch Him as He drank the bitter cup and as He remembered the bitterness that it represented. I closed my eyes, and we drank it together. The Lord's word for His children as they take communion is *"What was the cup of bitterness and death to Me is the cup of life to you."*

The value of Yeshua's blood is beyond our ability to imagine, but we trust in it even if we cannot fully understand it. This was an incredibly sacred and special moment to me, and I will never forget it.

THE BLOOD SACRIFICE

Leviticus 16 gives us the most detailed biblical description of the high priest's responsibilities on this exacting and arduous day of Yom Kippur.

In addition to this account, there are other passages that add a more complete picture of this set-apart day. We see the requirement of sprinkling blood on the horns of the incense altar in Exodus 30:10. The golden atonement cover is described in Exodus 25:17-22; this passage explains that the same piece of gold used to make the atonement cover also formed the golden cherubim, whose wings stretched upward and overshadowed the cover. The Day of Atonement is also found within the chronological calendar of all the feasts, laid out in Leviticus 23:26-32. More details on the normal sin offerings are given in Leviticus 4:13-21. The Lord Yeshua's fulfillment of this feast is beautifully detailed in Hebrews 9 and 10:1-18. The next section of this chapter will expound on this teaching from Hebrews, in which this feast finds its fulfillment in the Lord's blood, sprinkled on the atonement cover in Heaven.

I will provide here a brief summary of the extensive priestly activities found in Leviticus 16, and the motivated reader can study the biblical passages described above for more detail.

The high priest performed his normal morning offerings in his priestly robes and breastplate. However, on this one day of the year, he was then required to change his clothing, and to put on special garments made of white linen. Before he put on these white garments and turban, he needed to first bathe his body in a laver of water, located outside of the Holy Place, in the court of the priests.

Throughout the day, the high priest needed to immerse his body in water on two occasions (see Lev. 16:4,24). However, according to rabbinic literature (the Mishnah), the high priest immersed himself a total of five times during Yom Kippur's services.[2]

Wearing his white garments and turban, he would enter the Holy of Holies, sprinkle the blood, and burn incense; this created a cloud that concealed the atonement cover from view (see Lev. 16:11-14). This Scripture states that if it were not concealed from his sight, the high priest would die. This means that to behold the Presence of God is to die, as it is written, "No one may see Me and live" (Exod. 33:20).

He sacrificed a bull for his own sins, and sprinkled its blood on and before the atonement cover. This slab of pure gold was the covering of the Ark of the Covenant, located in the Holy of Holies. The New King James Version calls this covering, "the mercy seat." In Hebrew, only one word is used, which means both covering and atonement, *chaporet* (see Exod. 25:17).

The Lord often uses the image of *covering* our filth with His righteousness and *covering* our sins with His mercy. The golden lid of the Ark was of the same piece of gold as the cherubim, whose wings stretched over it. Between these angelic forms dwelt the very cloud of God's living Presence, called the *Sh'chinah*, meaning, the "dwelling." Some Christians refer to this overwhelming manifest Presence of God as the "Shekinah Glory," taken from this Hebrew word, *Sh'chinah*. There is no pleasure or fear on this earth that compares to the terrible ecstasy of feeling the Lord's manifest Presence upon us. You feel as if you might die, and yet your life is spared, and you want *more!*

The blood of the bull was also taken outside the curtain and sprinkled on the horns of the altar of incense, the Tent of Meeting, and the altar of sacrifice (see Lev. 16:15-19; Exod. 30:10).

After making atonement for his own sins with the blood of the bull, the high priest went back out from the Tent of Meeting to cast lots over two goats, each of which had a different role to play in making atonement for the sins of the people. Thus, he determined which goat was to be slaughtered and which one was to be designated the "scapegoat."

After the high priest slaughtered the goat the Lord chose, he returned to the Holy of Holies and sprinkled its blood on the atonement cover and on the horns of the altar, just as he had done with the bull's blood for his own sins.

Then he went back out to lay his hands on the head of the "scapegoat." The term literally means, "The goat who escapes." However, we now use the term to mean one who is loaded down with other people's guilt, one who is blamed for every problem. One historical example of "scapegoating" involves the Jews of medieval Europe, who were blamed for the epidemic of plague, although, as we saw in the first chapter, they had no actual guilt in this matter. They conveniently became the scapegoat for society's ills; this was the case in Hitler's Germany with its economic woes.

On a more personal level, some dysfunctional families develop an unspoken agreement that one particular family member is to blame for the whole family's problems. Often, the weakest member will "act out" the dysfunction of the family unit. For example, one of the children might be suicidal, while the other members of the family seem normal and well-adjusted. Actually, the whole family has a problem, but it is easier to focus on the troubled one. This is a subtle kind of blame, also called scapegoating.

The priest would confess all of Israel's sins upon the head of that living goat. God transferred all the filth, blasphemy, idolatry, and wrath onto its head. In one sense, this goat was not slaughtered and thus, escaped death. Yet, after all the sins of Israel were confessed and laid on this poor goat's head, he was led out into the wilderness where he would surely die slowly, without food or water.

So contaminated was this goat after the transfer of sin that the man who led him away had to bathe and wash his clothes outside the camp before returning to his people. The high priest also had to bathe again after handling the scapegoat.

This requirement really gives us a sense of how associating with sin can contaminate us. This does not mean that we are to avoid all sinners, since we might be able to lead many to salvation. We ourselves are redeemed sinners and often live in the midst of sinful environments and families.

Even so, it does mean that we need to cleanse ourselves spiritually after any sin we have committed, or after we have been unwillingly exposed to pornography, idol worship, or blasphemy. Our cleansing through prayer is similar to the priests washing their bodies in water after handling the scapegoat.

Sometimes, our own family members will bring unclean influences into our homes, through music, television, books or objects of witchcraft, wizardry, occult religion, computerized violence, or pornography. This feels like a horrible betrayal to a believing parent, spouse, or child. Due to the Lord's enormous kindness, the believer in the family does not have to carry inadvertent defilement. He or she can go to the Lord privately and pray a cleansing and covering prayer for his or her own purity and protection. He or she can also repent on behalf of the family member who is sinning, whether deliberately or in blind ignorance of God's holy standards.

This repentance and intercession does not excuse the sin, but covers the believer and the household with a large degree of mercy and protection. I have seen this mercy many times, and the Lord is very faithful, even for the sake of one righteous person within a family unit. Of course, each individual sinner must repent and receive the Lord to be saved. And we, the believing member, must bathe in the pure water of God's Word and prayer after handling the sin-infested goat.

DANGLING BETWEEN ATONEMENT AND WRATH

It is hard to express how fearful the Israelites felt during this one and only day on which they could be forgiven. All of their lives hung in the balance, as their trusted high priest went about his sacred duties for hours, coming in and out of the Holy of Holies.

The families of Israel stood outside of the Tent of Meeting all day, not permitted to enter. Even the children, hungry and tired though they were, stopped their chatter and whining as they saw the breathless anxiety on their parents' faces. There were no activities or refreshing drinks to break up the hours, which passed slowly in hunger, thirst, and suspense. The soul was afflicted on this most unpleasant day.

Some of the priest's activities were public, such as the confession over the head of the live goat, its terrible exile into the wilderness, and the burnt offering. Other activities were partially visible as the priest's shadow moved behind a screen, bathing and changing his garments. But within the Tent of Meeting and its holiest inner chamber, the Israelites could see nothing of his progress or God's acceptance of his work.

The reader may recall the New Testament account of Zechariah the priest, burning incense in the Holy Place, where he encountered the angel Gabriel, who announced the coming birth of his son, "John the Baptist." Actually, the child's name was Yochanan, which means "God is Gracious." He later received the title, "The Immerser," because of his ministry of immersion in water for repentance of sins. Most translations use the word "Baptist," from the Greek *baptizo,* instead of the more descriptive word, "Immerser."

The people waited anxiously outside the Temple as Zechariah was so delayed in coming out, not knowing what was happening to him. He could have been struck dead, not merely struck mute, and they would not have known right away. The suspense was like this with the high priest as well, on the Day of Atonement.

While wearing his normal priestly attire, there were golden bells on the bottom of his robe, which enabled the people to hear his movements. However, the Scriptures do not record any such bells on his white linen garments used on Yom Kippur.

When he would enter behind the curtain, into the Holy of Holies to sprinkle blood, they would know nothing of his well-being until he emerged and lifted up his hands to bless them. If he could exit the Holy Place and bless them, Israel knew that God had accepted the priest's offerings and sprinklings of blood. He would speak this blessing over the people:

> *The Lord bless you and keep you; the Lord make His face*
> *shine upon you and be gracious to you; the Lord turn His*
> *face toward you and give you peace* (Numbers 6:24-26).

It was a matter of life and death for the priest to carefully obey all of the Lord's instructions. If he were to neglect any of his duties, or if he were to presumptuously add activities that were not commanded, he would be struck dead in the Holy Place. But there was far more at stake than merely the life of one man.

The atonement of all of Israel hung on his obedience. If he were to be rejected by the Lord for failure to adhere to His commands, the sins of Israel would not be removed, covered, or forgiven.

To put ourselves in their place for a moment, picture this scenario: you knew that you had just committed a grievous sin. You wished that the Lord Jesus could forgive you, but you somehow knew that His kindness and forgiveness was totally exhausted. There was no chance He would take you back one more time, no possibility that He would extend mercy to you once more. You knew it was over, and you could never get back into His grace again. This sin was absolutely irrevocable, unforgivable; you were doomed to physical death within the coming year and would suffer the eternal fires of hell. Can you imagine the horror, anguish, and regret you would feel?

This is exactly how the people of Israel would feel if the priest's Yom Kippur sacrifices were not accepted by God. Horror would grip them, and their atonement would not be accomplished. They were doomed and damned souls, like the sin-laden scapegoat.

Now you can imagine the joy and relief the people would feel when the exhausted high priest would successfully complete the scapegoat ceremony and begin his final work on the burnt offerings.

Shortly before sunset, the priest bathed again, cleansing himself from the contamination of the scapegoat. He changed into his normal priestly garments one more time, and went out to offer the two rams as burnt offerings for himself and for the people.

At last, he had discharged his duties; the merciful God of Israel had accepted his work and his heart, and the people of Israel were covered and forgiven for one more year. As the sun descended in rosy splendor over the Mediterranean Sea, this faithful servant was now permitted to return to his wife and family, eat and drink a joyful and much-needed meal, and collapse in his tent, full of relief and thankfulness at the mercies of a Holy God.

In our safe position as blood-bought children of the Lord, we do not have to live out the terrible scenario described above. We need not doubt that His love and mercy will continue to cleanse and forgive us as we continually confess our faults to Him. We should not agonize that we have lost all hope of His mercy when we fall into sin once again. His mercies are new every morning, and we never have to feel like doomed and damned souls ever again. On the other hand, we must *never* take His kindness for granted, nor use it as a license for deliberate, presumptuous sin. This would not bode well.

A HIGHER ACCOUNTABILITY

The stakes were high for the high priest that day; for twenty-four hours, he needed to be perfectly obedient, and could not yield to temptation even once. His own life and the forgiveness of all of Israel hung in the balance.

Can you imagine how high the stakes were for the ultimate High Priest, Jesus the Messiah? He had to walk and talk on this earth for thirty-three years. He needed to be perfectly obedient and could not yield to temptation even once. The tempter was extremely active in devising enticements and snares for this righteous man, on whom the fate of all living souls rested. If Yeshua had sinned *one time*—one hateful thought, one vengeful word, the momentary satisfaction of one lustful stare, one moment of self-pity, one self-serving boast—what would have occurred?

To make atonement, our High Priest had to be *perfect* all the time, every moment of every day, for thirty-three years. *Do not suppose it was easy because He was the Son of God!* He was tempted in every way as we are, yet without sin (see Heb. 4:15). If He were not tempted, He could not identify with our weaknesses and struggles in this flesh, surrounded by the corruption of this world.

The tempter threw everything he could at this man, far worse than anything we have known. He would wait for an opportune moment when Yeshua was exhausted, or famished, or had just endured hours of unjust accusations from His own leaders who knew better. The devil would use the disciples to hurt and disappoint Yeshua, even to betray Him. The tempter knew that all of humanity's souls were at stake, and he wasn't going to let this perfect little Lamb just walk away with the prize. Consider the accountability of Yeshua's every word and deed, and consider the difficulty of His assignment.

Oh, beloved reader, had He sinned *once*, can you imagine the outcome? None of our sins would be atoned for. In anguish and fear, we would stumble through this existence with the dreaded certainty of eternal torment and irrevocable separation from God.

The higher the calling, the higher the accountability. The higher the priesthood, the higher the risk for the population he atoned for. Yeshua's priesthood was of a higher order than that of Aaron. We will now look into the Book of Hebrews to understand how a man from the tribe of Judah could become the High Priest of Israel.

A HIGHER PRIESTHOOD

The writer of the Book of Hebrews was a Jewish believer who had a deep understanding of the temple sacrificial system and an extensive knowledge of the Torah. Scholars are not certain who wrote this book; it might have been Joseph, a Levite from Cypress, whom the apostles called Barnabus, which means Son of Encouragement (Acts 4:36). It is also possible that Paul wrote this letter, but did not identify himself to the readers. He may have remained anonymous in order to shield the Messianic Jewish recipients, many of whom were still within the synagogues, from persecutions at the hands of Judean leadership.

One of the most vital and comprehensive doctrines found in Hebrews is the priesthood of the Lord Yeshua. However, He is not descended of the priestly tribe of Levi, but rather of the kingly tribe of Judah. Therefore, His priesthood was not according to the original descendency of priests.

The Lord's greater office is compared to that of a priest who lived four hundred years before the Levitical priesthood was established: his name was Melchizedek, king of Salem (Jerusalem) and priest of God Most High (see Gen. 14:18-20; Heb. 7:13-17).

The writer of Hebrews teaches about Melchizedek in the seventh chapter, but the identity of this man remains a mystery. The writer then quotes Psalm 110, which establishes that Yeshua's priesthood was higher and more permanent than the Levitical order; in fact, it was eternal (see Heb. 7:15-17).

This High Priest, Yeshua, would accomplish for mankind what even Aaron could not accomplish for his people Israel: the gift of permanent, irrevocable, perfect atonement for all the sins ever committed by men on the face of earth, for all time. This statement is so huge that it would take another entire book to teach it fully. We will now summarize the most important points, and the reader is encouraged to pursue it thoroughly.

We learn about the Day of Atonement and the tabernacle structure in Hebrews 9.

> *But only the high priest entered the inner room, and that only once a year, and never without blood, which he offered for himself and for the sins the people had committed in ignorance.*
>
> *When Christ came as high priest of the good things that are already here, He went through the greater and more perfect tabernacle that is not man-made, that is to*

say, not a part of this creation. He did not enter by means of the blood of goats and calves; but He entered the Most Holy Place once for all by His own blood, having obtained eternal redemption.

Nor did He enter heaven to offer Himself again and again, the way the high priest enters the Most Holy Place every year with blood that is not his own. Then Christ would have had to suffer many times since the creation of the world. But now He has appeared once for all at the end of the ages to do away with sin by the sacrifice of Himself.

Just as man is destined to die once, and after that to face judgment, so Christ was sacrificed once to take away the sins of many people (Hebrews 9:7,11-12, 25-28a).

Moses made the earthly tabernacle according to the pattern he was shown on the mountain (see Heb. 8:5). His model was the true tabernacle in Heaven. This is where the Lord Yeshua entered, and applied His own blood on the Atonement Cover in Heaven.

There are six billion people on the earth now, and another six billion have lived from the beginning until this present generation. How can one human sacrifice of sinless blood take away all the sin that mankind has ever committed? Can you conceive of the value of those five quarts of blood, which were able to take away that ocean of filth?

THE SCAPEGOAT

Both of the goats in Leviticus 16 represent an aspect of Yeshua's sacrifice. We have now looked at His blood as being applied to the atonement cover in Heaven, which is a fulfillment of the role of the slaughtered goat.

But how did He represent the scapegoat? The sins of the people were laid on this goat's head, and He bore them and carried them outside of the camp. He died with our sins on His head. He staggered away from the community, alone and accursed, so that we would never encounter our sins again. That goat died slowly.

When Adam and Eve sinned, the Lord told them that they would surely die. After they had eaten the forbidden fruit, they did not physically die at that moment. In fact, they lived for a long time after that. But at that point, they began to die slowly. Spiritually, they were instantly separated from God, and their bodies began the slow and inevitable process of death and decay.

The Lord spent forty days in the desert with no food or water. As a man, He walked as one of us. As a great and merciful High Priest, He was also tempted by evil and felt all that we feel.

> For we do not have a high priest who is unable to sympa-thize with our weaknesses, but we have one who has been tempted in every way, just as we are—yet was without sin (Hebrews 4:15).

He carried our sins away, as far as the west is from the east. Like the scapegoat, we never have to see our sins again. They are not only covered and atoned for, but they are also taken away. This scapegoat function clears us of our guilty conscience, which can separate even believers from God. Whenever we feel guilty or ashamed, we must run into His arms and not hide from Him. He bore it all so that we would never have to suffer shame or separation from Him again.

Our High Priest had to be made perfect through obedience, suffering, and temptation. As He wrestled with His terrible ordeal in the Garden, the stench of all of our sins was laid upon His head, and He carried our guilt and shame.

> Surely He took up our infirmities and carried our sorrows (Isaiah 53:4a).

THE LORD'S HEART

I was asking the Lord if He would give me a word for this chapter. I would like to share the word I received while still in the process of writing it, which fits in very well with the teaching on the scapegoat we have just concluded.

I AM the High Priest. I AM the greater High Priest than was My servant, Aaron. He went into the Holy Place and offered blood on behalf of himself and on behalf of his people. He could not behold the face of My Father, and so he required a cloud of sweet smoke to hide My face from him.

I honored him and did him no harm for all the years that he brought Me these offerings. His sons did not respect Me or fear Me when they came in with their presumption. The smoke and fire they burned before Me was not authorized by Me. Much presumption goes unpunished in the camp of My people, in the midst of My Church.

Many presume to speak for Me, to represent My thoughts and My desires. Many have offered Me strange and unauthorized fire and much smoke. These have not yet been punished for their presumption, for I wait patiently for their repentance and the understanding that they have not offered Me the kind of hearts I have requested, even required. My blood on the altar has covered their presumption, and still I wait for those who will ask Me what I desire and press in to know what I AM thinking.

When they find out what I AM thinking, it will surprise them, and many will be sorry for their presumption to misrepresent Me.

My white robes were made filthy, spattered with blood, just as Aaron's white robes were spattered with blood. His robes were stained with animals' blood. My robes were stained with My own blood. When I appeared before the altar in Heaven, I was a crushed and filthy scapegoat. Every filth and abomination was on My head and clung to Me like leprosy. I was too unclean to appear before My Father, and I collapsed before Him, covered in My own blood, and the stinking filth of the peoples of the earth.

Because I overcame, this filth was removed from Me, and I was given clean robes to wear. I was washed with pure water, strengthened with the food of angels, and a crown was placed on My head, a turban of pure gold.[3]

I was "Joshua," Yeshua, the High Priest. I made atonement in the Holy Place. It would never have to be repeated again, and there is no more atonement ever to be made by men again.

The Day of Atonement is a memorial, a holy memory that we observe by fasting and doing no regular work. But woe to anyone who attempts to offer the sacrifices of atonement for sin on this earth.

It has been made; it is finished. The atonement is complete and permanent. My blood still lies fresh and alive on the Atonement Cover on the Ark of the Covenant in Heaven. My Father's face is reflected in the blood that lies on that cover, His shining face perfectly reflected in that pool of blood.

Tell My people that I AM the High Priest, and I have stained all My garments.

You may fast for Me; it is still a sacred memorial of what I have done. But let no one make atonement for themselves or for any sin they have committed. This will be seen as strange fire. Let them confess their sin to Me first, and then one to another, and the blood of Messiah will cover and cleanse and remove it from their record book.

I AM Yeshua, even the "Joshua" in Zechariah. I was filthy for your sakes, but now I AM clean and pure, glorified and exalted at the right hand of My Father! Amen.

It is important for both Jewish people and Christians to understand that we are not fasting to atone for our sins. Some Jewish people feel that by fasting, they are earning another year of health and life. They desire to be inscribed in the Book of Life for another year, but most Jewish people do not think about an eternal perspective. This thinking is a misunderstanding of the concept of atonement, for which blood was always necessary. The Lord sees and rewards the Yom Kippur fast, but it simply cannot atone for sin.

If a Gentile believer chooses to fast on Yom Kippur, it will often be as a sign of solidarity and identification with the Jewish people; it could also be to intercede for deliverance from their enemies or for their spiritual salvation. Once again, this is wholly voluntary; neither the Lord nor any person judges you for choosing not to participate. Even so, I am convinced there is a serious blessing for those Gentiles who willingly fast on this day that is extremely holy to the Lord.

While Passover celebrates our individual salvation, the Day of Atonement represents a day of Israel's national salvation. Of course, this national revival will be comprised of millions of individual Jewish people who have recognized the identity of their Jewish Messiah.

The prophet Zechariah speaks of a day of national mourning for the nation of Israel:

> And I will pour out on the house of David and on the inhabitants of Jerusalem a spirit of grace and supplication. They will look on Me, the one they have pierced, and they will mourn for Him as one mourns for an only child, and grieve bitterly for Him as one grieves for a firstborn son. . . .
>
> On that day a fountain will be opened to the house of David and the inhabitants of Jerusalem, to cleanse them from sin and impurity (Zechariah 12:10; 13:1).

The Day of Atonement for Israel, as a nation, is still a future event. There are tens of thousands who believe, even hundreds of thousands, but in that day, there will be millions. This holiest of days is a rehearsal for the salvation of the nation of Israel. Let us intercede for Israel as we fast on this day.

The apostle Paul will give us the final word of intercession for this chapter:

> Brothers, my heart's desire and prayer to God for the Israelites is that they may be saved.
>
> I do not want you to be ignorant of this mystery, brothers, so that you may not be conceited: Israel has experienced a hardening in part until the full number of the Gentiles has come in. And so, all Israel will be saved, as it is written:
>
> The deliverer will come from Zion; He will turn godlessness away from Jacob. And this is my covenant with them when I take away their sins (Romans 10:1; 11:25-27).

Chapter 8

THE FEAST OF TABERNACLES

The last and greatest feast in the yearly cycle of seven holidays is the Feast of Tabernacles. Another biblical name given is the Feast of Ingathering, which refers to the culmination of the summer harvest and the gathering of the crops into the barn before winter. The end of this seven-day period also commences the rainy winter season of plowing and planting, in anticipation of the spring harvests of barley and wheat. The first and eighth days of this week are sacred assemblies on which we do no regular work.

> *Celebrate the Feast of Tabernacles for seven days after you have gathered the produce of your threshing floor and of your winepress. Be joyful at your feast—you, your sons and daughters, your menservants and maidservants, and the Levites, the aliens, the fatherless and the widows who live in your towns.*
>
> *For the Lord your God will bless you in all your harvest and in all the work of your hands, and your joy will be complete.*
>
> *Three times a year all your men must appear before the Lord your God at the place He will choose: at the Feast of Unleavened Bread, the Feast of Weeks and the Feast of*

Tabernacles. No man should appear before the Lord empty-handed: Each of you must bring a gift in proportion to the way the Lord your God has blessed you (Deuteronomy 16:13-14;15b-17).

This passage in Deuteronomy provides a summary of the three essential feasts, in which all Israelite men were required to travel to Jerusalem to celebrate. The seven feasts are condensed into these three, which required pilgrimage to God's temple in the spring, summer, and fall: Unleavened Bread, Weeks, and Tabernacles.

Once again, when a pilgrimage feast comes around, the Lord impresses on us His enormous burden for the poor. As we recall from the Feast of Weeks chapter, God's heart was turned toward the poor and the disenfranchised at these seasons in particular. Just as Israel was happily scooping up the harvest and storing great piles of grains and fruits, just when her celebration was at its zenith, the Lord was always reminding them to share with the poor from their abundance.

I recorded a personal word from His heart at the conclusion of Chapter 5, as you may recall. I myself was somewhat stunned at His weighty emphasis on the poor during these feasts. Somehow, I did not grasp the degree of emphasis the Lord desired until He graciously poured out that word to me from His heart. If I missed this point so readily, even while writing a book on the feasts, it is likely that others who celebrate the feasts and write books about them have also missed it. I pray that this fresh revelation will ignite readers' hearts, as well as my own, to become more purposeful in our giving to the poor at these seasons of the year. It will please our Father greatly!

NOT A VISIT, BUT AN INDWELLING!

This joyful seven-day festival contains many themes, but probably the heart of God can best be captured by the word *indwelling*. This word speaks of the relationship between God and man; it represents the Lord's desire to dwell with His people, even to dwell *in* His people. He has made Himself available to camp in their midst, to spend intimate times of fellowship with them, and to refresh them in the camp as they are preparing for coming seasons of marching out. Difficult assignments await them, and without camping times, the marching times of conquest will not be successful. *First comes intimacy, and then comes warfare.*

We see from Genesis to Revelation that it was always the Lord's desire to dwell with us on earth, with His sons and daughters.

> *Then the man and his wife heard the sound of the Lord God as He was walking in the garden in the cool of the day* (Genesis 3:8).

> *Then I saw a new heaven and a new earth, for the first heaven and the first earth had passed away...and I heard a loud voice from the throne saying, "Now the dwelling of God is with men, and He will live with them"* (Revelation 21:1-4).

We long to dwell in Heaven with the Lord, and this desire was certainly placed in us by Him. Even so, the Bible contains many more references to His desire to walk with man on the earth than to His desire to bring us to Heaven. The Lord actually yearns to tabernacle with us more than we desire to be with Him. The Lord has demonstrated this yearning throughout Scripture but has displayed it most dramatically and painfully when He became a man and dwelt on the earth among His beloved ones.

> *The Word became flesh and made His dwelling among us. We have seen His glory, the glory of the One and Only, who came from the Father, full of grace and truth* (John 1:14).

> *Every spirit that acknowledges that Jesus Christ has come in the flesh is from God, but every spirit that does not acknowledge Jesus is not from God* (1 John 4:2b-3a).

A Prophetic Calendar: The Feasts of Israel

The Lord Yeshua the Messiah has come in the flesh. But He has also come in *our* flesh. When He lived on the earth, we beheld His glory in mortal form. Now He indwells us and tabernacles in our fleshly tents by His Holy Spirit.

> *Do you not know that your body is a temple of the Holy Spirit, who is in you, whom you have received from God?*
>
> *And in Him you too are being built together to become a dwelling in which God lives by His Spirit* (1 Corinthians 6:19; Ephesians 2:22).

Where Is Our Permanent Home?

> *On the fifteenth day of the seventh month the Lord's Feast of Tabernacles begins, and it lasts for seven days....after you have gathered the crops of the land, celebrate the festival to the Lord for seven days; the first day is a day of rest, and the eighth day is also a day of rest. On the first day, you are to take choice fruit from the trees, and palm fronds, leafy branches and poplars, and rejoice before the Lord your God for seven days. Live in booths for seven days: All native-born Israelites are to live in booths so your descendants will know that I had the Israelites live in booths when I brought them out of Egypt* (Leviticus 23:34;39b-40;42-43b).

The Lord has commanded us to dwell in primitive and temporary structures for seven days. These are somewhat like tents, but there is a different biblical word that could have been used for "tent" (*ohel*). This Hebrew word is closer to a "booth" or "hut," and is the word *succah*. Thus, the Jewish people call this feast by its plural form, *Succot*.

Notice that the primary reason given for living in booths is to commemorate the wanderings in the desert. For forty years, the Israelites had no permanent homes. They could not settle in and raise children, "each one eating from his own vine and fig tree" (see Isa. 36:16). They were forced to live a nomadic existence, dwelling in tents, and always hoping to reach a more permanent and settled status. Even so, the Lord found them beautiful as He tenderly gazed upon their encampments in the desert.

> *How beautiful are your tents, O Jacob, your dwelling places, O Israel! Like valleys they spread out, like gardens beside a river, like aloes planted by the Lord, like cedars beside the waters* (Numbers 24:5-6).

The Lord desired to bring them into a better situation in their own land. Nevertheless, He used this period of temporary dwellings to train them to find their security only in God. There are certain attitudes of godly dependency that cannot be learned in a comfortable, permanent environment. We must be trained in the wilderness, and Israel went through a most difficult boot camp, which lasted far too long.

Our father Abraham dwelt in tents in the land of Canaan to which God had called him. He could not take a wife for his son from among the Canaanites and had to send for a relative in his father's country. His son Isaac and grandson Jacob also dwelt in tents all of their days, and Jacob died in Egypt, though he was buried in Israel. Joseph, too, was forced into foreign slavery and died in Egypt, but his bones were carried back to his fathers by Moses when they finally left Egypt (see Gen. 49:29-32; 50:12-14; 24-25; Exod. 13:19). Jacob's and Joseph's bones finally found a "permanent" resting place in the Land of Promise. However, even the grave cannot keep them much longer, and their bones are only dwelling temporarily in the earth until the much-awaited resurrection of the righteous dead (see 1 Cor.15; Rev. 20:4-6).

David spent many years running from Saul's jealous rage, moving from place to place like a hunted animal. It was approximately fifteen years between his anointing by Samuel and his ascension to the temporary throne of Judah in Hebron. Seven years later, he was finally installed as Israel's king.

During the second century before Messiah's birth, the faithful Israelites suffered a time of severe tribulation under Antiochus

"Epiphanes" IV (168-165 B.C.). During this persecution, they hid in caves and holes in the ground as they were hunted down. Many were tortured and killed by Antiochus' cruel officials.

After the Jews drove the foreign armies from Jerusalem, they rededicated the Temple to the Lord and celebrated for eight days, as if they were recapturing Tabernacles, which they had been unable to celebrate while in hiding.

Both the Book of Hebrews and the Book of Maccabees refer to this period. We will study more about this remarkable persecution and its end-times correlations in the next chapter on Hanukah and the original antichrist. Hanukah falls seventy-five days after Tabernacles.

> They went about in sheepskins and goatskins, destitute, persecuted and mistreated—the world was not worthy of them. They wandered in deserts and mountains, and in caves and holes in the ground (Hebrews 11:37b-38).

The Lord Yeshua remarked: "Foxes have holes and birds of the air have nests, but the Son of Man has no place to lay his head" (Matt. 8:20). As a man of faith following in the footsteps of His fathers—Abraham, Isaac, Jacob, and David—our Lord, having entered His public ministry of preaching and healing, never enjoyed the comforts of a normal life in a permanent home. He was looking forward to a better place, like His fathers before Him.

> By faith Abraham, when called to go to a place he would later receive as his inheritance, obeyed and went, even though he did not know where he was going. By faith he made his home in the promised land like a stranger in a foreign country; he lived in tents, as did Isaac and Jacob, who were heirs with him of the same promise. For he was looking forward to the city with foundations, whose architect and builder is God (Hebrews 11:8-11).

Even God Himself commented on not having a permanent home on earth! Do you remember the passage when David was absolutely determined to build a house for the Lord? At first, the prophet Nathan told him to do whatever was in his heart. But then the Lord spoke to Nathan and gave him this message to take back to David:

> *You are not the one to build Me a house to dwell in. I have not dwelt in a house from the day I brought Israel up out of Egypt to this day. I have moved from one tent site to another, from one dwelling place to another.*
>
> *Wherever I have moved with all the Israelites, did I ever say to any of their leaders whom I commanded to shepherd My people, "Why have you not built Me a house of cedar?"*
>
> *I will raise up one of your offspring to succeed you, one of your own sons, and I will establish his kingdom. He is the one who will build a house for Me* (1 Chronicles 17:4-6,11-12).

It is amazing how the Lord identified with the wanderings of His people. He never asked for a house while His people lived in tents. He was humble, content to move from tent site to tent site. The pagan gods were imagined to desire huge and ostentatious shrines, which their worshipers slavishly built for them. The temperamental and vengeful "gods" needed to be appeased, usually with the blood of children.

Not so with our gentle and respectful God. Out of His great love for David, the Lord allowed David to compile all the financial and architectural arrangements for God's house, and then permitted his son Solomon to build Him a temple in which His very Sh'chinah Presence would dwell. It meant so much to David that the Lord granted this desire, but who knows if He would have asked for a house?

As we celebrate the Feast of Tabernacles, we are rehearsing the unsettled condition of strangers in a strange land, of wanderers looking forward to something better.

Of Booths and Branches

The Lord describes this climactic festival in the seventh month as an everlasting ordinance. Since "everlasting" means "everlasting," it should not surprise us to learn that during the Lord's future Millennial Reign, the Feast of Succot will be celebrated in Jerusalem by all nations, and not only by Israelis. We will examine this shortly.

The passage we read in Leviticus 23 instructed an exuberant worship celebration, in which the worshipers waved branches and fruits before the Lord. Not only did they create their semi-open roofs out of tree branches, but they also used them as worship banners, waving them high in the air, and singing to the Lord. In the days of the Temple, the Scriptures describe vast priestly choirs and instrumental ensembles singing the Psalms of Ascent, and waving leafy boughs with unparalleled joy.

In modern Israel, the temperate climate allows families to camp out in these booths for seven days. They take their meals under a canopy of willow and myrtle and fall asleep beneath the stars, shining through the branches. The cold rainy season begins soon after we have packed up our huts for the winter, if the Lord blesses us with the needful autumn rains.

Israeli families usually dwell in apartments, and try to build their family succot in the courtyards or flat roofs of their buildings. Synagogues might have a small property on which to build one. Jewish people who live in colder regions might only eat their meals in the Succah, but not attempt to sleep outside. In the U.S., some regions are quite cold in October, and camping out would be a bit punishing.

The four species of plants that are currently imported from Israel at this time of year to be waved in our worship services are the willow, the myrtle, the palm, and a yellow citrus fruit called a "citron." It is much like a lemon, and in Hebrew is called an *etrog*.

Some synagogues will order a group of these plants from Israel right before the holiday, and individual families can order them in advance from the synagogue. Some people might be able to gather their own branches from comparable trees and can wave a lemon as well as an *etrog*. While there is something special about holding the fruits of the land of Israel, these branch-packages are a bit expensive, and those who have access to a variety of leafy branches are certainly free to gather their own.

On the other hand, I like to support the synagogues who order these packets. If they did not perform this service to the community, neither Jews nor non-Jews who wish to celebrate this holiday would have the privilege of waving these exact species of Israeli plants before the Lord.

Once again, we owe this ancient and covenant-bound people a great debt. They have both knowingly and unknowingly preserved God's Word, and taken His name and reputation into all the nations where they have been scattered. Where else could you get these branches, but from a synagogue?

As believers, we love to celebrate Tabernacles by waving these particular branches during our times of worship. In a later section, we will learn more about the priestly celebrations and receive more practical help and details on holding a worship service.

The poor willow leaves dry up very fast, and it is hard to keep them moist enough until the day of waving them arrives. These branches were not meant to be cut down and shipped halfway around the world, cut off from their roots and water supply. Does this sound like a parable of the Church? You decide.

THE OFFERINGS AND THE GLORY

These seven days were a time of great quantities of animal sacrifices. We see a detailed account of these sacrifices in Numbers 29:12-39. The totals of each type of animal were always multiples of the number seven. In summary, during the seven days of Tabernacles, seventy bulls were sacrificed, fourteen rams, seven goats, and ninety-eight lambs, if I have calculated correctly. There were others on the eighth day, but the number did not follow the same decreasing numerical pattern as the first seven days.

We see an almost unbelievable scenario in Second Chronicles 5:2-7. Solomon had now succeeded his father David, and had built and furnished the first permanent temple for the God of Israel. He conducted the dedication service in his eleventh year as king, on the Feast of Tabernacles,

959 B.C.[1] Levitical leaders brought up the Tent of Meeting the Ark of the Lord's covenant and all the sacred furnishings from the City of David into the new temple. When they were all gathered around Solomon before the ark, they "sacrificed so many sheep and cattle that they could not be recorded or counted" (see 2 Chron. 5:6). It is hard to imagine the effort and expense of that number of animals.

The priests brought the ark into the Holy Place and then withdrew, while the Levitical musicians worshiped, playing many instruments and singing with one voice:

> *"He is good; His love endures forever."*
> *Then the temple of the Lord was filled with a cloud,*
> *and the priests could not perform their service because of*
> *the cloud, for the glory of the Lord filled the temple of God*
> (2 Chronicles 5:13-14).

King Solomon then blessed his father David, whose heart was moved to build a house for the Lord; he prayed for God to be responsive to all sincere prayers that would be offered up from this house, and the Lord responded to his prayer with fire from Heaven. I recommend that you take the time to read aloud to the Lord this prayer that Solomon prayed, found in Second Chronicles 6:12-42. We could learn much about God's character and the type of prayer that pleases Him from this chapter. How does the Lord respond to these offerings and this prayer of thanksgiving and dedication?

> *When Solomon finished praying, fire came down from*
> *heaven and consumed the burnt offering and the sacri-*
> *fices, and the glory of the Lord filled the temple. The*
> *priests could not enter the temple of the Lord, because the*
> *glory of the Lord filled it.*
> *When all the Israelites saw the fire coming down and*
> *the glory of the Lord above the temple, they knelt on the*
> *pavement with their faces to the ground, and they*

worshiped and gave thanks to the Lord, saying, "He is good; His love endures forever" (2 Chronicles 7:1-3).

The same God whose glory filled Solomon's temple desires to fill our houses of worship as well. Do we desire the same manifestation of His glory to the point that we cannot enter the building due to the Presence of God? What are the sacrifices and offerings that will move His heart to respond as He did to Solomon's offerings?

In the New Covenant, we obviously no longer offer animal sacrifices. The offerings of our heart are sincere praise, thankfulness, worship, holiness of lifestyle, generosity to the poor, and humility toward one another. When we pour out our hearts of love in an intense and purposeful unity, His glory will surely fall upon our meetings. He will consume our songs, declarations, and tears of repentance with His jealous fire and will cover us like a cloud. Our acceptable sacrifice is our hearts. Our God is jealous for *all* of our hearts. What we give to the Lord is for Him only, and not for human consumption.

WATER ON THIRSTY GROUND

One of the major themes of Tabernacles is the ancient, joyful Water-Drawing Ceremony and the prayers for rain. This ceremony dates back to the time of Ezra, and we see it celebrated in the New Testament in John, chapter 7. It may have originated from the following passage in Isaiah, in which the Hebrew word for "salvation" is our Lord's name, "Yeshua."

With joy you will draw water from the wells of salvation (Isaiah 12:3).

The biblical year contained a cycle of priestly rotations of service. These two-week periods of service were assigned by casting lots for the clans of Aaron and Levi. The schedule of priestly and Levitical service is detailed in First Chronicles 24. In all, there were twenty-four divisions, covering the entire calendar year.

A PROPHETIC CALENDAR: THE FEASTS OF ISRAEL

During the Feast of Tabernacles, all twenty-four divisions presented themselves for service in Jerusalem. This celebration involved hundreds of Levites, who would gather around the high priest every morning for the water ceremony. Carrying a golden pitcher, he would walk down from the Temple to the Pool of Siloam, as the Levites formed a processional, singing and playing musical instruments to Psalms 113-118. This cluster of psalms is known as the *Hallel*, which means "praise." The Israelites sang these hymns during the major festivals and at new moon celebrations. Psalm 118 has so much Messianic significance that we will examine it more closely in the next section.

After the high priest filled the pitcher with water, the joyful throng would ascend to the temple courts, waving willow branches from the water brooks and palm fronds before the Lord. When they arrived at the inner court of the Temple, the high priest poured the water into the basin of the altar designed for this drink offering. During normal services, a drink offering of wine was poured out into another basin, but this unique water offering was only poured out at Tabernacles. They recited Isaiah 12:3 as he poured out the water, and prayed for the autumn rains to begin for the planting season.

In a sense, this water offering was a type of first fruits offering, because the priest was "wasting" precious water by pouring it out to the Lord and praying for a large "harvest" of rain to come in the immediate days and weeks that followed the feast. In Israel rain is scarce, even in a good year. By the time of the fall feasts, it has been a long dry summer, and rain is badly needed.

During the days of Elijah, Israel experienced a three-and-a-half-year drought with severe famine. The drought was a curse brought upon the land by Baal worship, the killing of the Lord's prophets by Ahab's foreign wife, Jezebel, and the horrific demonic cult of child sacrifice.

Because Elijah announced the curse, Ahab blamed him, and called him a "troubler of Israel." Elijah responded that he didn't trouble Israel, but the king's wickedness had brought this curse upon Israel by worshiping foreign gods.

The divine showdown between the God of Israel and the prophets of Baal and Asherah took place on Mount Carmel in Haifa, and is recorded in First Kings 18. To me, one of the most interesting aspects of this story is that in a severe drought, Elijah demands that a huge amount of water be poured on the sacrificed bull and the wood. So much water was hauled up that mountain and wasted that it ran down and filled a trench he had dug around the altar. The trench reminded me of the basin of the altar, which also received a drink offering at a time when water was in short supply. Men and beasts were dying of thirst, and Elijah was pouring gallons and gallons of water on a dead bull and soggy wood. Was he just making it "hard" for God to set the offering on fire? Or was there something more important than that?

I believe that Elijah knew that once the prophets of Baal and Asherah were exposed and executed, the curse of demon-worship would be broken over Israel, and God would finally open the windows of Heaven and send rain. Elijah knew that he could waste a lot of water, because God could give it back many times over, once the curse was broken. This was an act of enormous trust, believing that God's supernatural fire would vindicate Elijah's authority in the name of the Lord.

The fire fell, the false prophets were seized and killed, and Elijah prayed seven times for rain. When the small rain cloud appeared, he told Ahab that the rains were coming so fast and hard that his chariot would get stuck in the mud on the way to Jezreel. What we think is wasteful can bring incredible blessings and multiplication.

As with the first fruits offerings, Israel poured out water as they were praying to God for more water. This was a foreshadowing of the extravagant, "wasteful" worship that the Lord desires of His people today, just as He did in biblical times. No burnt offering or precious drink offering was ever wasted on the Lord. He sees every sacrifice and the motivation with which we offer it to Him; He returns to us more than what we have given away. What looks wasteful to the world looks precious to our God.

Two days before the Lord Yeshua's death, a woman came into the house where He was dining, broke an alabaster jar of very expensive perfume, and poured it over His sweet head. The guests complained that this perfume was worth more than a year's wages and should not have been "wasted" when it could have been given to the poor. The Lord defended the woman's act of love, telling them that this sacrificial offering was a preparation for His burial, and that a memorial of what she had done would be recorded for all time (see Mark 14:3-9).

WHOEVER IS THIRSTY, LET HIM COME!

During the Lord's final celebration of the Feast of Tabernacles, He injected an amazing statement into the water-drawing ceremony on the last and greatest day of the feast. The priests and the Levites had just sung, "With joy will you draw waters from the wells of *Yeshuah* [salvation]," for the seventh time that morning. Now they watched breathlessly as the golden pitcher of water was being poured out for the final time, praying that the Lord would graciously send the soaking rains early enough to prepare the ground for a ripe barley crop before Passover.

In this astonishing and forceful revelation, Yeshua irrevocably linked His Messianic identity and life-giving authority to the Feast of Tabernacles. Months earlier, He had also revealed this mystery to a Samaritan woman, although Israel's leadership would not have had opportunity to hear her report, due to the social stigma of being both a Samaritan and a woman.

> [During Tabernacles]: *"If anyone is thirsty, let him come to Me and drink. Whoever believes in Me, as the Scripture has said, streams of living water will flow from within him"* (John 7:37-38).

> [To the Samaritan woman at the well]: *"If you knew the gift of God and who it is that asks you for a drink, you would have asked Him and He would have given you living water....Everyone who drinks this water will be thirsty again, but whoever drinks the water I give him will never thirst. Indeed, the water I give him will become in him a spring of water welling up to eternal life"* (John 4:10,13-14).

The claim that Yeshua made during the Water Ceremony would resonate with anyone well-versed in the Torah and Prophets. The theme of living waters was a very familiar one to the Jewish people. Yeshua's claim would have sounded precisely like a fulfillment of these well-known prophecies, which is why many declared Him to be the Messiah after He spoke this "Tabernacles Surprise." The Lord God had offered His people living waters through the prophets Isaiah and Jeremiah, along with numerous other references to the river of God, the river of life, the river of justice, and the unfailing stream of righteousness.

> *With joy you will draw water from the wells of salvation.*
> *Come, all you who are thirsty, come to the waters;*
> *and you who have no money, come, buy and eat! Come,*
> *buy wine and milk without money and without cost...*
> *and your soul will delight in the richest of fare.*
> *My people have committed two sins: they have*
> *forsaken Me, the spring of living water, and have dug*
> *their own cisterns, broken cisterns that cannot hold water*
> (Isaiah 12:3; 55:1,2b; Jeremiah 2:13).

In addition to the declarations about water in the Old Covenant, the last promises in the Book of Revelation bear witness to the eternal waters of life, found only in the deep springs of Yeshua's heart:

> *To him who is thirsty I will give to drink without cost*
> *from the spring of the water of life. Whoever is thirsty, let*
> *him come; and whoever wishes, let him take the free gift*
> *of the water of life* (Revelation 21:6b; 22:17b).

Yeshua told the truth about Himself. May we learn to drink deeply and regularly from His inexhaustible source, and may rivers of living water spring up from our innermost being to water the parched and panting souls around us.

I AM THE LIGHT OF THE WORLD

Each night of Tabernacles was celebrated with a spectacular light ceremony, more awe-inspiring than our ambitious fireworks displays on the

Fourth of July. Four huge lampstands were lit in the temple courts, so tall that the young priests had to climb ladders to fill their bowls with fresh olive oil every evening. The wicks of these *menorahs* (lampstands) were made from worn-out linen garments of the priests.[2]

The lights blazed over the Temple and bathed the surrounding streets of Jerusalem in flickering radiance. Even the families eating supper in their little *succot*, which dotted the hillsides of Judea, could see the torches and hear the music of the Levites and the shouts of the people. The choir and musicians played the fifteen Psalms of Ascent (Psalms 120-134), which were part of each pilgrimage festival. This seven-day light ceremony was the highest moment of joy in the biblical calendar of holidays, a culmination of extravagant jubilation for the people of Israel and her leaders.

We have seen that on the seventh day of this feast, the Lord announced that He was the source of living waters, just as the morning service was concluding with the pouring out of water into the basin of the altar. John notes that the Lord went out that evening to stay on the Mount of Olives, and He appeared in the temple courts the next morning. It was on this occasion, when the memory of the seventh light show was still fresh in the minds of the worshipers, that He made this statement:

> *I am the light of the world. Whoever follows me will never walk in darkness, but will have the light of life* (John 8:12).

It is interesting that the Lord Yeshua did not call attention to Himself during the spectacular and impressive light show. He waited until the quietness of dawn to walk into the temple courts, and when He began teaching the people, He truthfully stated that He is the Light of the World. Later on that very day, He healed a blind man, saying, "While I am in the world, I am the light of the world" (John 9:5).

The Lord once again linked His Messianic identity and ministry to the Feast of Tabernacles: He came as a man and tabernacled among us; He fulfilled the water ceremony by proclaiming that He is the spring of living waters, which will so satisfy us that we will never thirst again; He received worship with the waving of palm branches, to shouts of "Hoshiana! Blessed is He who comes in the Name of the Lord!"; He used the image of blazing torches, illuminating all of Jerusalem, to create the picture of Himself as the light of the world, a banner to the nations, the Star of Jacob (see Isa. 11:10; Num. 24:17); and He promised to spread His tent over us, to protect us from the scorching sun, and to wipe every tear from our eyes (see Rev. 7:15-16).

"*HOSHIANA* TO THE SON OF DAVID!"

One of the greatest messianic psalms in Scripture is Psalm 118, the conclusion of the *Hallel* Psalms, 113-118. Interestingly, this psalm happens to be the central chapter of the Bible, with an equal number of chapters before and after it. These verses also refer to the Feast of Tabernacles, and are quoted in the New Testament concerning Messiah's role as the cornerstone of Israel's "house."

Just as the land of Israel dwells in the "center of the earth" (Ezek. 5:5; 38:12), so this psalm, connecting the Messiah to Tabernacles, dwells in the center of God's written Word. These verses speak of light, of leafy branches, of the joyful throng ascending to Jerusalem for the feast, and of the great "Hosanna," with which Yeshua the Messiah was welcomed into Jerusalem by joyful worshipers.

> *O Lord, save us, O Lord, grant us success. Blessed is He who comes in the name of the Lord. From the house of the Lord we bless you.*
>
> *The Lord is God, and He has made his light shine upon us. With boughs in hand, join in the festal procession up to the horns of the altar* (Psalm 118:25-27).

The plea, "O Lord, save us" is the Hebrew word, *Hoshiana*, which our Bibles usually write as "Hosanna!" It literally means, "Please, save us!" In the Jewish mind, this worshipful exclamation could only be made to the Messiah, as He would be the only one with the power, goodness, and authority to save Israel.

During the final week of His earthly ministry, the Lord Yeshua rode into Jerusalem on a donkey, as had His kingly father Solomon before Him. The whole crowd began to cut down palm branches, waving them before Him, in recognition of the fulfillment of Psalm 118. As they declared His kingship, the crowds praised God for all the miracles they had seen, quoting this beloved festival psalm, and applying it to Yeshua of Nazareth (see Luke 19:37).

> *Hosanna to the Son of David! Blessed is He who comes in the name of the Lord! Hosanna in the highest!* (Matthew 21:9b).

For the crowds of Israel to address Him as the "Son of David" was a clear declaration of His kingly identity and function. This unique and exalted title was reserved only for the Messiah, the Crowned Prince of Israel.

Although the season was Passover, the Jewish people waved the leafy branches of Tabernacles. Although the majority of the Sanhedrin rejected Yeshua as the Messiah, a significant number from Israel did *not* miss the day of their visitation.

As Yeshua warned the spiritual leaders of His people Israel, "*You will not see Me again until you say, 'Blessed is He who comes in the name of the Lord.'*"

Why did He say that, since the crowds had just welcomed Him with precisely this greeting? It is because the Lord will require this welcome from the chief rabbis, the restored Levitical leadership, the Orthodox authorities, and the other branches of Jewish leaders and religious educators. In the end, the reconvened modern Sanhedrin must acknowledge Yeshua a long-overdue recognition, to say the least.[3]

Was Yeshua Born on Tabernacles?

We have already seen that the biblical calendar was divided into twenty-four rotations of priestly service. The yearly order of these priestly divisions is detailed in First Chronicles 24.

The Gospel of Luke often provides wonderful details that the other Gospels do not include. From Luke's precise account of the Lord Yeshua's birth, we learn that John the Baptist's father and mother were both descended from Aaron, the brother of Moses and the first high priest of Israel (see Luke 1:5). His father Zechariah belonged to the priestly division of Abijah (see 1 Chron. 24:10). The division of Abijah served in late June or July on our calendar.

While on duty conducting his priestly service, Zechariah was visited by the angel Gabriel at the time of burning incense. Gabriel announced that Zechariah's wife, Elizabeth, would conceive a son in her barren old age, and this child would become the Spirit-filled forerunner of the Messiah's birth. After completing his two-week rotation, knowing that the Lord would now give him a son, Zechariah returned home, and his wife conceived John in this season.

We know that six months into Elizabeth's pregnancy, Gabriel was sent to visit Mary, whose name was actually "Miriam," a descendant of King David; the angel announced to her that she would conceive and give birth to Israel's Messiah, although she was a virgin.

Since John the Baptist was conceived in approximately July, the Lord Yeshua would have been conceived six months later, in approximately December. It is interesting to calculate that from the last day of Hanukah, which falls in December, to the first day of Tabernacles is 280 days, which happens to be the exact length of a pregnancy. Motivated readers can "do the math." The Word became flesh and *tabernacled* among us. It makes perfect sense that the Lord would cause His Son to be born on the Feast of Tabernacles, the feast that depicts God's desire to dwell in the midst of His people.

THE BIBLICAL TYPES OF TABERNACLES

As we conclude this teaching, let us highlight several pictures of the Tabernacle found in Scripture.[4]

The Tabernacle of Moses was also called the Tent of Meeting, which Moses had built and furnished according to the heavenly pattern he was shown on the mountain.

A Prophetic Calendar: The Feasts of Israel

The Lord camped with His people in the desert, and His *Sh'chinah* Presence dwelt between the wings of the golden cherubim over the Mercy Seat. So overpowering was God's glory that even Moses could not enter the Tent of Meeting (see Exod. 40:34-35). *Sh'chinah* means "dwelling" and through this picture, we see God's intense desire to dwell among His people on earth.

The Tabernacle of David was a preserved and refurbished tabernacle of Moses. By the time of Samuel, it had been set up in Shiloh, which is where Hannah received God's assurance that she would bear Samuel, a son for the Lord's service. Later, after David had become king, he had it moved to Jerusalem, where it became the center of Israelite worship and the celebration of the feasts. The Lord's presence and protection were seen and felt in David's tabernacle.

> *I have seen You in the sanctuary and beheld Your power and Your glory.*
> *For in the day of trouble He will keep me safe in His dwelling;*
> *He will hide me in the shelter of His tabernacle and set me high upon a rock* (Psalm 63:2; 27:5).

Several hundred years later, when David's tent had fallen into disrepair, the prophet Amos wrote of a day in the future when David's tabernacle of praise would be restored, not only to Israel, but to all the Gentiles (nations) who carried God's name (see Amos 9:11-12).

The apostle James quoted this prophecy from Amos to settle a dispute among the Jewish believers in Jerusalem, concerning the inclusion of the Gentiles into the salvation offered by Yeshua. James proved from this verse that it was always God's intention to make His house of prayer accessible to all nations, without the need to convert to Judaism.

> *After this I will return and rebuild David's fallen tent. Its ruins I will rebuild, and I will restore it, that the remnant of men may seek the Lord, and all the Gentiles who bear My name* (Acts 15:16-17).

The Feast of Tabernacles

The Lord Yeshua Himself, as He walked the earth, was a picture of a fleshly tabernacle in which God's glory was pleased to dwell in its fullness.

> *The Word became flesh and made His dwelling among us [literally, "tabernacled" among us]. We have seen His glory, the glory of the One and Only who came from the Father, full of grace and truth* (John 1:14).

On the Mount of Transfiguration, Peter, James, and John saw Yeshua's true glory revealed, although this heavenly glory was normally hidden during the Lord's earthly ministry.

The Lord's Body of Believers is a corporate dwelling place for His glory, as was the Lord's earthly body. His Spirit dwells in us, both individually and corporately. Peter tells us that we are like living stones, being built into a spiritual house to be a holy priesthood (see 1 Pet. 2:5). Paul also affirms that the Lord dwells in our bodies and in our corporate expressions of worship.

> *Do you not know that your body is a temple of the Holy Spirit, who is in you, whom you have received from God?*
> *And in Him you too are being built together to become a dwelling in which God lives by His Spirit* (1 Corinthians 6:19; Ephesians 2:22).

The Feast of Tabernacles reminds us that our spirits dwell in a temporary structure, our mortal flesh. We are strangers in a strange land, and this world does not feel like our home. The Lord warned us that the world can love its own, but it cannot love those who belong to Him because it hated Him first (see John 15:18-19). We are sojourners on this earth, and we are looking forward to a better home.

> *Now we know that if the earthly tent we live in is destroyed, we have a building from God, an eternal home in heaven, not built by human hands. Meanwhile we groan, longing to be clothed with our heavenly dwelling,*

because when we are clothed, we will not be found naked.
For while we are in this tent, we groan and are
burdened, because we do not wish to be unclothed but to
be clothed with our heavenly dwelling, so that what is
mortal may be swallowed up by life (2 Corinthians 5:1-4).

In this earthly tent, we wither as quickly as those poor little willow leaves, cut from their roots in Israel. Our lives are fleeting, and we must put our trust in our heavenly dwelling, where springs of living waters will restore us to permanent and eternal life. Let us labor while it is still day, redeeming the time we have left. Let us use every moment to tabernacle with our King, so that we will not be found unclothed on that day.

The Millennial Tabernacle is a supernatural tabernacle that will be established on earth. Scripture teaches that when the Lord Yeshua returns, He will reign over the earth for a thousand years from Jerusalem. This thousand-year period is called "the Millennium." Isaiah refers to this millennial tabernacle, using the very word *succah* in His amazing description.

(Note: So that the reader will not be confused by this end-time teaching, let me clearly state that in my understanding of the Scriptures, the Lord's thousand-year reign will take place *after* the Rapture, or "Catching Up" of the righteous dead and the living believers. It is not this book's purpose to cover the Lord's return in depth. Even so, the combined teachings in First Corinthians 15:22-28, First Thessalonians 4:15-17, 5:1-5, Second Thessalonians 2:1-12, and Revelation 20:1-10, along with the Old Covenant passages presented in this chapter, give us a helpful composite picture of His return. Those who are resurrected or caught up alive at the time of the Rapture, will return to earth with the Lord and will reign with Him, in their resurrected and glorified bodies.)

Now, returning to Isaiah's prophecy:

Then the Lord will create over all of Mount Zion and
over those who assemble there a cloud of smoke by day and
a glow of flaming fire by night; over all the glory will be
a canopy. It will be a shelter and shade from the heat of

the day, and a refuge and hiding place from the storm and rain (Isaiah 4:5-6).

Because this passage mentions rainstorms and shade from the sun, we can understand that this tabernacle is a shelter on this earth. In Heaven, there will not be any scorching sun or damaging storms (see Rev. 21:22-24; 22:5). The "shelter" that Isaiah describes is the word *succah*, and the word he used for "canopy" is *chuppah*, the very bridal canopy under which a bride and groom marry. The *succah* and *chuppah* seem to be combined into one structure, a huge tabernacle over one of Jerusalem's mountainous regions.

Isaiah 4 also refers to "survivors" of either war or catastrophic events, who will be purified by fire and turn to the Lord wholeheartedly. Again, this is not a particularly heavenly scenario.

The Lord will create over Mount Zion a cloud of smoke by day and a flaming fire by night. Isaiah's prophecy reminds us of Moses' testimony of the Lord's cloud and fire that Israel witnessed in the desert as they fled from the Egyptians, and as the Lord came to speak with them in their camp (see Exod. 13:21-22; Num. 12:5-6; Deut. 31:15-16).

This millennial tabernacle will likely be a supernatural glory-covering over the Lord's city and the remnant of His people during His reign from Jerusalem.

Zechariah also prophesied an end-time attack on Jerusalem by many nations, and at that time, the Lord's pierced feet will stand again on the Mount of Olives. He tells us that all the nations will celebrate the Feast of Tabernacles during this period of the Lord's earthly reign. Likewise, Zechariah also uses the word "survivors."

> *On that day his feet will stand on the Mount of Olives, east of Jerusalem....On that day, living water will flow out from Jerusalem, half to the eastern sea and half to the western sea, in summer and in winter. The Lord will be king over the whole earth. On that day there will be one Lord, and His name the only name.*

A Prophetic Calendar: The Feasts of Israel

> *Then the survivors from all the nations that have attacked Jerusalem will go up year after year to worship the King, the Lord Almighty and to celebrate the Feast of Tabernacles. If any of the peoples of the earth do not go up to Jerusalem to worship the King, the Lord Almighty, they will have no rain* (Zechariah 14:4a,8-9;16-17).

At that time, not only Jews but all the nations will be required to go up to worship the Lord and to celebrate this feast, or they will not receive rain for the coming year. As we have seen, the pouring out of water and prayers for rain are integral parts of this celebration. The fact that the nations will still need rain for their crops to grow is another indication that this millennial period takes place on the same earth that we know and love.

Finally, Tabernacles will be the international holiday God meant it to be. It will be for all nations and individuals who love the Lord and His feasts! When we wave our branches in our worship services, we wave them to the North, the South, the East, and the West. We are rehearsing for the day that the four corners of the earth will be covered with the Lord's glory! We are blessing the whole earth. All believers deserve the chance to bless the whole earth by celebrating this joyful festival!

The prophet Ezekiel gives us a third witness about this earthly reign and millennial temple. The last nine chapters of Ezekiel are about the new earthly temple in Jerusalem, which the Lord will inhabit. This temple, shown to Ezekiel in a vision, has never yet been built in Jerusalem.

> *Then the man brought me to the gate facing east, and I saw the glory of the God of Israel coming from the east.. ..The glory of the Lord entered the temple through the gate facing east. Then the Spirit lifted me up and brought me into the inner court, and the glory of the Lord filled the temple....He said, "Son of man, this is the place of my throne and the place for the soles of my feet. This is where I will live among the Israelites forever"* (Ezekiel 43:1-2; 4-5,7a).

After the soles of His wounded feet land on the earth, He will live among the Israelites "forever." He will gather in His Bride from all the nations, and many will come up, year after year, to celebrate Tabernacles. We'll be doing it then...why not start rehearsing now?

The Heavenly Tabernacle is disclosed in Hebrews 8:5. Moses was shown the real tabernacle in Heaven and was told to build the earthly one in the same way. It was this heavenly tabernacle that the Lord Yeshua entered, offering His own blood on Heaven's Mercy Seat.

> *When Christ came as high priest of the good things that are already here, He went through the greater and more perfect tabernacle that is not man-made, that is to say, not a part of this creation* (Hebrews 9:11).

The waving of the palm branches will continue for eternity, in the very Tabernacle of God's Throne. This feast is, indeed, an *everlasting* ordinance. Everlasting means everlasting. The following passage from Revelation contains so many references to the elements of this feast, it is impossible not to connect it to the Feast of Tabernacles.

> *After this I looked and there before me was a great multitude that no one could count, from every nation, tribe, people and language, standing before the throne and in front of the Lamb. They were wearing white robes and were holding palm branches in their hands. And they cried out in a loud voice:*
>
> *"Salvation belongs to our God, who sits on the throne, and to the Lamb."*
>
> *Then one of the elders asked me, "These in white robes—who are they, and where did they come from?"*
>
> *I answered, "Sir, you know."*
>
> *And he said, "These are they who have come out of the great tribulation; they have washed their robes and made them white in the blood of the Lamb. Therefore,*

they are before the throne of God and serve Him day and night in His temple; and He who sits on his throne will spread His tent over them.

Never again will they hunger; never again will they thirst.

The sun will not beat upon them, nor any scorching heat.

For the Lamb at the center of the throne will be their shepherd; He will lead them to springs of living water.

And God will wipe away every tear from their eyes" (Revelation 7:9-10;13-17).

Here we see the joyful throngs of worshipers waving branches and declaring the salvation of our God, as in Psalm 118. They are serving day and night in God's temple, and He has spread His tent over them. It is a shelter from the scorching heat that they endured on the earth. They will never again suffer hunger or thirst, as we read in Isaiah 55, John 4, and Revelation 21 and 22. He will lead them to springs of living water, as Yeshua promised His people in John 7, during the Water Ceremony. All of our mourning is turned to joy on the Feast of Tabernacles, and God will wipe every tear from our eyes.

When we depart from these mortal tents, we will find our city whose builder and architect is God. We will dwell permanently in His tabernacle, never to be separated again!

The Lord has always desired to dwell with us, to walk with us in the cool of the day, and to enjoy the fellowship of a meal with us. Even a cup of coffee!

Now the dwelling of God is with men, and He will live with them. They will be His people, and God Himself will be with them and be their God. He will wipe every tear from their eyes. There will be no more death or mourning or crying or pain, for the old order of things has passed away (Revelation 21:3-4).

CELEBRATING TABERNACLES

In Chapter 6, I provided a structure for a worship service for believers in Yeshua to celebrate the Memorial of Blasting (the Feast of Trumpets). You may recall that I also suggested that you could follow a similar pattern for the Feast of Weeks, the Day of Atonement, and the Feast of Tabernacles, along with Purim and Hanukah, which will be covered in the next two chapters. Since Tabernacles does not usually appear on our normal calendars, the dates for the years 2009-2012 are 10/3/09, 9/23/10, 10/13/11, and 10/1/12.[5]

Here are a few differences that will help you create a service that is unique to this feast.

1. The shofar would normally be blown only on Trumpets and the Day of Atonement. However, sometimes believers simply wish to blow the shofar as a declaration of freedom, or a call to arms, or a prophetic act of summoning Israel or another nation to repentance and revival. This is fine, and if the Lord's Spirit leads, you can insert this penetrating sound at any sacred gathering; but biblically speaking, a Tabernacles service would not normally include the shofar.

2. It is very important to wave branches before the Lord on this feast. As I mentioned in this chapter, you can order them from a synagogue if your region has a Jewish community that orders these packages from Israel. If not, you may cut down leafy branches of any tree or bush, although willow, myrtle, or palm would be desirable. (Obviously, it is not permissible to cut branches off your neighbor's trees without permission; that would be called "stealing.") You would wave them to the four directions of the earth, as a prophetic covering of the earth with God's glory. You can also

wave them during the worship songs and dance with them. Just be careful that you don't poke someone with them, because the dried palm leaves have very sharp tips, and personal injury will detract from the worshipers' joy!

3. A number of wonderful Scripture verses pertaining to Tabernacles were shared throughout this chapter. Feel free to use any or all of these to have the participants read aloud as part of the service. I strongly encourage you to read Psalm 118 and the verses from John 7, which the Lord injected into the Water Ceremony. Add any messianic songs you like, from the musical resources provided in the other chapter, or any other worshipful music you love.

4. If you are able, actually build a succah for your family, church, or congregation. I cannot provide the architectural instructions, but I will say this: it should be a rectangular hut, at least large enough for a family to sit in around a small table and have a meal. It should have at least three sides, although it is more common to have four sides, with a tent-flap opening to get in and out. The frame can be constructed of wooden tent poles, and the "walls" can be canvas or plastic, or any material you wish to use. You can even make plywood walls if you wish. The roof should be partially open to the sky, at least enough to see some stars. You can lay branches across the roof poles. We add a clear plastic cover over our roof, in case it rains, and we don't want the table or carpets to get soggy. Often, families will hang fruits or gourds from the roof, string electric lights across the top (I will *not* call them Christmas lights, but

you know what lights I mean!), and decorate the walls with their children's artwork or paper fruits. You can be as creative as you wish! Perhaps you can google the word *succah* and find some Web sites that support building your own succah or purchasing a pre-fabricated succah kit. Some families just pitch a tent, if they cannot build one.

5. If desired, you can hold a Water-Pouring Ceremony, by filling a pitcher with water and pouring it into a basin placed on the altar of your church. One year, we (the crazy intercessors) went down to the river, filled a pitcher with water, and walked through the town, pouring the water out on the streets and sidewalks of our town, while reciting verses and prayers for revival. We greeted people who saw this strange procession, and even got to pray for a few. This was a very powerful prophetic act, and I believe the Lord was delighted with our "offering."

THE LORD'S HEART FOR A DRINK OFFERING

When I finished writing all the teachings in this chapter, I asked the Lord to insert His word about this feast, and this is what I received:

I see drops of water, drops of rain, drops of tears, falling from heavenly clouds. I see the tears of God watering the earth, falling into rivulets and gullies, forming streams and leading down into rivers, forming flowing rivers in dry riverbeds, and flowing down into a mighty ocean, the drink offering of tears, the tears of My people, the tears of God, the tears of Messiah, the tears of those who thirst for justice but do not find it, the tears of those who weep for the victims of lawlessness, but find no comfort on this earth.

207

I AM the Lord, and I AM looking for My drink offering to fall from the skies, fall from the eyes, the eyes of men and angels, the eyes of women and children, the eyes of the wealthy and successful, the eyes of the complacent and the satisfied, the eyes of laborers who float through each work day in a trance-like stupor, sleepwalking and unfeeling, completing their daily assignments like robot-slaves.

I AM looking for passion, for tears, for shouts, for extravagant rivers of water to be poured out and wasted before Me. Waste your sleep! Waste your meals! Waste your spare time on Me. Waste your night hours in silent meditation upon My heart. Waste your tears on My crucifixion, and on what My love for you cost Me!

I want a drink offering. I do not desire the blood of your children! Stop shedding the blood of My children and start shedding the tears of pity and repentance. These will be poured out at the basin of My holy altar in Heaven; these will run down over the souls of the martyrs, who cry out under My altar, who themselves were poured out as drink offerings before Me as they were killed for My testimony.

I see raindrops falling from Heaven, autumn rains, needful rains, the rains of crop growth, the rains of fertility, the rains of restoration, renewal, and revival of the earth and its inhabitants.

Let all the nations come up and celebrate the Feast of Tabernacles with My people Israel! Let them wave their branches to Me and shout with loud voices My praise. Let them celebrate with all their might and provoke My people to envy and desire, that they might desire Me and crave My face. Then will I open the windows of Heaven, and the river of water and fire from My throne will both water the earth and burn jealously all the pride and greed of men, even My Church.

I will send down fire on your sacrifice as you water it
with your tears, as Elijah soaked his sacrifice before I came
and consumed it with fire. I will consume your offerings
as I consumed Solomon's offerings, if you will mingle your
tears with Mine, the very tears of God.

This is My drink offering, and this is My heart for the
Feast of Tabernacles this year, as you write My book.
Amen.

As I pondered this word from the Lord, I was perplexed that He was
asking for *tears* as part of His drink offering. Since Tabernacles is a very
joyous festival, we would not normally weep.

I sat before the Lord several days after receiving this word, and I told
Him that I was confused about why He would wish for weeping on the
most joyous festival of the calendar. To be honest, I did not expect Him to
answer me. But the Lord is faithful, even when I doubt. He answered me
with a question: *"When do the autumn rains begin?"*

I realized by this amazing question that when we pray for rain, we are
always hoping the rain will not begin until Tabernacles is over! It would not
be good for rain to fall while we are camping out in our rugged and open
booths.

I answered the Lord, "After Succot." I then knew that He was asking
for weeping to take place after this festival was over, rather than during our
joyful celebration. Therefore, I say to the reader, "Go and do likewise!"
Celebrate this feast with all your heart for eight days, and when the season
of the fall feasts is concluded, offer the Lord the drink offering He has
requested in this prophetic word.

This concludes the teachings on the fall feasts. *Amen!*

PART III

THE FEASTS OF DELIVERANCE FROM OUR ENEMIES

Chapter 9

HANUKAH AND THE
ORIGINAL ANTICHRIST

Of the seven biblical feasts we have studied, Passover was an example of a feast of deliverance from our enemies, because God rescued us from the Egyptians with great power from Heaven's arsenals. Throughout the Seder meal, we celebrate the supernatural acts of deliverance that God accomplished for His covenant people, against all odds.

It is very dear to the Lord's heart and enriching to our hearts for us to remember and recount these moments of deliverance. In fact, we give a party in the Lord's honor, expressing our thankfulness that He saved us from our enemies, who were stronger than we.

The other two festivals that are specifically commemorations of the Lord's physical salvation are Hanukah and Purim. These two holidays are not among the seven Feasts of the Lord laid out in Leviticus 23. Both are celebrations of historic deliverances of the Jewish people from their enemies, which occurred well after the books of the Law and most of the Prophets were written.

The Hanukah deliverance took place during the four hundred years between the last writing of the Old Testament and the Gospels. The Purim deliverance took place in the fifth century B.C., when the Jews were subject to the Persian Empire, and is taken from the Book of Esther. Although

Esther's is the earlier history, I have written about Hanukah before Purim, due to their timing on the calendar. Hanukah comes seventy-five days after Tabernacles, usually in December; Purim occurs about one month before Passover, just at the end of the biblical calendar, usually in late February or March.

There is an old Jewish saying about these types of holidays: "They tried to kill us. We won. Let's eat!" These holidays are corporate acts of gratitude, very joyful and precious in the Lord's eyes. As with Passover, we have a feast!

It is also noticed and appreciated by God when individuals give a public testimony or celebration for a wonderful deliverance He has granted them, ending a terrible season or crisis in their lives. Sometimes, when the ordeal is finally over, we breathe a sigh of relief, but do not take the trouble to go back and celebrate His great salvation. However, the Lord loves a joyful and worshipful banquet in His honor as we remember what He has done. It makes His heart glad. Now, to the history books!

A KING DREAMS THE FUTURE

There is a great deal of prophecy and history that goes into the story of Hanukah. I will try to present the enormous significance of this festival, while keeping the explanations and the lengthy histories concise.

We must begin with the Book of Daniel. During the period that Judah was taken into captivity by Babylon (c. 600 B.C.), Nebuchadnezzar, King of Babylon, had a disturbing dream. He saw a statue with a golden head, with chest and arms of silver, belly and thighs of bronze, legs of iron, and feet a mixture of iron and clay. He then saw a rock strike the statue, and the entire statue was broken to tiny pieces, which were swept away with the wind. But the rock became a huge mountain that filled the whole earth.

The king ordered his wise men not only to interpret his dream, but also to tell him what he had dreamed, and threatened to execute them if they could not do so. As the astrologers could not accomplish this impossible task, God raised up the Hebrew captive Daniel to pray for information that no man could know. The Lord answered Daniel, and he received both the dream and its interpretation (see Dan. 2:1-45).

The four parts of the statue represented four successive Gentile empires that God would permit to rule the earth for limited periods of time. The first was Babylon, which was the head of gold. The second would be Medo-Persia, which was represented by the chest of silver. The third would be Greece, pictured in the belly of bronze. The fourth would be Rome, symbolized by the iron legs. Apart from Babylon, of which King Nebuchadnezzar was the ruler, none of these other kingdoms had yet come to power. The Lord had shown this Gentile king the future, hidden in the mysterious language of dreams. The rock that broke all the worldly empires was God's coming Kingdom, which became a huge mountain, filling all the earth.

FOUR BEASTLY SUPERPOWERS

History later fulfilled Daniel's interpretation. The Medo-Persians conquered Babylon in 539 B.C.; Alexander the Great established the Greek Empire in 330 B.C.; and the Roman Empire rose to power in 63 B.C. It was into the Roman Empire that God chose His Messiah to be born and to die.

All four of these Gentile superpowers inflicted great harm upon the land of Israel and its inhabitants or persecuted the Jewish people who were scattered throughout their regions of influence. The briefest summary of these persecutions is as follows:

1. Babylon concluded its lengthy invasion of southern Israel in 586 B.C. They killed thousands, burned the Temple and the royal palace, razed Jerusalem, carried away the gold and silver vessels, tables, and candlesticks of God, as well as Solomon's laver, and took into captivity the Jewish survivors, leaving a remnant behind.[1]

2. Under the Persian reign of Xerxes, son of Darius (486-465 B.C.), an official named Haman was elevated to power. He devised a genocidal scheme, born out of his vengeful rage against one Jewish man who would not

show him sufficient honor, to annihilate all the Jews throughout the Persian Empire. This story is contained in the Book of Esther and will be discussed in detail in the next chapter.

3. After the death of Alexander the Great, his Greek Empire was divided into four regions, which were ruled by four lesser kings. One of these four rulers became the cruel tyrant whose campaigns of persecution are the subject of this chapter.

4. The Roman Empire's beastly brutality against Jerusalem and the Jewish people during the first and second century has already been noted in Chapter 2 of this book.

COVENANT OR ASSIMILATION?

During and after Alexander's reign, the Greek language, philosophies, religion, and culture exerted enormous influence over the vast territories he had conquered. The spread of Greek influence over conquered territories was called "Hellenization."

Two of the regions under Greek rule were Egypt, ruled by Ptolomy Soter, and Syria, ruled by Seleucus Nicator. These rulers founded dynasties that continued in power for close to two centuries. Syria and Egypt were continually striving against each other for dominance, and the tiny land of Israel was sandwiched between their ambitions and armies. In fact, Israel was the central route linking Arabia to Europe and Asia to Africa. The Jewish people were caught in the middle of a geo-political struggle, which resulted in much oppression and persecution for their adherence to God's covenants.

This period was marked by much political intrigue. In 175 B.C., Syrian king Seleucus IV was murdered by his minister, Heliodorus, and the king's younger brother usurped the throne. His name was Antiochus IV, but he blasphemously called himself "Antiochus Epiphanes," which means, "the manifestation of God." Not only was there treachery and murder in the Syrian corridors of power, but Israel's priestly families were also caught up in this life-and-death battle for power and control.

By the time of Antiochus IV's reign, a bitter schism had arisen among the Jews in Israel, over the issue of Hellenization. There were two severely divided groups: the Jewish worshipers who clung to the faith of their fathers and the Law of Moses; and those Jews who wildly embraced everything Greek, from their names to their gods to their foods and customs. Those who wanted to become Greeks curried favor with Antiochus, bribing him for positions, and requesting permission to introduce Greek customs to Jerusalem. Through much wickedness, some within Israel's priesthood were corrupted with every form of greed, idolatry, power-mongering, and even murder.

At that time, Israel's high priest was a righteous man named Onias III, whose priesthood was from 196-175 B.C. His brother Joshua was a Hellenist, who sought to radically reform Israel's customs to the Greek way of life. Joshua changed his name to Jason, a Greek name, and offered Antiochus a large bribe to appoint him as high priest instead of his godly brother.

As high priest, Jason enlisted Israelites as citizens of Antioch and built a gymnasium in Jerusalem's Tyropoeon Valley where the men performed naked. Some of the Hellenists underwent surgery to cover their circumcision, so that they would look like Greeks when naked.

Several years later, a Benjamite who was called Menelaus bribed Antiochus with a larger sum and wrested the priesthood from Jason.[2] As if a pagan king could appoint God's chosen priests for a sum of money! Menelaus stole gold from God's temple to pay Antiochus the bribe. Onias learned what he had done and tried to make public Menelaus' crime. However, Menelaus conspired with one of the king's officials, and through deceit and treachery, Onias was murdered.

For a while, Antiochus continued to make friends with the Jewish leaders who wanted nothing to do with Moses; they continued to flatter Antiochus and bring him revenues that should have gone to the Lord's house.

These Jews prostituted themselves before an idol-worshiping king to suit their goals. They desired to reshape Israel from a monotheistic nation under God's law to a one-world Greek government, with its language, currency, and religion. They made deals with the king and received power and authority to spread their political and social agenda into every level of Israeli life.

The godly Jews grew more and more despised; they were considered to be antiquated religious zealots who were too stubborn to realize that Greek culture and religion were far more sophisticated and civilized than ancient covenants with the Hebrew God. As we will now see, Greek culture was not as "civilized" as it was purported to be.

THE TRIBULATION

The event that triggered a full-blown tribulation for the godly Jews was Antiochus' decision to invade Egypt in 169 B.C. He would have conquered this region, but Rome sent a dispatch to force his withdrawal from Egypt. Antiochus was enraged and humiliated by Rome's exercise of authority. He needed to display his wrath and frustration against a defenseless people, since Rome had thwarted his simmering aggression. Unsuspecting Jerusalem lay directly in his path northward, and instead of continuing on his journey back to Syria, the demonized tyrant ordered his soldiers to destroy Jerusalem's center of worship and murder its inhabitants. Within three days he had slaughtered forty thousand Jews, not sparing women, children, or the elderly. Another forty thousand were sold as slaves.[3]

He broke into the Temple of God with much destruction and stripped the Holy Place of its sacred articles. [4] On the 25th of Kislev, 168 B.C., he erected a statue of Zeus in God's Holy Place, with his own face on the idol. He sacrificed a pig and sprinkled its blood on God's altar. He poured the broth over the Torah scrolls and then burned them with fire.[5] The prophet Daniel had prophesied that a wicked ruler would set up an abominable idol in the Holy Place and would leave Jerusalem desolated of her worshipers (see Dan. 11:31).

Harsh laws were decreed, forbidding Jews to circumcise their infant sons, observe Mosaic dietary laws, or keep the Sabbath; they were required to participate in the daily sacrifice of pigs on Greek altars in every village and town, and to eat the sacrificed flesh.

These laws were enforced and policed with house-to-house searches. Those found owning Torah scrolls or observing any aspect of Judaism were tortured and killed. Women who circumcised their sons were crucified with their babies hung from their necks, strangling them both. Many faithful Jews were mutilated and burned alive in boiling cauldrons.[6] There are a number of chilling and inspiring stories from this hideous period in which Greek soldiers offered "deals" to the stubborn Jews to entice them to avoid the slow torture with a face-saving pretense.

In one case, a beloved and elderly scribe named Eleazar was refusing to eat sacrificed pork, although they were about to scourge him to death. The officers then tempted him to bring in some "lawful meat" and eat it, so that the people would think he was obeying Greek law, even though the meat would not actually be pork. Eleazar refused, stating that he would not wish to mislead the young men, who would think he had gone over to the foreign religion. Under the final blows of the sharp instruments, he said, "The Lord in His holy knowledge knows that, while I might have escaped death, I endure dreadful pains in my body from being flogged; but in my heart I am glad to suffer this, because I fear Him."[7]

In another terrible case of the martyrdom of a mother and her seven sons, one of the children spoke these words to his tormentors just before he died: "It is better to die at men's hands and look for the hopes God gives of being raised again by Him; for you will have no resurrection to life."[8]

The writer of Hebrews made several references to this time of tribulation in Hebrews 11, the memorial to the faithful ones:

> *Others were tortured and refused to be released, so that they might obtain a better resurrection* (Hebrews 11:35b).

For the Jews who complied with Antiochus' decrees, there was favor and promotion. The Hellenized Jews could not understand why the stubborn worshipers would undergo such horrific deaths, they and their children, when they could have simply acquiesced to a new culture and religion and received great rewards. It must have seemed like sheer madness to the compromisers, who were glad to become just like the nations. It apparently did not occur to them that their fellow Jews were being butchered by the most sophisticated and "civilized" one-world religion on the earth. What is wrong with this picture? Is there tolerance for everyone, except for those who worship the God of Israel?

These histories of martyrdom have often made me wonder if I would hold up under such a tribulation and test of my integrity; to say that these martyrs have inspired me is an understatement. They are a part of that "great cloud of witnesses" who will cheer us on when our moment arrives to show Heaven where we really stand. May we stand indeed.

The Resistance Arises

At this time there was a priest named Mattathias, a well-respected citizen of Jerusalem with five sons. When the Greek officers came to his hometown of Modi'in, a village about seventeen miles northwest of Jerusalem, they wanted Mattathias to set a "good" example for the townspeople. The officer commanded him to slaughter a pig on the altar before the town. Mattathias refused, but immediately, a fellow Jew stepped forward and "obediently" slaughtered the pig. Zealous anger rose up in Mattathias, who ran forward, killed the officer with his own sword, and then killed the traitorous Jew. He tore down the pagan altar, and then he and his sons fled to the Judean desert, taking none of their possessions with them. Many others followed them and fled the persecution with their wives and children; they dwelt in caves and dens like hunted animals.

This was a terrible time of hardship and hiding, also honored in the eleventh chapter of Hebrews:

> They went about in sheepskins and goatskins, destitute,
> persecuted and mistreated—the world was not worthy of

them. They wandered in deserts and mountains, and in caves and holes in the ground (Hebrews 11: 37b-38).

On one occasion, the soldiers tracked the fugitives to a cave where a thousand of them were hiding. It was the Sabbath day, and the Jews chose not to fight on that day. The soldiers lit a fire in the cave, and the unresisting Jews all perished in the smoke and flames. From this terrible incident, Mattathias persuaded them that it was better to fight for their lives on the Sabbath than to let the soldiers always choose the easiest day to kill them all, when they would never resist. From then on, his ragtag army was willing to fight and to die, even on the Sabbath, rather than to be slaughtered like helpless sheep.

About a year later, Mattathias died of illness, and his son Judah continued to lead the resistance against the Syrian army. His nickname was "Maccabee" which means "Hammer." Despite being greatly outnumbered, Judah and his men, largely through prayer and fasting, managed to gain many astonishing victories over larger and larger forces of foreign soldiers. Much is written about these battles and strategies in the comprehensive writings of the historian Josephus, and also in the respected histories in the first book of Maccabees. However, we must summarize these points and move into the Feast of Hanukah.

THE REDEDICATION OF THE TEMPLE

Judah Maccabee was an incredibly brave and inspiring leader to his tiny army of exhausted and hungry soldiers, who lived as fugitives in poverty for several years. As the Syrian forces would regroup each time, with an even larger army against the Jews, Judah would stir up their hearts with courage to die for the Lord's covenants. As William Wallace ("Braveheart") was to Scotland, so Judah Maccabee was to trampled Israel. Due to this uncommon determination, victory after unlikely victory was granted by the Lord to these godly men.

After a particularly large defeat of Antiochus' soldiers, Judah gathered the multitude to go up to Jerusalem to offer sacrifices to the one true God.

When they arrived, and saw the degree of desecration and destruction, they tore their clothes and mourned aloud at the condition of God's house.

They then began to purge the Temple, bringing in new vessels, tearing down the pagan altar, and bringing in new and uncut stones for the altar, as the Law of Moses required. They replaced the altar of incense, the tables, and the candlesticks. After much work, they completed the repairs on the 25th day of Kislev, exactly three years to the day after the abomination that wrought desolation upon Jerusalem had been erected.

When all things were set right, the grateful and joyful worshipers celebrated the dedication of the Temple unto the Lord. In Hebrew, the word for "dedication" is *Hanukah*. They lit the lamps with sacred oil and offered sacrifices to God, singing songs with harps, flutes, and cymbals, and worshiping the Lord for granting them victory over their enemies. They also considered this victory to be so miraculous that they encouraged Jews everywhere to continue to celebrate this day as a lasting memorial to God's faithfulness, for He recovered what the enemy had stolen and trampled. We serve a redeeming God. Surely, His Holy Place was redeemed, at great cost in Jewish blood, on that unique and excellent day.

Seventy-five days earlier, they had missed the Feast of Tabernacles for the third year in a row, due to the relentless persecutions and hiding. Their joy was so great at being able to worship the Lord again that they celebrated for eight days, waving branches and singing psalms, recapturing the joy of the eight-day feast that had been denied them for so long. The Maccabees recorded their eight-day celebration in this passage, in which "Tabernacles" is translated as "the Camping Out Festival":

And they celebrated it for eight days with gladness, like the Camping Out Festival,[the Feast of Tabernacles], and recalled how, a little while before, during the Camping Out Festival they had been wandering in the mountains and caverns like wild animals.

So carrying wands wreathed with leaves, and beautiful branches and palm leaves too they offered hymns of praise to Him who had brought to pass the purification of His own place. And they passed a public ordinance and decree that the whole Jewish nation should observe these days every year.[9]

There is also a rabbinic tradition concerning the lighting of the lamp on the 25th of Kislev that falls approximately in December on the Roman calendar. According to tradition, the Jews found only one small flask of consecrated olive oil among the ruins of the Temple, only enough to burn for one day. However, when they lit the golden Menorah, the oil miraculously burned for eight days. It is for this reason that we light eight candles for the eight nights of Hanukah.

Since the multiplication of the oil is neither recorded in Josephus, nor in the books of the Maccabees, it is hard to be certain of this account. Those who were accomplishing the repairs were working vigorously to bring in new sacred articles, furniture, and stones for many days. Therefore, there is no reason that they could not have also brought in a sufficient amount of consecrated olive oil to burn continually, as the Law prescribed. Even so, since our God is a God of multiplication, it is very possible that He multiplied the oil until fresh oil could be consecrated and burned.

However, the historical accounts all agree that they celebrated this event for eight days, as they would have for the Feast of Tabernacles. Therefore, we joyfully light our Hanukah candles for eight days, and sing inspiring songs of God's deliverance of those who fear Him and do not consider the threats of wicked men.

THE DEATH OF JUDAH MACCABEE

After the miraculous Israeli victory and the rededication of the Temple, other foreign armies were stirred up to attack the Jews and Jerusalem, in addition to repeated attempts by Syrian forces. Judah Maccabee's battles with these hostile people groups continued for many years. Among them were the Ammonites and the Idumeans (Esau's descendants, who became the ancestry of Herod and his dynasty).

It is hard to exaggerate the courage and perseverance of this priestly warrior, Judah, son of Mattathias, who was forced to lead his people through fierce battles for almost ten years. When this remarkable hero finally fell in battle with a Syrian general, even his death was a feat of great courage and nobility, such as has rarely been seen in the pages of history. It saddens me to think that people can celebrate Hanukah without deeply honoring the sacrifices of men of character, like Judah, who gave us this victory.

It also saddens me that because this history took place during the four hundred years between the Old and the New Testament, it is not widely known by most Christians.

Modern and ancient biblical historians, including Flavius Josephus, often cite the detailed histories recorded in the books of the Maccabees, which are found in the Apocrypha. The books of the Apocrypha were included in the Septuagint, the Greek translation of the Old Testament most often used by New Testament writers. They were also included in the Authorized King James Version of the Bible until 1827, when the Protestant British and American Bible Societies removed the Apocrypha from the books of Scripture.[10] Even so, scholars agree that Maccabees is a reliable historical record; without these documents, we would not have the story of Hanukah, and we would lose a significant source of inter-testamental history. The books of the Apocrypha are still included in Catholic Bibles.

Josephus was a first-century Jewish diplomat, general, and historian, and is considered the most cited writer in the world of biblical scholars. Without his comprehensive writings, the biblical reference books in seminary libraries and universities, as well as our own Bibles' text notes and commentaries, would be much reduced in quantity and quality.[11]

THE DEATH OF ANTIOCHUS IV

Throughout Antiochus' infamous reign, there were at least three times when he set out to destroy the Jewish people and Jerusalem, in particular. We saw the results of two of these invasions in the previous sections, although I compressed the narrative. The third attempt brought the wrath of God upon him, and he died in great agony, as he had tormented so many victims during his life.

During the wars of Judah Maccabee, Antiochus was traveling through Persia, and learned of a wealthy city where the temple of Diana contained great valuables to be plundered. He attacked, but was driven back as far as

Babylon by the fierce pursuit of the city's defenders, losing many of his troops. He was angry and humiliated.

At the same time, Antiochus was told of yet another battle that Judah Maccabee's forces had won in Judea, and he was enraged. Once more, he vowed to punish the Jews with great slaughter. But as he was charging back to Jerusalem, he was suddenly struck with worms in his intestines, which caused a lengthy and exceedingly painful deterioration of his health. The reader may recall that about one hundred and fifty years later, King Herod was also suddenly struck down with intestinal worms after a proud and blasphemous stance toward the Lord (see Acts 12:21-23).

As his suffering grew more intense, Antiochus began to belatedly humble himself and acknowledge that God was punishing him for his affliction of the Jews. He hastily converted to Judaism and wrote an amicable letter to the Jews in Jerusalem, as if they were the oldest of friends. Obviously, he was desperate for healing, but it was too late for the arrogant butcher, who had devised unspeakable tortures for the faithful Jews. Finally, his body was destroyed by such a foul and hideous disease that even his own soldiers could not get near him. Thus did God put an end to a lawless one, who dared to defile God's Holy Place with idolatry and innocent blood.

WHAT WOULD YESHUA DO?

We see in John 10:22 that the Lord Yeshua was in Jerusalem for the Feast of Hanukah. In English, it is called the Feast of Dedication. Although we see many references to Jewish feasts throughout the New Testament, this passage is the only one where the Feast of Hanukah is specified.

The victories of the Maccabees had occurred only one hundred and fifty years before Yeshua's birth, and several issues would have been on the minds of the religious leaders at this season. One would be the miracles that God did for the faithful Jews who stood firm in the face of terrible persecution. It is interesting that on this occasion, the Lord spoke of His miracles, stating that the miracles He did in His Father's name validated His claim to be one with the Father (see John 10:25,30,38).

Another issue that would have been on their minds was martyrdom and the resurrection of the dead. Their recent ancestors in this very city had submitted to painful deaths, while trusting that eternal life awaited those who remained faithful. At this feast, the Lord declared to them that He gives eternal life to those who listen to His voice, and that no one can pluck them out of His hand (see John 10:28-29). In saying this, the Lord was likely recalling His ancestors' determination to endure the destruction of their bodies, while bravely declaring their resurrection to their tormentors. Soon, the Lord would endure martyrdom for the joy set before Him, a martyrdom more costly and terrible than that of His earthly fathers.

Finally, the Jewish leadership was aware of the corruption of the priesthood that had occurred during and after that period, as well as the political and religious prostitution of their leaders with Greek rulers. Now, the Jewish nation was under Roman rule, and it would be tempting to cut deals with the Roman authorities to obtain favorable positions or to avoid persecution. Herod was a Roman client, a ruler without integrity or living faith in God.

The Sadducees were of the priestly lineage and controlled temple politics. Some were more motivated by a desire for power than for faith, repentance, and humility. Hanukah may have been something of an embarrassment to the Sadducees in particular, or even to the Pharisees, who worked with them. Both groups were, in fact, already plotting to kill Yeshua, although He had committed no sin (see John 10:31,39).

Hanukah may have reminded them of the shameful behavior of their priestly fathers who sold out their brothers and sisters to martyrdom. Or, they may have told themselves that they were as faithful as priestly Mattathias and his sons, and would never have compromised their faith to protect or advance themselves.

CELEBRATING HANUKAH TODAY

I believe that in the Lord's generation, they would have celebrated Hanukah by reading aloud the stories of bravery and martyrdom from the books of the Maccabees in the temple courts or reciting them from memory in their homes. They also would have sung stirring hymns and psalms about the resolve needed to lay down our lives for the worship of the one true God, Adonai. They would have lit special oil lamps in their homes, but those who lived near Jerusalem might have come to the temple courts to participate in the Feast of Lights (as it was also called) and enjoy the corporate lighting of special Menorahs.

Today, Hanukah has become somewhat of a parallel holiday to Christmas because both holidays occur in December. I am convinced that whether or not a Christian chooses to celebrate the Lord's birthday on December 25, the Lord would be very pleased if all believers honor the Feast of Dedication as their Lord Jesus did. After all, many of His most important teachings took place in the temple courts, and had the Temple not been reclaimed from pagan soldiers and rededicated, neither He nor any other Jewish worshipers could have gone up for the Feasts of the Lord, year after year, as was His custom.

For the years 2009-2012, the dates of Hanukah are 12/12/09, 12/2/10, 12/21/11, and 12/9/12.[12] Once again, the first candle would be lit on the night *before* each date given.

Many Jewish families give gifts to each other, particularly to the children, for eight nights. Our family did this as well, when the children were young. Other Hanukah customs include the following:

1. Recounting the desecration of the Temple and persecutions of Antiochus, the martyrdom of the faithful Jews, the bravery of Judah and his ragtag army, and the miraculous victories God granted them as they cleansed and purified the Temple after such great suffering.

2. Eating fried potato pancakes, called "latkes" and jelly doughnuts, which remind us of the oil in the sacred lamps (some of us can only eat a tiny bit of fried foods, but we still love God!).

3. Singing special songs about Hanukah. Some of these are found on my worship CD, *Remember Me*.[13]

4. Playing a game with a special spinning top called a "dreidel," and "gambling" with chocolate gold coins.

5. Lighting a nine-branched candelabra, called a "Menorah." We light one additional candle each night for eight nights, and we sing special Hanukah blessings as we light them (see the next section for more detail).[14]

EIGHT LITTLE CANDLES

To me personally, the singing of Hanukah songs and the lighting of candles are by far the most joyful and inspiring parts of this feast. Although I love the potato pancakes and the chocolate coins, they mean nothing to me when compared to the awe of worshiping the Light of the World with my family! I play the piano for hours, and as we sing, the candles burn low, illuminating our living room with a beautiful glow of flickering lights.

The special candelabra, which we use only at Hanukah, is different from the seven-branched lampstand found in the ancient temple, and which is still a symbol of modern Judaism. Because our people celebrated for eight days, we use a special menorah with nine branches. There is one central branch, with four branches on either side, one for each of the eight days.

On the first night, we light the central candle with a match. This middle candle is called the *shamash*, which in Hebrew means "the servant." We then use this servant candle to light the first candle, placed on the *right side* of the menorah. Each night, we put in the correct number of candles, according to which day it is, from right to left. We always use the shamash to light the other candles. This servant candle clearly represents Yeshua, the Servant of the Lord, who gives light to all the other little candles in the house. We cannot light our own lamps, but we require His oil and light to give light to the whole world. He was the light, shining in the darkness, and the darkness has not overcome Him!

Each night, we sing Hebrew blessings as we light the candles. I will provide the words to these blessings here, and you can also obtain the proper Hebrew pronunciation and the sung melodies from my CD, *Remember Me*, or from the resources listed in the endnotes to this chapter. On the *first night*, we say or sing:

1. *Baruch Ata Adonai, Eloheinu Melech HaOlam Asher kid'shanu b'mitz'votav V'tzivanu l'hadlik ner shel Chanukah.*

2. *Baruch Ata Adonai, Eloheinu Melech HaOlam Sh'asa nisim l'avoteinu Bayamim hahem, laz'man hazeh.*

3. *Baruch Ata Adonai, Eloheinu Melech HaOlam Sh'hechianu, v'kiamanu, v'higianu laz'man hazeh.*

On *all other nights*, we only sing the first two blessings, but not the third one. This is their translation:

1. Blessed are You, O Lord our God, King of the universe who has set us apart by Your commandments and has instructed us to kindle the light of Chanukah.

2. Blessed are You, O Lord our God, King of the universe who has done miracles for our fathers in those days, at this time.

3. Blessed are You, O Lord our God, King of the universe who has given us life, sustained us, and has brought us to this time.

After this, we might eat treats, play the dreidel game, or just sing many other worship songs while the candles burn down. I think gift-giving should not be over-emphasized, because it can take away from the awe of this celebration and cause the children to be too consumed with the gifts. Of course, this problem also occurs with Christmas, and we should keep our priorities fixed on the Lord's Person and Presence!

THE ORIGINAL ANTICHRIST

We began this chapter by studying Nebuchadnezzar's dream and Daniel's interpretation of the four parts of the great statue, as well as the Rock of God's Kingdom that would shatter these Gentile superpowers in pieces.

Antiochus IV was a boastful and blasphemous tyrant who arose out of the Greek Empire, the third portion of the statue. He is called a "little horn" in Daniel 8:9-14. A horn in the Bible signifies power, authority, and strength. His small horn grew out of the larger horn of Alexander the Great, which was divided into four parts.

The reason that I have called Antiochus "the original antichrist" is because his beastly reign of terror over the godly Jews was a foreshadowing, or a picture, of a lawless world leader who will arise on the earth in these last days. Throughout the Book of Daniel, there are some prophecies that were fulfilled in the reign of Antiochus IV, and yet other prophecies that seem to refer to a future antichrist.

For example, Daniel 8:9-14 and 11:21-35 describe Antiochus in amazing detail, even though he would not come to power for another four hundred years. However, Daniel 7:7-27, 9:27, and 11:36-45 describe the future antichrist, who will oppress the saints, speak blasphemy against the Most High, and try to change the appointed times (God's calendar) and God's laws (see Dan. 7:23-25).

This latter-day ruler will resemble Antiochus in a number of ways, and we would be well-advised to learn from history so that we might be found faithful in the day of trouble.

The main similarities between these past and future lawless ones are:

1. They are both godless and lawless men, who have no respect for the one true God of Israel or His righteous standards.

2. They both are rulers who desire to unite the world under one language, currency, culture, and religion.

3. They appear to be civilized and sophisticated, and have tolerance for all people, with the exception of one population: the stubborn and zealous worshipers of the God of Abraham, Isaac, and Jacob, the Creator of the Universe.

4. They are both deceptive and subtle and mislead many believers as to their true motives and intentions.

5. They appear to be men of peace, but some event on earth will trigger the manifestation of their demonic rage, hatred, and merciless brutality to all who love God and refuse to bow the knee to an idolatrous system of false worship. Their cruelty will be so severe that many believers will be tempted to give up, so great is the cost of perseverance.

6. They both set up some sort of abominable idol in Jerusalem's temple area, which causes severe destruction in the city and the killing and scattering of Jerusalem's inhabitants.

7. They both come to a miserable end, but not before they have tormented and killed many righteous ones, which God will permit for a season.

Daniel prophesied that "the abomination that causes desolation" would be set up in the temple area, and Antiochus fulfilled this prophecy about four hundred years after Daniel wrote it (see Dan. 11:31).

However, the Lord Yeshua reminded us that this prophetic word was yet to be fulfilled in Matthew 24:15-22. When He spoke these words, Antiochus had already been dead for almost two hundred years. In this passage, He was warning His disciples about the soon-coming Roman destruction of Jerusalem and also the future antichrist, who would set up an abomination that would cause Jerusalem to be desolated (depopulated). Paul also warns us about this coming lawless one in Second Thessalonians 2:1-12, and John speaks of him in First John 4:1-3, Revelation 13, and Revelation 19:19-20.

I have now summarized the key parallels between Antiochus IV, the tyrant of the Hanukah story, and the coming antichrist who will persecute both the Jewish people and the true Christians in the days leading up to the Lord Yeshua's return. These teachings on the endtimes would be a very large topic, and it is not the purpose of this book to cover it thoroughly.

While a number of books have been written on this subject, I have not found many that take into account the whole counsel of Scripture. One book that admirably tackles this very difficult task is *The Pre-Wrath Rapture of the Church,* by Marvin Rosenthal.[15] In addition, Bible teacher Mike Bickle (International House of Prayer, Kansas City, MO) has produced an extraordinarily clear and accurate teaching series on the Book of Revelation. Serious students of the endtimes would greatly benefit from this biblically sound revelation.[16]

THE LORD SHARES HIS LIGHT

I have come to crave and pray earnestly for the closing prophetic words, which the Lord has shared with me for each of the feasts. As I completed the research and teachings in this challenging chapter, I asked the Lord if He would show me His heart for this feast. As I waited patiently for the Lord, He shared this word with me:

> "My oil fills My lamps, My golden vessels. My oil is over-flowing over the heads of My people, My priests who wait upon Me in humility and gentleness.

> "I will fill the lamps that know they are empty. I will give light to the lampstands that require extra oil to burn brightly after the midnight hour has fallen.

"I AM the Bridegroom, coming in the darkest hour to look for faith, living faith, upon the earth. My lampstands must be burning continually; as the Eternal Flame was never to go out, day or night, so My bright ones, My shining ones, My radiant ones must let their light shine before men, even before their enemies in the darkest corners of humanity and on the fringes of the populations who live in seclusion and darkness. A candle penetrates every corner of a room. How much more must My people's light permeate every crevice of society, even the dark and disenfranchised people groups.

"Woe to those who are not found to be with extra oil in their lamps when I come in the darkest hour. Woe to those who could have bought oil from Me, sitting in My Presence and allowing My oil to drip down their heads and over their outspread hands for the healing of the nations!

"I would have filled them," says the Lord! "I would have given them **all** that they needed and **more**, if only they had asked Me! Woe to My churches whose lampstands are found to be empty and dry when I pass by them for the last time, the final examination! I will remove these lampstands," says the Lord. "I will come and take away their lampstands, and no one will ever receive light from them again, nor will they ever burn brightly the lights of truth and conviction in their streets and cities and towns. They will be darkened holes, and how great will be their darkness.

"These churches will be as black holes in the heavens, sucking the light and life out of all who draw too near to their cores, and never emitting My light again!

"Get your oil from Me now! Do not wait and say, 'I will make time for intimate waiting in the Lord's presence when things settle down, when this crisis is over, when the kids are older, when the crazy season passes by.' That moment will not come in time! Get up early, and wait upon Me for oil in the anointed atmosphere of quiet worship music, tears, praise, humility, gentleness, and a broken and contrite heart. My oil can **only** be purchased with this currency. There is no counterfeit currency that can purchase the oil of intimacy with Me. There is no other price you can pay with later. I will not accept it, and you will find Me harsh and unyielding.

"I stretch out My hands to you now in gentleness and humility. Come to Me, and fill your lamps with extra oil. While there is time, come to Me with outspread hands and open and tenderized hearts. This is My heart for the Feast of Lights, the Feast of Dedication. Dedicate your temples to Me now, in complete and utter holiness. Thus says your God and Savior. **Amen.**"

Chapter 10

PURIM
(ESTHER'S FEAST)

Legends and fairy tales have been born out of noble themes that stir and inspire the human imagination. One such theme is that of a beautiful but obscure orphan girl, who grows up to become the queen of a great empire. The king notices her, finds her beautiful, and marries her. Justice reigns in the land, and they live happily ever after.

The Book of Esther is a remarkable book of the Bible, in which the secret of Esther's Judaism simmers quietly beneath a suspenseful tale of political intrigue, pride and prejudice, prayer and fasting, and genocidal madness. The name of God is not named in this book, but His unseen hand is obviously at work behind the scenes, causing events to unfold with purpose and intelligent design. God is glorified in the Book of Esther, although He is not explicitly mentioned.

Unlike a fairy tale, it is precise in its historical detail, the reporting of names and dates, and the geographic and political facts of the Persian Empire during the fifth century B.C. Thus, the Book of Esther commends and acquits itself as a reliable historic document, though it is "stranger than fiction." I am so exceedingly thankful that it has been included in our Bibles, so that all believers can know and understand the urgent end-time prophetic message of this book.

LIKE FATHER, LIKE SON

As we did with Hanukah, we look again to the Book of Daniel for the overview of the four Gentile superpowers who ruled over the Middle East from the Babylonian captivity until the fourth century. The second of these empires was Medo-Persia, and the Book of Esther is set in the Persian capital of Susa, under King Xerxes, son of Darius the Mede. Darius reigned from 522-486 B.C. and his son Xerxes, from 486-465.

We saw King Darius elevate Daniel to one of the highest positions in the Persian government, on a fast track to becoming prime minister (see Dan. 6:1-3). Other jealous officials conspired to destroy Daniel, and because they could find no fault with his leadership, they resorted to trapping him in matters of Hebraic worship. These deceptive men convinced the king to sign into law a new decree stating that no one in Persia could worship any other god but Darius; they deliberately did not mention the identity of their intended victim. Darius trusted them and sealed this decree into Persian law, making it irrevocable.

Since Daniel continued his normal prayer life, he was caught breaking the law, arrested, and thrown into a den of lions. As most readers know, the king was distraught that he had been tricked into signing this law, and he spent the night in prayer and fasting. The Lord saved Daniel's life, and the perpetrators were then thrown into the lion's den and immediately torn apart.

Darius' son, Xerxes, was also tricked into signing an irrevocable Persian decree, suggested to him by an ambitious and ruthless minister named Haman. Xerxes also displayed a grieved conscience when the realities of this law became clear to him, and he realized that innocent lives were at stake. Like his father before him, he had not carefully studied the implications of the new law he was about to sign; he trusted his officials to behave wisely and ethically. When a leader is surrounded by wicked advisors, the innocent suffer, while the king drinks wine. This principle holds true in our society as well; even a good and benevolent president can agree to counsel given to him by advisors who do not acknowledge God's covenants. Later, this president will regret the consequences of his signature, though he did not foresee them at the time. May God surround our leaders with godly counsel!

It is this story of miraculous deliverance that we celebrate each year, usually falling in the month of March. It is the Feast of Purim, and it holds much blessing and spiritual treasure for Christians who choose to honor this commemoration.

A NEW QUEEN

During a particular banquet, Xerxes' queen Vashti exhibited public disrespect for her husband, and he was humiliated before all his officials. Thus, he banished her from her royal position, and three years later, he began to search for a new queen.

Many beautiful virgins were brought into the king's harem, and after a year of preparation, each one was brought before the king for a one-night encounter. One of the girls was a Jewish orphan named Hadassah, who was raised by her cousin Mordechai after the death of her parents. *Hadassah* is the Hebrew name for the myrtle tree, whose branches were gathered on Tabernacles (see Neh. 8:15). Mordechai was a fourth-generation descendant of the Babylonian captivity, and was of the tribe of Benjamin (see Esther 2:5-7). The apostle Paul was also descended from this tribe.

Mordechai had instructed Hadassah not to reveal her Jewish background as she entered the king's lengthy selection process. Since she loved Mordechai like a father, she continued to follow his instructions, even after being moved into the harem in the palace complex.

There was something special about this girl, whose Persian name was Esther. The eunuchs who took care of the harem gave her special attention, and were intent on helping her obtain the king's approval. All the girls were beautiful, but there was something about Esther's spirit that caused her to find favor. When her night finally arrived, the king was very drawn to her, and he crowned her as his new queen (see Esther 2:17).

A LIFE-SAVING NETWORK OF COMMUNICATION

Mordechai seems to have served in some capacity as a civil servant in the Persian capital, since the Scriptures often refer to him being "in the king's gates," a reference to the court of public affairs. One ancient Babylonian text describes an accountant or scribe named "Mardukaya," who served in Xerxes' court.[1] Based on his literary skills as the probable author of the Book of Esther, he may well have been a scribe for the king.

During the months and years that followed, Mordechai remained close to Esther, and they communicated frequently through trusted messengers, who moved daily in and out of the king's gates and returned to the palace complex with his messages to Esther.

One particularly critical communication that took place was Mordechai's warning of an assassination attempt on the king's life. Mordechai overheard two guards plotting this murder and sent a message to Esther, who reported it to the king's officials. The conspirators were tried and hanged (see Esther 2:21-23).

In the case of Persian executions, the English word *hanged* actually refers to being impaled on a stake, common also in other near-eastern cultures. To be impaled means to be either nailed to a structure or to be thrust against a sharp stake and left hanging until death occurs. In Genesis 40:22, an Egyptian baker was "hanged," meaning impaled. During the eighth century B.C., the Assyrians impaled tens of thousands of Israelites; King Darius recorded in his chronicles that he impaled 3,000 Babylonians when he conquered Babylon.[2] Roman crucifixions were also a form of hanging on a stake. This is why our Lord's death fulfilled the verse, "Cursed is everyone who is hanged from a tree" (see Deut. 21:23; Acts 5:30; 10:39; Gal. 3:13).

Although it was Mordechai's warning that saved the king's life, he was given no reward or recognition for his role in this thwarted attack. The invisible hand of God would use this hidden factor later, to save His people from the slaughter that would be decreed against them.

HAMAN'S "FINAL SOLUTION"

In time, a Persian official was elevated to prime minister under Xerxes. He was Haman, the Agagite. Haman was a descendent of the Amalekites, from whom King Agag was descended (see 1 Sam. 15:20). The Lord said

that He would "be at war with the Amalekites from generation to generation," due to their treatment of Israel as they journeyed through the desert
(Exod. 17:16).

As Haman, in all his pomp and position, would come and go through
the king's gates, many officials would show fear and reverence toward him.
Mordechai, however, did not show honor to this man, whose spirit emitted
contempt and arrogance. Enraged at Mordechai's lack of homage, Haman
learned that he was a Jew and plotted to destroy every Jew in the Persian
Empire. He approached the king with a veiled suggestion of destroying the
Jews, without identifying his intended victims.

> *There is a certain people dispersed and scattered among
> the peoples in all the provinces of your kingdom whose
> customs are different from those of all other people and
> who do not obey the king's laws; it is not in the king's best
> interest to tolerate them. If it pleases the king, let a decree
> be issued to destroy them, and I will put ten thousand
> talents of silver into the royal treasury for the men who
> carry out this business* (Esther 3:8-9).

King Xerxes gave his signet ring of authority to Haman and granted his
request. Haman and his advisors cast lots to determine the date of the
impending slaughter of the Jews, and the lot fell to the thirteenth day of the
twelfth month, the month of Adar. They cast lots in the first month (April),
and the lots "happened" to fall on the last month (the following March).
This was another example of God's invisible hand at work, giving the Jews
the maximum time to pray, fast, and obtain Heaven's strategy against this
demonic slaughter. In the Akkadian texts, the word *pur* means "lot." This is
why the feast came to be called "Purim," which is the plural form of *pur*.

"IF I PERISH, I PERISH"

As far back as the Assyrian invasion of Israel in 722 B.C., the Jewish
people were exiled among the provinces of the Medes and the Persians. The

Babylonian exile (605-586 B.C.) also sent many more into Babylon, from which some continued to migrate eastward. There are archaeological records of significant Jewish populations living throughout the Persian Empire as far as India. It is hard to estimate how many Jews would have been slaughtered by this terrible decree, but I would estimate in the hundreds of thousands.

Some Jewish people had begun to return to Israel in 536 B.C., about seventy years before the story of Esther and Mordechai took place. However, only about 50,000 had returned by Esther's time, perhaps only a tenth of the widely-dispersed nation.

The decree of death was disseminated in many diverse languages, carried by messengers to Persian provinces as far as India and Africa. When the widely-scattered Jewish populations heard this unthinkable death warrant, they went into mourning and wailing, as did the Jews of Susa, the Persian capital. Mordechai put on sackcloth and wailed loudly in the streets, stunned by the horror of this murderous and irrational decree against an innocent people. He could not enter the king's gate clothed in sackcloth, and Esther sent a messenger to learn why he was in mourning.

He sent her a copy of the edict, pleading with her to go before the king and ask him to stop this event. She sent him the reply that it was against the law to enter the king's palace without being invited, and that the penalty for such presumption was death. Esther added that the king had not requested her presence for some thirty days, and that she was afraid to go to him, unbidden. The final reply that Mordechai sent her was stark, even fierce with God's urgency and resolve:

> *Do not think that because you are in the king's house you alone of all the Jews will escape. For if you remain silent at this time, relief and deliverance will arise from another place, but you and your father's family will perish. And who knows but that you have come to royal position for such a time as this?* (Esther 4:12-14)

Esther's spirit was provoked to courage by her beloved cousin's desperate words, and she told him to call a three-day fast for all the Jews in Susa; she and her maids would fast as well. After that, she would approach the king. Her resolve conquered her fear of death, and her final words to Mordechai still resonate through the ages: "And if I perish, I perish." If we have not come to this point of resolve, we are not worthy to be called His disciples.

On the third day, Esther put on her royal robes and entered the palace. The king was facing the entrance, and upon seeing her unexpected entry, he extended his golden scepter of mercy; at this gesture, she could safely approach him with her request. The king knew it must be very urgent for his queen to risk her life to approach his throne, uninvited.

He asked, "What is your request?" Esther did not reveal the life-and-death matter that had brought her to this terrible moment. She merely asked the king if he and Haman would attend a banquet that she had prepared for them. The king agreed, and they joined her immediately for a feast.

The king and Haman were untroubled as they enjoyed their food and wine; they did not notice that Esther was not eating, and that she was silent. As the meal was winding down, the king addressed her again, knowing there was still something important she needed to ask of him. "Esther, what is your request? It will be given to you, even up to half of my kingdom."

Esther was not ready to reveal Haman's evil, or her identity. The moment was not right. She asked the king if he and Haman would be so kind as to attend a second banquet the next day, and then she would tell him her request.

THE SECOND BANQUET

Haman left the banquet in high spirits, particularly flattered that Queen Esther had invited only him to accompany the king to the second day's banquet. But when he observed Mordechai near the king's gate, head bowed, dressed in sackcloth and paying him no homage, his elation turned to bitter rage. Although *all* the Jews would be dead soon enough on his "legal" day of slaughter, Haman could not rest until this disrespectful Jew was exterminated.

Arriving at his house, he shared with his wife and friends all that had happened, and how intolerable was Mordechai's presence. His wife suggested that he build a gallows and hang Mordechai on it the next morning; then he could enjoy his banquet with the king and queen. Haman was pleased and had the gallows built. As we saw earlier, the "gallows" would actually have been an execution stake to which the criminal was nailed or thrust through. The higher the stake, the more visible the body would be to the surrounding villages, and thus, the horror and deterrence factor would be greater.

In one of the greatest plot twists in the Bible, we see the hand of God stirring the heart of a Gentile king during the night between the two banquets.

> *That night the king could not sleep; so he ordered the book of the chronicles, the record of his reign, to be brought in and read to him* (Esther 6:1).

It was found during these lengthy readings that Mordechai had saved the king's life several years earlier and that no reward had been given to him. Hoping for advice, the king asked his attendants who was in the court. At that moment, Haman had entered to ask the king's permission to hang Mordechai. The king ushered him in and asked, "What should be done for the man the king delights to honor?"

Haman assumed the king must be referring to himself, and replied that this man should be given a kingly robe, seated upon the king's horse, and led around the city of Susa by a trusted prince who would continually shout the king's delight and praise over this individual. The king appreciated this suggestion and ordered Haman to do this for Mordechai the Jew, who sits in the king's gate.

Mordechai was a broken man that morning as his arch-enemy placed him on a royal steed and walked for hours around the city, proclaiming, "This is what is done for the man the king delights to honor!" Mordechai had been fasting for four days without food or water, and was unwashed and sleepless, with dust thrown on his filthy hair in mourning for the imminent slaughter of his people. When the horseback ride was over, he was unmoved and returned to his place of mourning at the king's gate. Haman, however, was humiliated and rushed home to tell his family of the shame that had befallen him. *In this astonishing scene, we see the difference between humility and humiliation. Mordechai was humbled through fasting; Haman was humiliated, due to his arrogance.*

His wife, who only twenty-four hours earlier had so helpfully told him to build a gallows for Mordechai, now gave him completely different advice: "Since Mordechai, before whom your downfall has started, is of Jewish origin, you cannot stand before him; you will surely come to ruin!" (Esther 6:13).

As she was announcing this new bit of wisdom, the attendants came and hurried him off to the banquet. After the king and Haman had eaten and were drinking their wine, the king turned to Esther and again asked, "Queen Esther, what is your petition? What is your request?"

Finally, the moment had come for Esther to expose the evil. "If I have found favor with you, O king, grant my life—this is my petition. And spare my people—this is my request. For we have been sold for destruction and slaughter and annihilation" (Esther 7:3-4).

The king was shocked and bewildered by such a statement from his gentle queen. Who would slaughter his own queen? And who are her people, that they would be sold for destruction?

"Who is he? Where is the man who would do such a thing?" (Esther 7:5).

Esther turned toward the astonished prime minister, whose wine glass was suspended inches from his speechless lips, and pointed her trembling finger at him. The moment of the Lord's deliverance was upon her! Strength rose up within her weakened body as she poured out her bitter accusation: "The adversary and enemy is this vile Haman!" (Esther 7:6).

The stunned king stormed out in a rage, while the terrified Haman fell on Esther's couch to plead with her for his life. Just then, the king returned to see his prime minister's head groveling upon his queen's bosom, and he shouted, "Will he even molest the queen while she is with me?" At this, one of the eunuchs helpfully told the king about the gallows Haman just had built for Mordechai.

The king ordered him hanged on it, and Haman the Agagite was no more (see Esther 7:9-10).

The Irrevocability of Persian Law

If this had been a fairy tale, Haman's death would have ended the wicked plot, and all would be well. But when a Persian king sealed an edict, it was irrevocable; even the king himself could not reverse it. Xerxes' father, Darius, had run into this same Persian complication when he realized that his beloved Daniel was to be the victim of his ill-conceived law. Even Darius could not rescind the law he had sealed, and the guilt-ridden king could only fast and pray for his friend throughout that terrible night in the lion's den.

Mordechai washed and dressed, took some food, and was strengthened. When he was brought before the king, Xerxes realized that this genocidal decree had been published in all known languages under his own seal, and that it would still be carried out by foreign armies on the thirteenth of Adar. The king appointed Mordechai to the position of prime minister and gave him authority to write a new edict, even though the onslaught of the hate-filled armies could not be cancelled. Mordechai wrote a new decree, stating that all the Jews in the Persian provinces were granted permission to assemble and arm themselves, and to kill all who would come against them on that day.

When the day finally arrived, the Jews gained victory over all the forces that came in to slaughter them. Many in the provinces turned to God and became Jews, for the fear of Mordechai's authority had gripped them. During these military victories, Haman's ten sons were killed in the city of Susa, and Esther was given Haman's estate.

Mordechai wrote one more edict to all the Jews dispersed throughout the Persian Empire: that we were to observe the Feast of Purim as a lasting memorial of God's great deliverance from this murderous, anti-Semitic scheme, hatched by those who hated us without a cause (see Esther 9:20-28).

The Church as Esther

Esther was an obscure Jewish orphan, hidden in the midst of the vast

Persian Empire. She was a fourth-generation Jewish exile, a humble and unrecognized vessel in a wealthy, worldly power system. God had an appointed moment in history when her beauty and worth were to be unveiled to the world.[3]

The Lord chose the vehicle of a national beauty competition to elevate Esther to the position of queen. Although thousands of beautiful teenagers competed for the king's attention, there was something about Esther that drew his heart. The Lord caused her to find favor with the king. Why did God elevate this particular girl and raise her up to royalty in one hour? Was she merely the prettiest girl in Persia? Why was Mordechai so adamant that she keep her Jewish identity a secret? For what higher purpose did the Lord bring her to royal position and give her power?

Although Esther knew nothing of her enormous destiny when she became queen, she was raised up to royal position for the physical salvation of her own people. The Lord foreknew that the Jewish people would be targeted for mass-slaughter about five years after Esther would be crowned queen.

When Haman's genocidal plan became law, Esther was suddenly thrust into a deadly chess game, whose strategic goals were devised in the unseen realms, both good and evil. *Esther was the queen on this chessboard of human destiny, the most powerful piece and also the most threatening player to the evil one.* For her to approach the king, uninvited, meant death; it is likely that without the corporate prayer and fasting of the Jewish community for three days, the outcome of her unsolicited entrance would have been immediate death.

The demonic forces of anti-Semitism, personified in the vile Prime Minister Haman, were determined to exterminate the Jewish people from the face of the earth. This would not only grieve the heart of God, but would also thwart His covenant faithfulness to keep the Jewish people, even in the nations where they had been scattered. This slaughter could easily have wiped out the ancestors of the Messiah Jesus; even if His ancestors were among the exiles who had returned, the land of Israel was very much a part of the Persian Empire, and the killings would have come upon these ones as well.[4]

The hosts of Heaven were fighting for the physical deliverance of the Lord's chosen people for a number of reasons: the Lord hates the slaughter of the innocent; the Lord had promised to preserve and guard them in the land of their enemies; the Lord required a living, thriving people among whom His own Son could be born and raised; and the Lord guaranteed a continued survival of the Jewish people until His return in the distant future, as a sign of His faithfulness to keep His covenants (see Exod. 23:7; Prov. 6:17; Lev. 26:44-45; Deut. 18:18-19; Jer. 31:35-37; Matt. 24:15-21; Rev. 11:1-2).

Although the Book of Esther is a true and historical account, it is also a symbol of the end-times Church.[5] The true Church was of Jewish origin; our Lord, the disciples, apostles, and the writers of both the Old and New Testaments were Jews. The Lord's New Covenant people are hidden among the kingdoms of this world, obscure and lowly. In the world's eyes, the Church does not appear as royalty, nor is she esteemed. Her Jewish origin has been hidden from the world, even from her own self-awareness. So foreign have the Church's customs become, that she does not appear to be Jewish.

Even so, when the day comes for God to unveil His bride to the world, her beauty and worth will be seen, and she will be elevated to a position of influence "for such a time as this." She will be thrust into a deadly battle for the souls of men and nations, and will need to offer her life, as Esther did, to intercede for the lives of the persecuted and hunted Jewish people.

God has brought us to royal position for such a time as this. *I believe that this is the moment for the Church to arise and identify herself as Esther, the queen whose Jewish origins must now be revealed to the world.* The Gentile church must begin to grasp the wave of evil now arising against the Jews on the earth. This dark cloud signals a terrible persecution that is being hatched and released, for while Antiochus, Haman, and Hitler are dead, the anti-Semitic spirit lives on in the hearts of men. Even now, in the streets of Europe, we see anti-Semitic incidents increasing, though greatly underreported. In Israel, violent missile attacks on Israeli cities continue to kill and maim, while individuals and public locations are constantly subjected to terror threats. In the corridors of power and the secret councils of lawless ones and rogue nations, the destruction of Israel is the highest priority.

The Church will soon be thrust into a choice of personal safety or high-risk intervention and intercession, which will cost many lives. However, the heavenly reward for blessing the Lord's Jewish people was sealed in Genesis 12, as pertinent in ancient Persia as it was during the Holocaust, and standing to this very day:

> *I will bless those who bless you, and whoever curses you I will curse; and all the peoples on earth will be blessed through you.*
>
> *Do not think that because you are in the king's house you alone of all the Jews will escape. For if you remain silent at this time, relief and deliverance will arise from another place, but you and your father's family will perish. And who knows but that you have come to royal position for such a time as this?* (Genesis 12:3; Esther 4:12-14)

CELEBRATING PURIM

It is wonderful to celebrate this great deliverance of the Lord, which usually falls in March. It is hard to find the date of Purim each year in our normal calendars, but you can find the date on a synagogue calendar, or on a calendar from a ministry connected to Israel or the Jewish people, such as Eagles' Wings,[6] or Vision for Israel.[7] To help you get started for the years 2009-2012, the dates of Purim are 3/10/09, 2/28/10, 3/20/11, and 3/8/12.[8]

The Jewish custom is to hear the entire scroll of Esther read aloud on Purim, usually in Hebrew. Those of us who wish to understand what we are reading are free to read it in English, of course. Each time Mordechai's name is mentioned, we cheer and shout. When the reader utters Esther's name, we all cry, "Blessed be Esther!" But when the vile Haman's name is read, we drown out his memory with a special kind of noisemaker, called a "grogger." It makes a loud, ratchet-like grinding noise, and is very annoying by the time we finish the book. Even though I have summarized the incredible story in this chapter, it is very enlightening to read the whole book, which only takes about 45 minutes to read aloud at a Purim party or prayer meeting.

Another biblical tradition is to give baskets of food to each other and gifts to the poor; this was part of the decree that Mordechai wrote to the Jews about how to celebrate Purim (see Esther 9:20-22). One of the foods we bake and give away is a triangular pastry called *Hamantaschen*. In the Yiddish language, this means, "Haman's Hats," because someone decided that Haman wore a triangular hat. You can search your Bibles for this piece of trivia, but I fear you will not find it. Would you like the recipe for the absolute best *Hamantaschen*, which I make every year?

The Dough (*double this recipe, unless you have a very disciplined and small family!*)

½ cup butter (if you use margarine, it will not taste anywhere near as good)

1 tsp orange rind

1 cup sugar

1 egg

2 Tbs orange juice

2 cups flour

2 tsp baking powder

¼ tsp salt

Cream the butter and sugar till smooth. Add egg, juice, rind.

Add all the dry ingredients and mix the dough. If I have doubled the recipe, I divide the dough in half, and make two balls of dough, which I wrap in waxed paper and chill in the fridge for at least 15 minutes. This makes the dough less wet and sticky, and easier to roll out.

Pre-heat oven to 400 degrees.

Roll out one ball of dough at a time, on a floured surface. Sprinkle the top with a little flour, so it won't stick. Roll it fairly thin, to about ¼ inch thickness. Then, get a small, circular bowl or large round cookie cutter about 4 inches in diameter. Use this circle to cut out as many circles as you can from the dough. Then lay the circles on a greased cookie sheet. Push together the extra dough, roll again, and try to make more circles till you run out of dough.

The Filling

You can use any pie or pastry filling you like. It is common to use cherry filling, apple, lemon, poppy seed paste, or prune. It depends what you or your family enjoy.

Take about a tablespoonful of filling and put it in the center of each circle on the cookie sheet. Then fold the circle together to form a triangle like this:

If the circle was a clock, go to ten o'clock, two o'clock, and six o'clock, and fold these three edges toward each other and press them together. You should end up with a triangular pastry, with some filling showing through the hole in the center. If too much filling is running out of the center, it will spill out when they bake, and the triangle will split apart.

Bake 10-12 minutes at 400, until golden brown but not too dark or crispy. They should be firm, somewhere between cookie and cake consistency. Totally awesome!

Aside from giving away treats, the Lord gave us the most wonderful idea for Purim, 2007, which we had never considered: an Esther Banquet! It took place on 3/3/07, and was one of the most joyful and prophetic banquets I have ever hosted or attended.

About six months earlier, a dear prophetic friend received a word from the Lord that He would like us to intercede and weep for Israel from Hanukah until Purim, and then to celebrate and honor the Lord with a feast for His Bride. When the king crowned Esther as queen, he gave a banquet in her honor. In the same way, I believe that this is the season for His Church to be unveiled as a royal, beautiful Bride, who will support, love, and intercede for Israel and the Jewish people. Thus, we gave a banquet in her honor, as well as the Lord's honor.

I got very excited, and we planned an elegant meal at our church, preceded by an anointed worship service. Our pastors were very supportive of this idea, and we decorated the church with an array of Jewish symbols, place settings, banners, flags, candles, and menorahs. The room looked amazing, our dress was elegant, the food was the highest quality, and the atmosphere was welcoming and heavenly.

One of the unique features of the table settings is that we left a seat for the Lord Himself. One special chair, placed in a central and honored position at the table was adorned with a prayer shawl, a crown, and a scepter. The place setting was like those of the other guests, and no one would sit in this seat but the Lord. Although we could not see Him, we trusted that He was with us, and that He felt welcomed and honored by this place setting reserved for Him. Likewise, no one presumed to sit on His right or left hand, but these two honored seats fell, by default, to the last ones to be seated, who were busy serving others before they sat down.

This is the ceremony that we created, so that you can do likewise if the Lord should request such a delightful celebration for your church or prayer group. The Scripture readings below would replace the need to read the entire Book of Esther.

THE ESTHER BANQUET

Appetizers can be served as the guests mingle, before they are seated for the service. Then they are seated, and the service begins.

Greetings: Here, the host or hostess can welcome the guests and explain the reason for this celebration.

Song: "Sh'ma Yisrael" from *The Road to Jerusalem,* track 1 (includes shofar blast). This track spills smoothly into track 2, which is Mordechai's spoken declaration/warning to Esther. As this concludes, fade the volume quickly before track 3 begins (see chapter six for more details on Messianic worship resources).

Scripture Readings (ask different volunteers to read these aloud):
Psalm 87
Esther 2:10-11;17-18

Esther 3:1-2;5-9
Psalm 130
Esther 4:1-3;12-16
Esther 7:1-6
Esther 8:11-13
Esther 9:20-22
Psalm 124
Isaiah 25:6-9
Blow the Shofars (if available)
Worship Songs: (all found on Paul Wilbur's anointed *The Watchman* CD)
"Lord God of Abraham"
"Adonai"
"O Shout for Joy"
"Shout for Joy"
"The Watchman"

These songs can be interspersed with the Scripture readings above, or can be played together as a concentrated time of worship music. You can use as many or as few songs as you like, and can add any others that you feel create the worship atmosphere needed for your service.

Dinner is served.

After the feast is over, it is important to seal the celebration and worship/warfare that was accomplished before people begin to leave. Call everyone's attention, and have the shofars blown once more as a solemn closing blast. Dismiss the people with gratitude, love, and blessings for sharing in this unique and precious evening.

If there is left-over food, I found it very fitting and joyful to give out "care packages" of food to the guests who could use a little extra food at home for their families, or for the next day. Giving gifts of food is part of the Purim celebration.

THE LORD'S HEART FOR PURIM

Once again, I asked the Lord to continue in His faithfulness to show me His heart for this feast. As I waited in His Presence, this is the word that came to me:

"Esther was caressed by silk scarves and veils. Her beauty was hidden from the Persian nobles and princes. Vashti before her had rejected her husband's demand that she display her beauty publicly.

"Esther's beauty was a quiet, inner beauty, a tenderness and humility of heart which she had learned from her dear cousin, and from the pain of being an orphan.

"My Bride is to be clothed in quiet dignity and authority, unlike the other women of worldly power and influence. My Bride is the industrious and obedient woman of Proverbs 31, a woman of valor, like a soldier among the flowers. Strength and dignity were Esther's clothes; courage and commitment were her portion.

"She rose up to intercede, to weep, to fast, and to plead. She rose up to judge and condemn the wickedness that had come up before her eyes to destroy her heritage, her roots, her people, her family tree, her worship, and her childhood. Such a great wickedness was placed before her, and she had to choose the hardest path, the place of death and vulnerability to a Gentile ruler who knew nothing of the true character of his bride or her people.

"The king had only heard evil gossip, rumors, and hearsay from Haman about the disobedience and rebellion of the Jews in the Persian Empire. He had heard the worst report, that this people caused trouble and were deserving of death. He did not think or pray, nor did he seek more information about what crime this people had committed to deserve death, such a great slaughter on one day.

"How easy it was for this slaughter to be set in motion, to be sealed into law. How little thought he took.

"Are not the nations the same as Ahashverus,[9] as they

take counsel together, and listen to evil whispers and lies about the Jewish people, about their greed and wickedness, their oppression of the innocent, their fault and blame in the hindrances to world peace? How much better off would these kingdoms and nations be if the Jews were eliminated, if Zionism was eradicated, if Israel were abolished as a nation among the nations! Would not the world be a better and brighter place?

"Such are the lies and whispers of the Hamans of the earth, the proud and the lawless, the hateful and the boastful, those who profit on the deaths of others. They convince the rulers of the earth to conspire to remove Israel from the map and to drive the Jews off of their land and into the sea of blood.

"I will come against these schemes," says the Lord. "They will not prosper, for I shall cause them to stumble and fail. I will expose them and bring them to shame and grief and humiliation.

"My Bride, My beautiful Esther will rise up to condemn them and put an end to their lying schemes. She will expose their ways to the kings and will plead for her people with tears and fasting. Then I will deliver My people from the snares of the evil one.

"Celebrate the feast of Purim with Me, with each other, with the Jewish people, even in their synagogues. Show them your solidarity, that they might know that the true Church, those who love Me and are called by My Name, love My people as I love My people. Tell her that all Israel will be saved. I have spoken this before, and I AM speaking it now. This is My heart for the Feast of Esther, the feast of My Bride. Amen."

PART IV

THE GREAT
LOVE
RELATIONSHIP
RESTORED

Chapter 11

THE SABBATH (SHABBAT)

All seven of the biblical feasts are laid out in Leviticus 23, but before they are listed, the Lord names the Sabbath day as the first feast of the Lord. Although I could have similarly begun this book with the Sabbath, I felt it might be best to place it near the end, connecting it to the restoration of all things.

The Sabbath comes once a week, fifty-two times a year; the other feasts only come once a year. Therefore, while the biblical cycle of seven festivals involves our yearly calendar, the Sabbath seriously affects our weekly calendar. Because of its relentless appearance every week, the Sabbath requires a more pervasive and costly lifestyle change within our culture for those who wish to honor it.

THE SEVENTH DAY IS HOLY

Several thousand years before the Law of Moses was given, the principle of the seventh day being a day of rest was established at Creation. This is a staggering truth to contemplate; many Christians assume that the concept of a seventh-day Sabbath is a Mosaic commandment given at Mount Sinai, and is therefore swept away as part of the "Old" Covenant. It is not deemed to be relevant to Christians, and has been reserved for the Jews alone.

However, when God spoke these words at Creation, there would not be any Jews for yet twenty generations (see Luke 3:34-38). Obviously, He was speaking to all of mankind, to every seed that would come from Adam and Eve.

> *By the seventh day God had finished the work He had been doing; so on the seventh day He rested from all His work. And God blessed the seventh day and made it holy, because on it He rested from all the work of creating that He had done* (Genesis 2:2-3).

Because our English Bibles say that God rested, we might get the impression that He was tired from the work of creation. This is a natural thought, but it does not line up with the Hebrew meaning. There are two different words used in the Bible for "rest." One word is *manoach,* which means to rest when you are tired. We see this word used in Genesis 8:9, where Noah sent the dove out of the ark, but she found nowhere to rest her feet. Because she was tired, she came back to the ark. It is also interesting that Noah's name comes from this same word, to rest.

The other Hebrew word is *shabbat,* which means to cease and desist. This word can include resting your body, but the primary meaning is to stop your normal activity.[1] Throughout this chapter, I will often refer to this day by its Hebrew name, *Shabbat.*

When the Lord brought His people out of Egypt, He spoke of the seventh day even before He gave them the Law on Mount Sinai. As He rained down manna from Heaven, He gave this instruction:

> *On the sixth day they are to prepare what they bring in, and that is to be twice as much as they gather on the other days.*
>
> *Tomorrow is to be a day of rest, a holy Sabbath to the Lord. So bake what you want to bake and boil what you want to boil. Save whatever is left and keep it until morning.*

The Sabbath (Shabbat)

Six days you are to gather it, but on the seventh day,
the Sabbath, there will not be any (Exodus 16:5,23,26).

The Israelites were commanded to gather fresh manna each morning, but not to keep it until the next day; if they kept the manna, it rotted with maggots. However, in the Lord's amazingly intelligent design, He told them to gather extra on the sixth day and store it until the seventh day, because He would not be raining down any bread on the Sabbath. Only on this one day did the stored manna not go bad, because the Lord made a distinction between the days of the week.

For forty years, the Lord performed this miracle every day, raining down bread onto the desert floor; for forty years, His manna-making machinery ceased and desisted from its work on Shabbat. The Lord served several million people breakfast every day for forty years, but never on Shabbat! Who can say that God considers one day just like another? Does He not make a distinction? The Lord has clearly stated that every day is *not* the same to Him.

When the Israelites came to Mount Sinai, the Lord gave them the Ten Commandments. It is rare to meet a Christian who does not consider the Ten Commandments to be binding on New Covenant believers. The fourth commandment is this:

> *Remember the Sabbath day by keeping it holy. Six days*
> *you shall labor and do all your work, but the seventh day*
> *is a Sabbath to the Lord your God. On it you shall not do*
> *any work, neither you nor your son or daughter, nor your*
> *manservant nor maidservant, nor your animals, nor the*
> *alien* [foreigner] *within your gates* (Exodus 20:8-10).

The Lord is very clear that He wants even the servants, the animals, and the Gentiles living among Israel to take this day of rest. Within this fourth commandment, the Lord gives the reason why this is to be a day of rest: because He rested from His work of creation on the seventh day, He blessed it and made it holy. Since He refers to Creation and instructs even the

Gentiles to observe this day, it seems clear that He intended this Sabbath rest for all of mankind, and not for the Jews only.

However, it was especially important to the Lord that Israel observe Shabbat. He mentioned it many times throughout the Law and the Prophets. It was also special to the Lord Yeshua, for the Bible states that "on the Sabbath day He went into the synagogue, as was His custom" (Luke 4:16); He also performed seven recorded healings on the Sabbath, and from other Scriptures we can infer that He did far more healings than these (see Matt. 4:23; 9:35; John 21:25).

We see it listed as the first appointed feast of the Lord in Leviticus:

> *There are six days when you may work, but the seventh day is a Sabbath of rest, a day of sacred assembly. You are not to do any work; wherever you live, it is a Sabbath to the Lord* (Leviticus 23:3).

Now you might think that a people who had just been rescued from four hundred years of slavery would be elated to receive a command to rest! To know that the One who created you *wanted* you to deliberately rest, should have been a very wonderful and freeing revelation.

You might also think that most people in our culture feel tired and overworked and would relish the opportunity to cease and desist. Didn't someone write a song that says, "Stop the world, I want to get off"?

Despite what you might think, the Israelites were continually tempted to break God's command about Shabbat. They were tempted to gather manna on the seventh day; they were tempted to gather firewood and cook on the seventh day; they were tempted to do business and commerce on the seventh day once they had entered their land; and they were tempted to plow and sow their fields in the seventh year, which God had commanded to be a resting year for the land (see Lev. 25:1-7).

And despite what you might think about our exhausted society, just mention the Sabbath to anyone, Christian or non-Christian, and you will hear every reason known to man why they cannot possibly consider resting on the seventh day. In fact, some will actually get upset with you for suggesting that they might benefit from resting on the seventh day. Some will think you are trying to put them in *bondage*!

But all you are saying is that their loving God, who created them, wants them to rest on the very day that He rested, the day that He considers set-apart. As you can see, this is a very difficult topic, although it really shouldn't be. Let's see if there is anything we can do to make it easier to consider.

A DATE DAY WITH GOD

All married couples know that the hectic routines and pressures of life can erode their relationship; communication and spending relaxed time with each other is needed to preserve any trace of genuine friendship. This is why some couples set aside a "date day" once a week, once a month, or at any interval that fits their schedules.

What if you thought about the Sabbath as a date day with God, one that He specifically requested when He made you? He is not necessarily saying, "Please lie on the couch, put on a good movie, make some popcorn, kick back, and chill." On the other hand, the Lord is not opposed to lying on the couch that day.

However, this is the very heart of what the Lord is saying to us: *"I want you to cease and desist from the endless distractions of your normal work, chores, routines, and worldly entertainments. I want to spend quality time with you, where we talk about our lives and feelings, and how much we love each other. Is that too much to ask?"*

About a year ago, the Lord gave me a dream that I think is relevant to this discussion. In this dream, I was sitting at a table in a restaurant, having lunch with someone. For the first part of this dream, I had no idea who I was dining with, because I never saw the person. I was turned to my right, observing a long line of people and activities passing by our table. I saw so many interesting people of all varieties, each one doing or saying fascinating things. Many, many people and activities passed by, and I was so captivated that I could not take my eyes off of them. Because of this, I was completely unaware of anyone else at the lunch table with me.

Suddenly, I heard a man's voice from the other side of our round table—pleading, urgent, calling me to attention: "Hey, we're having lunch here!" This caused me to turn to look at my companion, instantly feeling sheepish for having ignored him thoroughly for so long, without even realizing he was sitting there with me. I could feel his hurt that, although we were on a lunch date, I was looking at everyone and everything but him.

For the first time, I looked at my companion. He was a gentle, middle-aged man with sweet brown eyes, and he was looking at me with an expression I had never seen before. He was smiling at me with an expression of immense tenderness, joy, admiration, sweet affection, adoration, and a sense that he was consumed with the wonder of being with me. Since no one has ever looked at me that way, I felt a bit uncomfortable. I realized that his face was close to mine, and his relentless, joyful gaze never left my eyes. I felt he had invaded my personal boundaries, and I said, "Don't get so close."

The moment I spoke these words, he was instantly "transported" to a new location at the table, about two or three feet further away from me. However, his expression never flickered or altered. His face didn't reflect hurt or anger at my feeling that he was too close, but without physically getting up, he was just suddenly in a new location, a bit further away. Still, he gazed at me with the same radiant smile of concentrated adoration.

Then I woke up and realized it was the Lord, even though he had been disguised as a normal person. Had I known it was the Lord while I was dreaming, I would not have told Him that He was too close to me; this is probably why the Lord disguised Himself, so that I would reveal my true heart on the matter. I am afraid of intimacy.

Although this dream is not about Shabbat in particular, it is obviously a parable of our intimate friendship with the Lord. It exposes the vast array of distractions that pull us away from Him, even when we are supposed to be "dining" with Him. Once we give the Lord our full attention, we don't want Him to get too close; it makes us uncomfortable. If the Lord were to display the extent of His affection for us, it would make us feel awkward and self-conscious, as I felt in my dream.

The Lord has brought this dream to my mind many times, as I am constantly distracted from the focus needed to give Him my full attention.

Why is it so difficult to set aside our distractions, and give one twenty-four hour period to the Lord alone with all our hearts and souls? Can't we do our work six days a week as He commanded and give the seventh day completely to Him? And if we would like a day of rest with the Lord, does it matter which day of the week we choose?

I realize there are differing opinions about this matter, and I also realize that the Lord loves *any* and *all* time slots that we willingly devote to prayer, worship, Bible study, or fellowship with each other. He is a gracious God and can fellowship with us at all hours of the day or night, every day of the year. But does the Lord still hold His original feelings about the seventh day?

WHICH DAY IS THE SABBATH DAY?

As you may recall from the first chapter, the Lord Yeshua and early Jewish believers celebrated Shabbat on the seventh day, according to the original pattern given at Creation. In addition, a majority of Gentile believers were also observing this day until the fourth century, when new laws were created that changed the set times and seasons in God's Word.

Constantine declared Sunday to be a compulsory day of rest for all of his subjects, an official Roman holiday.[2] Between A.D. 343 and 381, the Council of Laodicea forbade Christians to observe the seventh-day Sabbath. Any Christian who continued to observe the Jewish Sabbath was considered "anathema," which means accursed, to Christ.[3]

Although Constantine deliberately changed and replaced the biblical Sabbath, there is no indication that New Testament believers replaced it with Sunday. There is one account in the Book of Acts in which the believers met to break bread on the first day of the week; on this one verse, some have based their claim that Sunday had replaced Shabbat (see Acts 20:7). There are three reasons why this is far-fetched.

First, Shabbat ends at sunset, and the first day of the week begins at that time; therefore, the phrase "met on the first day" may have referred to a Saturday evening meeting that went on all night long. We see that at midnight, Eutychus fell out the window, and after a quick interruption to resurrect the dead, Paul kept talking until morning.

Second, even if they were having a fellowship meal or communion service on a Sunday, it does not imply any replacement of the normal Shabbat worship.

Third, and this is the most compelling argument, there are numerous Scriptures that plainly state that the New Covenant believers continued to worship on the seventh-day Jewish Sabbath (see Acts 13:14,42,44; 17:2; 18:4).

The seventh day was blessed as far back as Creation. Biblically, it seems clear that the Lord intended it to be an eternal covenant with mankind, as long as there would be times and seasons. At the time of Creation, two ever-lasting covenants were established: the marriage between one man and one woman, and the seventh day of rest. These were established by the Creator long before there were a Jewish people, or a Law of Moses. *Therefore, I believe it is for all people, for all time, until time itself is erased by eternity.*

The Lord was not tired after He created the heavens and the earth. He felt a great sense of satisfaction and completion. His heart was full, and He rested to enjoy the goodness of what He had finished creating; the Lord was particularly joyful about His highest creation of man in His own beautiful image. Therefore, just as He stopped to enjoy His creation, the Sabbath is a good day for us to stop and enjoy His creation.

LEGALISM VERSUS BLESSINGS

Before looking at practical problems and helpful attitudes concerning Shabbat, it is important, once more, to establish the Lord's principle of blessing, rather than bondage. The Lord gave the Sabbath to mankind for a blessing. It was never meant to be a legal list of permissible and forbidden behaviors, as we have seen at times exhibited by the Pharisees in the New Testament. It was meant to be a peaceful and enjoyable day, spent in fellowship with the Lord and with His people.

Although the Pharisees were upset with Yeshua for healing on the Sabbath because it constituted "work," the Lord looked at it differently. While the ministry of healing is a type of work, even tiring work, He saw it as a wonderful day to set someone free from crippling pain or demonic oppression. He understood that human life and the relief of suffering took precedence over the rules of "work." The Lord Yeshua corrected them by saying, "Look, if your sheep falls into a pit on the Sabbath, would you leave it there to die, or would you rescue it? How much more valuable are God's people than sheep?" (See Matthew 12:9-11.)

Therefore, in the discussion that follows, please do not think that I, or anyone else, can tell you exactly what you should and should not do on this day. Perhaps protests will arise in your mind, saying, "Lord! You *know* I can't afford to not do this or that on Saturday. You know I have to [fill in the blank]. This would not work at all in my job, business, or ministry!"

If these concerns arise in your heart, please know that neither God nor any person is judging you for your legitimate concerns about time management. The Lord respects your choices and only desires to bless you; He is not laying on you one more chore, which will make your life more stressful and difficult. So hear my heart in the following section, without guilt or stress. He is aware of every detail and situation of our weekly schedules and how we use our time.

Then again, the poor widow gave her two mites. She was too poor to give to the Lord's work, but she gave anyway. This means that even if we are pressed for time, if the Lord Himself *desires* us to set this day apart for Him, then surely He is able to supernaturally provide for our needs. This is true of our money, and it is true of our time. They are both priceless commodities the Lord has given us, and He loves when His people "waste" their most precious commodities on Him. If your time is too precious to give to Him, maybe you are holding on too tightly to your own schedule.

Know that the Lord understands if you are in a ministry that involves working hard on a Saturday. Let me share an example of my own difficulties in ministry. I am often invited to speak or lead worship at Saturday meetings. This means I have to either pack and travel the night before and sleep in a motel, or get up very early on Shabbat and drive several hours to a meeting. Then I must either play keyboards and sing, or teach the Word, or both. In addition, when the meeting is over, I might need to continue standing for another hour or more to pray for people who come forward with needs. This is not a restful Shabbat for me, but I am doing the work the Lord has sent me to do.

In addition, I don't believe in doing commerce on the Sabbath. Nevertheless, sometimes I need to sell books and CDs while at a meeting; I will not be seeing these people again and to ship their materials later from my home would be costly.

When I return home from one of these ministry trips, I need to rest. Likewise, rabbis who work hard in their synagogues every Sabbath day might need to take a different day of rest each week. And for Christian pastors and worship leaders, Sunday is not a restful day, but it is an excellent day of needed ministry to His flock. The Lord is well-pleased when we serve His people with all our hearts, not thinking of our own comforts.

HOW SHOULD BELIEVERS KEEP THE SHABBAT?

As we learned in the first chapter, it is an uphill battle to maintain the biblical calendar in our culture. If this statement was true of the seven yearly feasts, it is even more painfully true concerning the weekly Sabbath.

Our culture is barely respectful of Sunday as a day of rest; how much less is its respect for the seventh day? We all know that for Americans, both Christians and non-Christians, Saturday is a day to mow the lawn, shop, go to the hardware store, move things and people, repair the car, hold fundraisers, do laundry, and all other chores we were too busy to do during the week. It is *almost* impossible to avoid all of these activities, to keep "Saturday" set apart.

In Israel, where we lived for seven years, the national culture was very conducive to keeping Shabbat. From Friday at sunset till Saturday's sunset, the buses didn't run, El-Al's flights ceased, and most cafés and businesses were closed. For our family, it was a day to worship in a congregation, take a walk, visit friends, or do family-related activities at home, preferably ones with some spiritual value.

However, it took a good deal of thought and preparation to be ready for Shabbat when the sun set. This is one of the secrets of keeping the Sabbath: you have to care enough about keeping it special that you make many special efforts and preparations the day before, even sometimes several days before. Many times, when the sun would set, I was not ready for Shabbat, or any of the feast days. I was either too busy, tired, or heedless to plan ahead at that time in my life, and these days often caught me in a state of unpreparedness.

One has to do extra on the sixth day to get ready for the seventh day, just as Israel had to gather twice as much manna on the sixth day to be ready for the lack of manna on the seventh day. For those readers who would consider this point before the Lord, it will take prayer and commitment to receive the Lord's personal strategy for your weekly schedule, which will allow you to set aside this day.

I will now share some activities that I do on Shabbat, and also those I try to avoid. These are my personal guidelines; the Lord will help you develop your own personal strategies that fit your lifestyle, your conscience, and your relationship with Him.

To Do:

1. Pray, worship to CDs or play musical instruments, and write in my journal about answered prayers, concerns, dreams, visions, or events in my walk with God.

2. Attend a small Shabbat prayer meeting, where we worship and intercede for Israel, America, or our region.

3. Eat, read the Bible, rest, drink coffee, or read any godly book that edifies me in the Lord.

4. Take a walk outside, go to a restaurant, or visit friends.

5. Watch a godly movie with the family, one that glorifies the Lord and is not merely secular entertainment. It is better for me to watch a video or DVD at home, because the movie theaters subject me to long, noisy,

over-hyped trailers with violent or unclean content, as well as loud, obnoxious commercials and announcements that make me feel unclean and separated from the Lord. The movie theaters are also very expensive now, as are their overpriced snacks.

6. Play a game with the children, like Scrabble or Pictionary. It should be a game that is interactive and makes you laugh.

7. If your sheep falls into a pit, by all means, pull it out, but don't injure your back!

Not to Do:

1. Computer work, including e-mails. This can be a distraction from the Lord, and it takes me into either business or ministry concerns, which I really need a break from. I turn off my computer on Friday at sunset, and I check my messages after the sun sets on Saturday night. If I am writing a book or songs for the Lord all week long, I do not do this on Shabbat. I cease and desist from even my godly assignments.

2. Laundry, grocery shopping, most cooking. Sometimes it is fun and relaxing to bake brownies or make a salad, but I try not to do a lot of work in the kitchen.

3. Lawn mowing, going to the mall, moving people into a new house, repairing the car, going to the bank, or taking any phone calls except for conversations with friends.

People often ask me if I think it is fine to garden on Shabbat. I think this and other similar questions are really between you and the Lord. If you are a landscaper, and you work hard in the dirt all week long, it is not a Shabbat activity to continue in your normal work. If you love planting flowers and you sit in an office all week, Shabbat might be a nice time to get out in the garden and commune with the Lord while you "work." It all depends on your heart, your week, and what you and the Lord enjoy doing together. Since I am not the policeman of Shabbat, ask Him; this is the bottom line!

WHAT ABOUT SUNDAY?

Keeping Shabbat does not imply that we should not worship on Sunday. The believers in the New Testament worshiped on many days of the week. Every day is a good day to worship the Lord. But not every day is the Sabbath. This day is different—it is set apart for holy purposes.[4]

I attend Sunday worship every week, and I feel the Lord's Presence with us as we worship and hear the teaching of His Word. The Lord loves to fellowship with His people on Sundays, and He comes where He feels welcome and honored, seven days a week.

If your region has a wonderful Messianic congregation that meets on Friday evenings or Saturday mornings, you can certainly attend that service as your corporate, weekly worship. This would depend on your preferences of style; some are very drawn to the Messianic flavor of worship, and others are more comfortable in a church setting.

If you continue to worship in church on Sunday, but also try to keep the seventh day holy, some might be offended that you believe the Lord still considers the seventh day to be special. Don't let anyone judge you if you try to keep the Saturday Sabbath set apart (see Col. 2:16). It is not unusual for some who misunderstand this to warn you of coming under bondage or "under the law." To keep the seventh day holy and obey God's Word is not bondage or heresy. It is called "obedience." *The Sabbath is the day where obedience encounters intimacy. Test the Lord, and see if He will not restore to you the time you have offered to Him.*

269

HOW DO THE JEWISH PEOPLE KEEP SHABBAT?

In a traditional Jewish home, we would welcome the Shabbat on Friday evening at sunset by lighting two candles at the table, and saying the blessing over the Sabbath candles. This blessing is very similar to one found in all Passover Haggadahs, and in the lighting of the Hanukah candles. After lighting the candles, the mother covers her face and says this blessing:

Baruch Ata Adonai, Eloheinu Melech HaOlam
Asher kid'shanu b'mitz'votav
V'tzivanu l'hadlik ner shel Shabbat.

Blessed are You, O Lord our God
who has set us apart by Your commandments
and instructed us to kindle the light of the Sabbath.

At the Sabbath meal on Friday nights, we serve a beautiful, braided bread called *challah*. This is available from some bakeries at grocery stores, or from other bakeries. You can also find a recipe for challah in cookbooks or online, but it takes time to make and braid this special dough. We also share a cup of wine, called the *kiddush*, which means "setting apart."

The bread and the wine remind us of the account given in Genesis 14, when Abraham rescued his nephew Lot and his household from captivity. Lot lived in Sodom, which had been defeated by four foreign kings; Lot, his family, and his possessions had been taken captive in this battle. Abraham mustered the men of his household, pursued the troops a great distance into Syria, and retrieved his relatives and their goods.

When Abraham returned from this successful battle, he was greeted by Melchizedek, king of Salem and priest of God Most High. This mysterious figure remains unknown to us, yet the writer of Hebrews compared his priesthood and eternal stature to that of the Lord Yeshua.

Melchizedek greeted Abraham with a gift of bread and wine and blessed Abraham in his God-given victory over his enemies. Abraham, in turn, paid a tenth of the plunder to Melchizedek. The greater blesses the lesser, and even the great patriarch Abraham tithed to this exalted priest (see Heb. 7:4-7). It is from this account of the bread and wine that the Sabbath tradition originated.

The blessing over the wine is this:

Baruch Ata Adonai, Eloheinu Melech HaOlam
Boray P'ri haGafen

Blessed are You, O Lord our God
Creator of the fruit of the vine.

The blessing over the bread is this:

Baruch Ata Adonai, Eloheinu Melech HaOlam
Ha Motzei lechem min haAretz

Blessed are You, O Lord our God
who brings forth bread from the earth.

After we have welcomed the Shabbat and the Lord in this way, we enjoy a lovely meal together. This begins the day of rest, and until the next day at sunset, we limit our activities to the ones described in the previous section.

In closing this section, I need to be transparent to the reader concerning my personal weakness in this area. Although I am writing about the ideal situation in a Messianic Jewish family, my own family was not able to consistently celebrate this Friday evening special dinner. I cannot in good conscience instruct others on the ideal Shabbat table, without being honest about the fact that we were far from an ideal family. As a couple raising three children in Israel and then later, in the States, we had many struggles concerning how to live a biblical Messianic Jewish lifestyle.

There were weeks when we succeeded at sitting down together in this atmosphere, but more often than not, we did not have a proper Shabbat dinner. There were a number of factors, which are not worth detailing. One reason was that I did not always make the effort needed to plan ahead, get the children organized, and make the dinner. Another reason is that my husband's job has been such that I have rarely known what time he would be home; this made it hard to plan around a certain time to have dinner ready for him and the three children. I have failed in other ways, as well.

In a real sense, I am not worthy to write this chapter on Shabbat. Perhaps the reason the Lord chose me to write this book is because I have not always kept these days perfectly and have no boasting to offer. Therefore, I can identify with anyone who has difficulty with this observance and do not dare to be judgmental. Even so, the Lord knows the ways I have honored this day, despite many failures. I know that in His kindness He will still greatly bless this chapter to your hearts; I know that He accepts me with all my shortcomings, with great love and delight. It is this way with all of His weak and failing children. Halleluiah!

As you read the Lord's word for Shabbat below, the Lord desires that you will see it as an invitation to blessing. This strong encouragement from the Lord is not meant to produce guilt. The Lord's love will never waver or diminish over you, whether or not you keep the Sabbath; in my understanding, this word promises special blessings to those who do, without condemning those who do not.

THE LORD'S HEART FOR SHABBAT

As I was waiting on the Lord for His heart on this special chapter, I felt He wanted me to read Isaiah 56. With that amazing word fresh in my mind, He gave me this word:

> My Shabbat is a resting place for all nations. My house is to be a house of prayer for all nations and a refuge to all people.
>
> I have spoken to My eunuchs, My foreigners, My love-servants, who have bound themselves to serve Me as one ties on a sash—who have honored My way above their own, above the customs of their people groups.

They have left their father and their mother and have joined themselves to Me, bound themselves to the things that are dearest to My heart.

What shall I say of these foreigners and celibate ones who are not physically fertile, nor can they marry? Shall I look at them as outsiders, or those eunuchs as damaged goods, blemished and unacceptable sheep? Even a sheep would have been unacceptable for an offering to Me, but these ones shall be honored in My house, and I will take away their reproach because they have honored My Sabbath day, and have chosen to set this day apart, and not to pursue their own crooked bent. I will choose these disciplined ones who daily crucify their own wayward lusts, rebuke the tempter, and determine to live their lives as holy eunuchs before Me. These ones will be honored, and foreigners will receive a name and a place in My house, better than sons and daughters.

Just as the Holocaust Museum is called "Yad VaShem"[a place and a name] as a lasting memorial, I will give **a place and a name** to those outside of Israel's responsibilities who hold fast to My covenant and keep My Shabbats without defiling them.

Shabbat is so dear to My heart, it would make you weep. My people, the Church, will be sad and will mourn when I show them how precious these Shabbats that I gave to them were to My heart, and when I remind them how they spent each and every precious Shabbat that I had numbered for them, according to their allotted days on the earth.

Shabbat is Paradise. Shabbat is the breathless stillness of the ecstasy of stopping—the pleasure of sitting, barely breathing, feeling My Spirit hovering, moving, blowing gently over a peaceful and quietly passionate soul, waiting, hoping, feeling the unutterable ecstasy of My joy, My pleasure, My delight in a day that is only ours.

It is for Me, and for My most treasured ones to run and hide in Me, to whisper their intimate love words, to feel the stillness come over them so that they can barely move their lips, so great is the delight of Shabbat I will pour over them like warm oil.

Let My beloved ones come to Me on Shabbat; let them step aside from all of their pursuits, works, chores, business, and catching up on the week's activities. Let My own ones come in My arms. Shabbat is for the outsiders, the foreigners, those who are not a part of the people of Israel. They will receive a Yad VaShem, a Name and Place and Hand in My Temple, a lasting name and memorial better than sons and daughters because they have bound themselves to My covenant of Shabbat; they have bound themselves to Me.

If a dear pastor needs to write his sermon on Shabbat, let Me propose this:

Sit in My Presence with very quiet anointed music in the background. Ask Me what Scriptures I would like you to read that day. Read whatever Scriptures I will show you at that moment. As you read them, I will so fill your mind and heart with My wisdom and insight and revelation, that the only notes you will need are the very passages I have you to read. You might simply write, "Numbers 10" in your notes, and on Sunday, when you get up and, in obedience, read this Scripture to My flock, I will so fill your mouth that My message will be given to you, and you will not lack words to preach. In fact, you will run out of time before you have finished sharing all of the insight and wisdom I poured into you on Shabbat. Wait on Me. This is your sermon. Honor My Shabbat, and I will honor your Sunday work, and your sermons will change and empower lives because you gave Me the fat of your offering, the choicest part of your week, even the Seventh Day.

This is My heart for the Gentiles who will honor My Shabbat: They will receive a Yad VaShem better than sons and daughters. Thus says your God. Amen.

Chapter 12

THE BRIDE HAS MADE
HERSELF READY

When the Bride of Messiah embraces these ancient paths in a Spirit-led response of loving obedience, the Word becomes flesh! Our lives become a testimony, both to the Church and also to Jewish people who do not yet know their Messiah. It is usually a pleasant surprise to Jewish people when they see Christians celebrating their holidays.

The Feasts of the Lord are not dry or academic, nor are they meant to be merely studied and mentally comprehended. In keeping with Hebraic thought, they are experiential behaviors and lifestyle choices; it is like laying muscle and flesh upon a skeleton of truth while the Lord's Spirit breathes life into them.

In the Passover service, we find this reading:

> "When your children ask you, 'Why do you eat unleavened bread?' then you will answer them, 'It is because of what the Lord our God did for us when we came out of Egypt.'"

Children need an object lesson, a physical reality, rather than a lecture. Scripture refers to all believers as "children"; we benefit from experiencing these realities just as literal children do.

A Prophetic Calendar: The Feasts of Israel

People need to experience the feasts, which was the Lord's original intention as He designed them. We need to *taste* the matzah-related foods, as we watch our friends eating their sandwiches and pizza, to *dip* our wine onto our napkin as we recite the ten plagues, to *hear* the penetrating blast of the shofar, to *feel* the discomfort of fasting one day a year, to *taste* the sweet apples and honey of the New Year, to *watch* the flickering Hanukah candles burn low as we sing songs of bravery and martyrdom for God, to *dip* our parsley into the salty tears, to *mingle the taste* of the bitterness of slavery and sweet promise of freedom for all of God's children.

When motivated believers begin to practice these festivals, the Church looks on in wonder, saying, "Why do you do these things? Surely, you are not under the Law anymore!"

Then the Bride will answer them, "We are remembering what the Lord our God did for Israel and for us. We are honoring Him in the commemorations He desired; we are accepting His invitation to the banquets that He has prepared for all nations. *Obedience brings intimate encounters with the Living God.*"

Not only will we provoke the Church to curiosity, but we will also provoke the Jewish people to envy, as they see the joy, healing, love, and life that permeate our extravagant celebrations and love-feasts.

The Jewish people have carried the Lord's reputation, deeds, and covenants into all the nations by keeping His calendar; even so, they are not experiencing the full measure of glory, healing, and intimacy that the Lord intended to experientially accompany His banquets. Once I was sitting in a church worship service while waiting to teach about the feasts, and the Lord spoke this concept to my heart, though I was not recording His exact words:

> Even My Jewish people are only keeping a skeleton of My feasts as they were intended to be celebrated. As Ezekiel saw the dry bones come together in the valley, the bones needed to be clothed with muscle, circulatory system, nerves, and skin; even then, they were but a beautifully clothed army of handsome, dead soldiers on the desert floor. Where is the breath of life, the breath of My Spirit?

I need to breathe life into this great army; when My feasts are celebrated with the life of My Spirit, it will provoke My people to envy.

These feasts are more than a ritual, more than a tradition. When we experience them, we encounter the Founder of the feasts in our hearts as well as our intellects.

THE RESTORATION OF ALL THINGS

A man crippled from birth had just been healed in the temple courts, to the astonishment of the Jewish crowd. As they gathered in Solomon's Colonnade to hear an explanation of this sign and wonder, Peter declared that it was not man who healed him, but it was the Name of Yeshua, the Jewish Messiah. He encouraged the people to repent in order that the following events could take place (see Acts 3:19):

1. Their sins may be blotted out.

2. Times of refreshing may come from the Lord.

3. God would send the Messiah, who has been appointed for the Jewish people.

Peter then revealed the end-time mystery of when God will send Messiah back to planet Earth:

> He must remain in heaven **until the time comes for God to restore everything**, as He promised long ago through His holy prophets (Acts 3:21).

The season of Messiah's return is linked to the restoration of all that was lost. When the Lord restores His ways and Torah to the Church, both Jewish and Gentile believers will look like a new creation, never before seen in the troubled history of the Church. We will neither be strangers to the Old Covenant, nor foreigners to Israel, nor will we be bound to any legalistic traditions. We will be "One New Man" in Messiah, as Paul wrote to the Gentiles in Ephesians 2 and 3.

> *Therefore, remember that formerly you who are Gentiles by birth ... remember that at that time you were separated from Christ, excluded from citizenship in Israel and foreigners to the covenants of the promise, without hope and without God in the world. But now in Christ Jesus you who once were far away have been brought near through the blood of Christ.*
>
> *He himself is our peace, who has made the two one and has destroyed the barrier, the dividing wall of hostility ... His purpose was to create in himself* **one new man** *out of the two, thus making peace.*
>
> *Consequently, you are no longer foreigners and aliens, but fellow citizens with God's people and members of God's household.*
>
> *This mystery is that through the gospel the Gentiles are heirs together with Israel, members together of one body, and sharers together in the promise in Christ Jesus* (Ephesians 2:11-14a,15b,19; 3:6).

The Lord Yeshua taught that the prophet Elijah is coming and will restore all things (see Matt. 17:11). Malachi also prophesied that Elijah's end-time ministry would be to restore the "hearts of the fathers to the children and the hearts of the children to the fathers."

> *See, I will send you the prophet Elijah before that great and dreadful day of the Lord comes. He will turn the hearts of the fathers to their children, and the hearts of the children to their fathers; or else I will come and strike the land with a curse* (Malachi 4:5-6).

While these verses literally refer to the restoration of family relationships, the Lord revealed a mysterious truth about them to my friend, David Michael; he shared this revelation with Messianic evangelist and teacher, Sid Roth, who published it in his outstanding book, *Time Is Running Short*.[1] Sid wrote that the implications of this passage are chilling because the earth will be under a curse unless this restoration takes place.

The revelation that David received was that the "fathers" refers to the Jewish people and the "children" refers to New Covenant believers. The people of Israel are often called the "fathers" or "patriarchs." Likewise, the New Testament frequently refers to believers as "children" (see Rom. 9:5; 11:28; Heb. 2:13; 1 John 2:1,12,18; Gal. 3:7).

The Lord requires that the hearts of the Jewish people and those of true Christians be turned toward each other in a bond of love and support. If the mutual hostility and mistrust continue as it has for many centuries of church history, it will bring the Lord's curse upon the earth; He died to make them one covenant people!

Blessed are the peacemakers, for they will be called children of God! (See Matthew 5:9.) When this loving relationship is restored, it will bring blessing and renewal to the earth. God's Name will be honored among both Israel and the nations. The earth will be filled with God's glory as the waters cover the seas (see Hab. 2:14). The Lord Yeshua spoke of this coming unity of Jew and Gentile as well:

> *I have other sheep that are not of this sheep pen. I must bring them also. They too will listen to My voice, and there shall be one flock and one shepherd* (John 10:16).

In addition to the hearts of Israel and the Church being restored to each other, what other related covenants will be restored in these last days?

1. God is causing the restoration of the Jewish people to their promised land. The Lord swore with uplifted arm this unconditional land grant to Abraham. We have seen the Jewish people regathered to the land of

Israel from the four corners of the earth in the last two generations.[2]

2. The Lord will cause the hearts of the Jewish people to turn back to their God. It causes the Lord unbearable anguish in His Father's heart that so many of His Jewish and Israeli people are not in a personal relationship with Him through His Son, Yeshua the Messiah.

    The unceasing grief that the apostle Paul described in Romans for his Jewish brothers is a small measure of the pain that the Lord feels for His people. There are so many Scriptures that describe His love and grief for the Jewish people, it would take another book to expound on them.

    > *I have loved you with an everlasting love; I have drawn you with loving-kindness.*
    >
    > *For a long time I have kept silent, I have been quiet and held myself back. But now, like a woman in childbirth, I cry out, I gasp and pant.*
    >
    > *For Zion's sake I will not keep silent, for Jerusalem's sake I will not remain quiet, till her righteousness shines out like the dawn, her salvation like a blazing torch.*
    >
    > *As a young man marries a maiden, so will your sons marry you; as a bridegroom rejoices over his bride, so will your God rejoice over you* (Jeremiah 31:3; Isaiah 42:14; 62:1,5).

3. The feasts will be restored to the Church. The Scriptural evidence for this statement is found throughout the chapters of this book. One example is found in

Zechariah 14, where the Lord describes the Gentile nations coming up to Jerusalem to celebrate the Feast of Tabernacles.

4. The Kingdom will be restored to Israel. While the risen Lord was eating with His disciples, they asked Him, "Lord, are you at this time going to restore the kingdom to Israel?"

   Yeshua answered, *"It is not for you to know the times or dates the Father has set by His own authority"* (Acts 1:7). He does not deny that this restoration will take place, but tells them that the *timing* of it is reserved for the Father alone. In that day, Israel will be a unified nation under the reign of the Son of David, never again to be trampled by Gentile superpowers.

Peter told the Jewish crowds in Jerusalem that Messiah would remain in Heaven until the time comes to restore everything. When these eternal covenants are restored, Messiah will not remain in Heaven any longer!

A FEAST ON THIS MOUNTAIN

On this mountain the Lord Almighty will prepare a feast of rich food for all peoples, a banquet of aged wine—the best of meats and the finest of wines. On this mountain He will destroy the shroud that enfolds all peoples, the sheet that covers all nations; He will swallow up death forever.

This is My blood of the covenant, which is poured out for many for the forgiveness of sins. I tell you, I will not drink of this fruit of the vine from now on until that day when I drink it anew with you in My Father's kingdom.

For the wedding of the Lamb has come, and His bride has made herself ready. Fine linen, bright and clean, was given her to wear.

A Prophetic Calendar: The Feasts of Israel

Blessed are those who are invited to the wedding supper of the Lamb! (Isaiah 25:6-8a; Matthew 26:28-29; Revelation 19:7b-8a,9)

Hebraic thought and practice were rich with the feasting of God's people. From Moses to the Prophets, from Yeshua's parables through the final pages of Revelation, we see a loving King in Heaven who is eager to provide an intimate banquet for a company of people who love Him. *It is a mystery that this feasting was always connected to the exposure of evil schemes, and to the victorious warfare of the righteous over lawless men.*

Isaiah 25 reveals that when we go up to the mountain of the Lord for this choice feast, the Lord will destroy the shroud that enfolds all people and the sheet that covers all nations. In the Book of Esther, it was at a banquet that the blinders were removed from Xerxes' eyes, and Haman's evil plot was exposed and cancelled. Revelation 19 describes the wedding supper of the Lamb, immediately before the Lord returns with His people to wage war and destroy the lawless one and his armies.

The last supper was a Passover feast; following this ceremonial meal, the works of satan would be forever exposed and defeated on the cross of our atonement. The veil would be removed from the eyes of the nations, and light would shine in the dark places of the earth.

We knew that fasting brought victory in times of war, but did we realize that feasting also destroys the works of the evil one? King David said, "You have prepared a table for me in the presence of my enemies."

In the seventh and final letter to the churches, the Lord Yeshua pleads with His own Church to open the door so that He can come in and dine with us.

Here I am! I stand at the door and knock. If anyone hears My voice and opens the door, I will come in and eat with him, and he with Me (Revelation 3:20).

Was the Lord Yeshua speaking to unbelievers when He asked them to open their doors to Him? No, He was speaking to His Church! The Lord eagerly desires to come into the midst of His people and dine with us; He considers this to be the sweetest promise of intimate fellowship.

God has appointed seasons on the calendar, and He has ordained the exact date for the Wedding Supper of the Lamb. When we celebrate His appointed feasts, we are rehearsing for the future Wedding Supper, the greatest and most desirable banquet ever given by a king on the earth or in Heaven.

HEZEKIAH'S PASSOVER REVIVAL

During the reign of King Solomon, Israel was divided into two kingdoms, the Northern (Israel) and the Southern (Judah). About two hundred years later, in 732 B.C., Ahaz was king of Judah, and he was unfaithful to the God of Israel. His Southern kingdom received much punishment from the Lord, at the hands of the northern tribes and also the Edomites.

One of the evils that Ahaz committed was to remove all the furnishings from God's temple and shut the doors of His sanctuary. The king set up pagan altars in the towns, but God's house was desolate and closed to His flock (see 2 Chron. 28:24-25).

When Ahaz died, his son Hezekiah became king. In the very first month of his reign, he was determined to restore God's house to the people of Israel, and to unify the two halves of the divided kingdom. He assembled the Levites and instructed them to consecrate themselves, remove the defilement from the Temple, replace, repair, and cleanse all of the sacred furnishings, and prepare God's altar to receive worship and sacrifice once again. Doesn't this scene remind you of the purification and rededication of the Temple that the Maccabees would accomplish, some five hundred years later?

It took the Levites sixteen days to consecrate the Temple and prepare it for holy offerings. They began their work on the first day of the first month (the month of Nisan) and completed the cleansing on the sixteenth day.

Then, Hezekiah assembled all the civil and spiritual authorities of Jerusalem, and they held a worship service of sacrifice to the Lord. They found the musical instruments that King David had made almost three hundred years earlier for the Levitical musicians and choir. Then, with praise, music, and burnt offerings, they worshiped Adonai as He had always desired to be worshiped. Thus, the service of the Temple was reestablished under Hezekiah's vision and leadership, and they rejoiced that this restoration had taken place so quickly (see 2 Chron. 29:15-36).

The godly Hezekiah realized that they had "missed" the Feast of Passover. They had not finished cleansing the Temple or consecrating the Levites in time to conduct a Passover service, which would have been on the fourteenth of Nisan. The Lord had already thought of this problem and had made provision in the Law of Moses; for those who wanted to celebrate the Passover, but were ceremonially unclean, they were permitted to observe it on the fourteenth day of the *second* month, instead of the first month (see Num. 9:9-11).

It was very important to Hezekiah to bring all of the tribes of Israel together for the Passover, and not merely the Southern kingdom. Hezekiah sent letters to all Israel and Judah, inviting them to come to the Temple of the Lord in Jerusalem to celebrate the Passover. His leadership had decided that they would celebrate it in the second month, since they had not been able to observe it at the proper time. He wrote a beautiful letter, in which he reminded them of the Lord's recent punishments and urged them to return to the Lord and receive His compassion and mercy (see 2 Chron. 30:6-9).

The gracious king in Jerusalem sent out an invitation to a banquet, inviting even the despised northern tribes to come up to God's mountain and celebrate the feast with the people of Judah. His desire for unity is remarkable, considering these northern tribes had recently slaughtered 120,000 of their Judean relatives in an attack during the reign of his father, Ahaz. That is forty times as many people as were murdered in New York City on September 11, 2001! To Hezekiah's generous invitation, we see a disappointing mixed response from the kingdom of Israel:

> *The couriers went from town to town in Ephraim and Manasseh, as far as Zebulun, but the people **scorned and ridiculed** them. Nevertheless, some men of Asher,*

*Manasseh and Zebulun **humbled themselves** and went to Jerusalem.*

*Also in Judah the hand of God was on the people to **give them unity of mind** to carry out what the king and his officials had ordered, following the word of the Lord* (2 Chronicles 30:10-12).

The proud and complacent Israelites scorned the invitation of the king. Why should they leave their farms and businesses to come to Jerusalem for a week to celebrate a feast of the Lord? They had no regard for the forgotten Law of Moses or the wishes of Israel's greatest king, David.

However, some of these men were of a nobler character, and something within them recognized the tug of God on their heartstrings. They humbled themselves and came up as guests to Jerusalem, despite being ceremonially unclean.

The people of Judah had unity of mind and came voluntarily. The righteous king did not force his subjects to honor God; he realized that if worship is not freely given, the Lord is not interested. A large crowd gathered, and the land of Israel was united again in this Passover celebration, for the first time in over two hundred years! This is a picture of the end-time Church, Jew and Gentile, coming together in unity and love to celebrate the feasts of the Lord. This is a picture of the revival of the last days.

The final amazing point about this story is that most of the participants from the north were not ceremonially clean and were legally forbidden to eat the Passover. But behold the mercy and kindness of our God, whose loving heart was the same in the days of the Old Testament as the merciful heart of Yeshua seen in the New Testament:

Although most of the many people who came from Ephraim, Manasseh, Issachar and Zebulun had not purified themselves, yet they ate the Passover, contrary to what was written. But Hezekiah prayed for them, saying, "May the Lord, who is good, pardon everyone who sets his

*heart on seeking God—the Lord, the God of his fathers—
even if he is not clean according to the rules of the sanctuary." And the Lord heard Hezekiah and healed the
people* (2 Chronicles 30:18-20).

Anyone who thinks that the God of the Old Testament was legalistic
and punishing, while the God of the New Testament was merciful and
forgiving, has certainly not read their Bibles. He is the same God, yesterday,
today, and forever. His heart and character have not changed, and He is able
to purify that which is impure; He is able to cleanse that which is unclean,
and He is willing to forgive and heal those who inadvertently break His
laws, when a righteous intercessor stands in the gap and prays for them.

We have much to learn from our beloved brother, Hezekiah, and from
the revival that his youthful zeal set in motion in the days of his reign in the
land of Judah. The unity he brought to Israel is a prophetic picture of the
Jewish and Gentile believers humbling themselves and celebrating the feasts
of the Lord together, with joy and gratitude, as One New Man in Messiah.

How Much Oil Is in Your Lamp?

*If the owner of the house had known at what time the
thief was coming, he would have kept watch and would
not have let his house be broken into. So you also must be
ready, because the Son of Man will come at an hour when
you do not expect Him* (Matthew 24:43-44).

The Lord Yeshua warned frequently of the urgent need to be ready for His
unexpected return. Many parables addressed this matter, and the most chilling
and sobering among them is the parable of the ten virgins. This warning is
clearly aimed at believers, rather than unbelievers, as we will examine now.

*At that time the kingdom of heaven will be like ten
virgins who took their lamps and went out to meet the
bridegroom* (Matthew 25:1).

288

All of the ten were actively waiting for the Bridegroom, and all had lamps. The three characteristics that identify them as Christians, or at least professing Christians in the last days, are these: they were virgins; they had a source of light; and they were expectantly waiting for the Bridegroom.

> *Five of them were foolish and five were wise. The foolish ones took their lamps but did not take any oil with them. The wise, however, took oil in jars along with their lamps. The bridegroom was a long time in coming, and they all became drowsy and fell asleep* (Matthew 25:2-5).

The only difference given between the wise and the foolish was that the wise had extra oil in jars, in addition to the supply in their lamps. Notice that even the wise ones became drowsy.

> *At midnight the cry rang out: "Here's the bridegroom! Come out to meet him!" Then all the virgins woke up and trimmed their lamps. The foolish ones said to the wise, "Give us some of your oil; our lamps are going out."*
>
> *"No," they replied. "There may not be enough for both us and you...go...and buy some for yourselves." But while they were on their way to buy the oil, the bridegroom arrived. The virgins who were ready went in with him to the wedding banquet. And the door was shut* (Matthew 25:6-10).

When the midnight cry rang out, the lamps of the unprepared virgins began to flicker and grow dim; their oil was insufficient. Notice that they could not meet the Bridegroom using other people's light, but needed their own source of light. As they rapidly found themselves in darkness, they begged for oil from their well-prepared companions.

At this point in the story, many Christians might think: "If they love Jesus, they will share their oil with the others." However, the wise virgins were not able to spare any extra oil for their sisters; they needed every drop of their own oil to light their way. Does this sound selfish to you?

Think of it this way: What if your neighborhood received warnings from the electric company that there would be a three-day power outage at some point in the near future, but they could not be sure on what date this outage would take place? The company told their customers to be prepared by stocking candles, generators, gasoline, water, and food. All the neighbors had equal opportunity to heed the warning and prepare for the outage. Half of the neighborhood spent time and money preparing, while the other half couldn't be bothered. They assumed they would figure something out when the time came.

On the day of the outage, the unprepared ones scurried around, requesting candles, food, and batteries from the prepared ones. The wise refused to share, pointing out that they needed what they had stored up for their own families; why didn't the others make the same efforts of preparation? Do you still think the wise virgins were selfish, or does this make perfect sense?

The secret treasures we have stored in our hearts for our own final battle against evil, or martyrdom, cannot be squandered on those who did not care enough to prepare. We will need *all* of what we have stored, and we will simply not have any oil to spare. All have received the same warning from the "Power Company," and all are equally accountable for preparedness.

> *"No," they replied. "There may not be enough for both us and you . . . **go . . . and buy some for yourselves."***
>
> *But while they were on their way to buy the oil, the bridegroom arrived. The virgins who were ready went in with him to the wedding banquet. **And the door was shut**.*
>
> *Later the others also came. "Sir! Sir!" they said. "Open the door for us!"*
>
> *But he replied, "I tell you the truth, **I don't know you**."*
>
> *Therefore keep watch, because you do not know the day or the hour* (Matthew 25:9-13).

Half of the neighborhood was unprepared. Five out of ten virgins were shut out of the Wedding Banquet. Those who are wise will stay connected to an inexhaustible source of oil. They are continually being filled with the oil that is only found in the secret place of waiting on the Lord, communing with Yeshua as a friend.

The oil represents the Holy Spirit, as well as the transformation of our inner being, which comes only by spending private time with Jesus. Knowing *about* Him is head knowledge, and does not transform our deepest motives. But knowing *His heart* and allowing Him to know our heart changes us from the inside out. We become more like Him and can even be joined to Him in holy union, by dying to self.

To make this more precise, I will try to identify several issues nearest and dearest to the Lord's heart. These are derived from Scripture in encapsulated form. Knowing Him as an intimate friend, and being known by Him, brings "oil" in our lamps, a reservoir of trust in His goodness, for the darkest hour we will face.

1. Loving the Lord with all our hearts and strength, above all other relationships and possessions. Yeshua told us this is the first and greatest commandment, and all are expected to pursue this great love relationship with every ounce of our motivation and determination (see Deut. 6:5; Matt. 22:37).

2. Knowing the Lord in a personal way through His Word, and allowing ourselves to be known by Him, through intimacy and transparent sharing with Him (see Ps. 139; Matt. 25:12).

3. Sharing His burden for the poor, the enslaved, the abused, and the murdered; and crying out in repentance and intercession against the great issues of injustice on the earth and innocent bloodshed (see Gen. 9:6; Amos 5:24; Rev. 6:10-11).

4. Knowing and appreciating the Lord's everlasting covenants with Israel, the Jewish people, and the appointed times on His calendar (see Gen. 12:3; Jer. 31:31; Rom. 11).

To understand His heart on this last matter, picture this: I might say to you, "I love you *so* much, but frankly, I can't stand your children."

You might answer me, "Thanks, but if you hate my children, you really don't love me that much. They are a part of me." In the same way, Israel is so near and dear to our Father's heart that to love Him is to share His feelings for His ancient covenant people.

The parable of the ten virgins is not directly connected to the Feasts of the Lord; even so, I have included it in this final chapter because I believe that when His Bride begins to celebrate His appointed festivals, she will receive extra oil in her lamp, causing her to shine as a light to Israel and the nations. There is an aspect of God's character and personality that cannot be acquired through any other channel. *The feasts of Israel are a conduit though which His oil flows and fills us with an intimate, experiential knowledge of His character.* The easiest example is Passover: once you have participated in the Passover, and not just heard about it, you understand the Lord's sacrificial death, atonement, and prophetic purposes in a far deeper way.

A society's calendar is a snapshot of the values and priorities that are dearest to their hearts. So it shall be with His true Church in these last days.

THE BRIDE HAS MADE HERSELF READY

Later the others also came. "Sir! Sir!" they said. "Open the door for us!"

But he replied, "I tell you the truth, I don't know you." Therefore keep watch, because you do not know the day or the hour.

For the wedding of the Lamb has come, and His bride has made herself ready. Fine linen, bright and clean, was given her to wear.

The Bride Has Made Herself Ready

Blessed are those who are invited to the wedding
supper of the Lamb! (Matt. 25:11-12; Rev. 19:7-8,9).

We would pay any price on this earth to ensure that we never hear those dreaded words, which the Lord Jesus spoke to the unprepared virgins: *"I don't know you."* The price is our time, our hearts, our very asking. He will fill us with His oil if we will but ask and wait. The word that the Lord gave to me at the end of the Hanukah chapter contained a similar reference, and was unsettling. He said, *"I would have filled them with My oil if they had only asked Me!"* Isn't it incredible what treasures we miss by not asking?

The spring feasts are a rehearsal of the Lord's first coming as the Lamb of God. The fall feasts are a rehearsal for the rapture, the catching up of the Bride, the return of the Lord Yeshua to set up His Kingdom over all the earth.

As we prepare for the sun to set on the eve of these holidays, we are thrust out of our sleep-walking routines, and into a state of present-tense readiness and alertness. Malachi tells us, *"Suddenly, the one you desire will appear in His temple."* Likewise, the apostle Paul warns us that many will be surprised when the Day of the Lord overtakes them *"like a thief in the night."* But Paul adds:

> *But you, brothers, are not in darkness so that this day*
> *should surprise you like a thief. You are all sons of the*
> *light and sons of the day. We do not belong to the night or*
> *to the darkness. So then, let us not be like others, who are*
> *asleep, but let us be alert and self-controlled* (1 Thessalonians 5:4-6).

We must be the ready ones, the vigilant ones, the watching ones. The Bride has made herself ready *before* the midnight cry rings out. We must purify our hearts and put away every unclean thing from before our eyes and ears. *Our eyes, ears, and mouth are the gates to our body. We must vigilantly keep our gates undefiled with impurity, for our bodies are the temple of the Holy Spirit.*

The following vision concerning the ten virgins was given to Messianic violinist, teacher, and prophet Maurice Sklar. It contains treasures of insight, concerning the type of fire that burns in our lamps, our lives, and our worship. As we will see, there is "authorized fire," and there is "strange fire." I believe this word connects to the restoration of the Lord's covenants, calendar, and biblically acceptable worship before the Lord:

Then I saw an old fashioned oil lamp that was lit with a flame coming out of the top of it. Then it suddenly became ten lamps that were lined up side by side. The five on the left of me suddenly started to flicker. The flame got smaller and smaller until finally it just fizzled and went out. But the lamps on the other side were fed by a lampstand that they were connected to that was previously hid in the darkness. They just burned brighter and brighter until finally I heard these words, "Come up here and escape the wrath to come, for you are found worthy. Behold, the Bridegroom comes!" Then they all disappeared.

The Lord then said to me, "Half of those that say they know Me in the time of the end are liars. They have never been lit with the fire from Heaven. They are burning with the strange fires of Mystery Babylon. They only pretend to know Me. Their lamp shall be put out in outer darkness, and there shall be weeping and gnashing of teeth. But those who are Mine shall shine forever and burn with the brightness of My glory as the stars. For they are lit from My throne and fed with my oil and shall never go out. These are My precious ones—My glorious Bride who shall always be true and faithful to Me. It is for her that I died and rose again. It is for her that I am returning in the midnight hour. Tell her that I have not forgotten her! She is My beloved, and I am hers! I love her with an everlasting love. I shall surely catch her up to My throne where she will rule and reign with Me in glory forever and ever at My right hand. Amen."[3]

In this amazing word from Brother Maurice, there is a warning about the "strange fires of Mystery Babylon." I would like to make the briefest of comments on this expression, so that the Church can be warned about what constitutes "strange fire" (this can also be translated, "foreign fire").

In Leviticus 10, Aaron's two sons, Nadav and Abihu, offered "strange fire" before the Lord, and were burned alive by the fire of the Lord. Although High Priest Aaron and his sons were authorized to burn incense before the Lord, it was not to be done at any time or in any way they desired. Nadav and Abihu burned incense at an "unauthorized time" and/or in an "unauthorized way," and the Lord killed them for it.

We too, in the New Covenant, need to worship the Lord in the ways and principles that He has desired, requested, and authorized in His Scriptures. We cannot just make up anything we like and assume that God will morph into any type of God we want Him to be. We cannot create God in our image! He is who He is and does not change His ways or character just because we want an "evolved" version of Judaism or Christianity. Here are a few of the dangerous elements that the Lord will see as strange fire, and that will deceive many Christians in these last days.

1. Changing God's unchanging standards of holiness and righteousness to conform to relative standards of morality dictated by society's wishes.

2. Chanting foreign words to other gods in the name of meditation.

3. "Channeling" messages we hear from inner "spirit guides"; some will tell us these voices are the voice of God. These "spirit guides" are often demons.

4. Removing the message of the blood of Yeshua, the Cross, and the issue of our sinfulness; denying our need for both forgiveness and atonement to be right with God. This will be a form of Christianity without the Cross, the blood, or atonement for sin, and will be seen by God as strange fire.

5. Labeling Jesus as one of many "avatars," or spiritual leaders, like Buddha or Mohammed, and denying His unique identity as the only Son of God.

A Prophetic Calendar: The Feasts of Israel

What I am briefly describing is a severely deceptive, counterfeit version of Christianity that is springing up with great popularity on the earth. The list of warnings above is not comprehensive but will give alert and concerned readers a reference point for guarding their fires of worship as acceptable offerings to the Lord.

Knowing your Scriptures in a whole and comprehensive way is a good safeguard against strange fire. It is important never to take one or two verses out of context, for they can be misused and misinterpreted. Know the *whole* counsel of God, both Old and New Covenants. The teachings in this book on the feasts will help with the bigger picture of scriptural truths.

The Lord Yeshua is more desirable than any pleasure the world has to offer. His presence and intimate companionship are so much more real and satisfying than any occult or new age religion, worldly entertainment, sports, addictions, pornography, soap operas, or the chatter of talk-shows.

We can choose to be with the Lord *at the speed of thought*, in the blink of an eye, by deliberately focusing our hearts on Him. In doing so, we receive the oil of intimacy He has promised us. Our lamps will not go out if we have spent precious time cultivating intimacy with the Lord, waiting expectantly in His Presence.

Let us fix our eyes on Jesus and turn our hearts toward Him with *purposeful passion*. The Lord loves us with great patience and affection; He wants us in His arms, not in front of the television. Every moment we spend entertaining ourselves is time that we will never have again; it is time we could have spent in the Lord's Presence, asking Him to fill us with His oil, to light our lamps in the darkest coming hour.

CHURCH, YOUR APRON IS FULL OF GRAIN!

> *When you reap the harvest of your land, do not reap to the very edges of your field or gather the gleanings of your harvest. Leave them for the poor and the alien [foreigner]. I am the Lord your God* (Leviticus 23:22).

In the Feast of Weeks (Pentecost) chapter, we learned that the Book of

Ruth is set in the grain fields of wealthy Israeli landowner, Boaz, at the season of the barley and wheat harvests. While the Book of Ruth is a true, historical account, the story of Ruth and Boaz is also a parable of the end-times Church.[4]

We see a picture of two widowed women, a Jewish mother-in-law and a Gentile daughter-in-law, who shared a bond of grief and loneliness. Although Naomi urged her to return to her people, Ruth clung tenaciously to the people of Israel. Her fierce love and loyalty for Naomi and the God of Israel drove her to leave her homeland forever. When the impoverished widow and her Moabite daughter-in-law returned to Bethlehem after the famine, Ruth gleaned in the fields to provide food for Naomi. Ruth had been instructed by Naomi that the Torah made provision for poor foreigners to glean from Israel's fields. She humbled herself and picked up the "crumbs" that fell from the Israeli table, the property of a Jewish landowner.

While Ruth began by gleaning crumbs, her extraordinary loyalty to her Israeli mother-in-law became known to Boaz, the owner of the fields. By the time he met her in his fields, he knew of her noble character and her devotion to the people of Israel. Boaz blessed Ruth at their very first meeting, saying, "May the Lord richly reward you, the God of Israel, under whose wings you have come to take refuge" (Ruth 2:12). This blessing released Ruth's destiny; she would be covered by Boaz's wing, and she would become his bride. It also released the Messiah's birth through their union.

Boaz began to show Ruth more generosity as time passed. Each time Ruth received a greater gift from Boaz, she immediately carried the blessing back to Naomi. The blessings grew, as did their love, and Ruth shared the multiplication with Naomi in a cycle of reciprocal blessings. Boaz (Israel) blesses Ruth (a Gentile); Ruth then blesses Naomi (Israel). Ruth represents the end-time Gentile Church: having originally received the Gospel from Israel's table, the Church now needs to respond generously to the Jewish people, giving from her storehouse of the bountiful mercy she has received (see Rom. 11:30-31).

As extravagant as Boaz was, there was a dramatic shift in the landscape halfway through the story. Once, as I was preparing to teach on Ruth, the Lord spoke to my heart:

What changed the equation from generosity to marriage? What was the key that transformed Boaz from being a very generous man to Ruth's husband?

Since I did not know the answer, the Lord provided the key:

Naomi taught Ruth the Torah, the Law of Moses; she explained to her the Law of the Kinsman-Redeemer. Naomi was not in a position to convince Boaz to consider marrying Ruth; rather, she sent her Moabite daughter-in-law to remind Boaz of his responsibilities according to the Law, as well as showing him the love in her heart. This would shift the equation from mere generosity to the full privileges of marriage.

I was overjoyed to receive this awesome key of understanding from the Lord, for my own sake as well as that of the teaching I was preparing.

When Ruth said to Boaz, "Spread the corner of your garment over me, for you are my kinsman-redeemer," she was citing the Law of Moses so that he would remember his legal responsibilities (see Ruth 3:9). When she lay at his feet, she was demonstrating her love for him. Less than a day later, Ruth's love for Boaz and for the Law of Moses resulted in Boaz taking Ruth to be His bride. Obedience encountered intimacy.

Once Boaz married her, it was no longer a case of generosity to a foreigner; rather, Ruth became a Mother of Israel, with all of the rights and property of her husband. Ruth became a full heir to all of the commonwealth of Israel, grafted into the fullness of the blessings. In the same way, Jewish and Gentile believers who love and serve Yeshua in His fields will feast with Him at His table as co-heirs with Messiah.

The result of Ruth and Boaz's marriage was the birth of the grandfather of King David, and in the fullness of time, the birth of the Messiah, who would bring salvation to all the nations of the earth.

The Lord's prophetic word that He gave me at the end of the Pentecost chapter included a reference to Ruth and Boaz. A portion of that word is repeated here:

A field full of ripe grain is like a banqueting table. I have spread out a table for the nations, a ripe field for all the peoples.

Do you see Ruth, following the servant girls of Boaz, behind the harvesters, picking up the kernels that the servant girls missed? She did not feel worthy to eat the crumbs that fell from Boaz's table, and even his dogs ate the crumbs. She followed behind, not even for her own hunger; she was thinking about Naomi's hunger, and how important it was for her to eat a nutritious meal and keep up her strength and spirit.

My people will raise up the poor Moabitess, spread the corner and the wing of My prayer shawl over her, and bless her to rise up to surpass them. She will become greater and wealthier than they who gave her of their crumbs and their gleanings. She will become a bountiful Mother of Israel, blessing her people in return.

As Israel showed kindness and mercy to Ruth, so now My Bride from the Gentile nations will become a mother to hungry and hapless Israel, and she will cover My people as they have covered her when she was still a nobody.

Israel's feasts are a field of ripened grain, and the Lord has made provision in His Torah for all the nations to feast at His table. It is no longer a matter of gleaning the crumbs; His Bride is the heir to the full covenant blessings of Israel, from whom she received salvation. As a farmer plows and sows his field with thousands of seeds, so these truths will spring up as a golden harvest in the Church's heart, a harvest of covenant love.

The Lord Yeshua is a Bridegroom in love. As His father Boaz had heaped grain upon Ruth's apron, so the Lord has filled you with good things. Standing and watching on the edge of His threshing floor, He lovingly sends you out to carry your grain to the nations and to the Jewish people. Though you were once a poor foreigner, now He has spread His garment over you and called you His own; you are in awe of His generosity.

How carefully you will carry these kernels, not letting even one fall to the ground without accomplishing its nourishing purpose for which He sent you out. Even one of them could become a barley loaf that will feed five thousand souls!

May the Lord reward you richly, the God of Israel, under whose wings you have come to take refuge. Your Kinsman-Redeemer has rewarded your humility and obedience to His ancient covenant, and your unconditional love for His people Israel, which could be likened to a bereaved Jewish mother. As with Ruth and Boaz, the first fruits of this One New Man marriage of Jew and Gentile will be the salvation of the Jewish people and the final harvest of the nations.

"Let Us Keep the Feast!"

On Passover, we will sing the song of Moses and the song of the Lamb. He is worthy, for with His blood, He has purchased sons and daughters from every nation! (See Revelation 5:9.)

During Unleavened Bread, we will remember the bread of affliction, and we will cleanse our hearts from the yeast of malice and envy (see 1 Cor. 5:7).

On First Fruits, we will celebrate the resurrection of our living Lord. Yeshua is the Bread of Life; death could not hold Him, and He will raise us up on the last day! (See John 6:35,54,57-58.)

In the Feast of Weeks, we will fill our aprons with grain and give generously to the poor, the foreigner, the orphan, and the widow. As we share our seed with the poor, we will see supernatural multiplication, until the banquet of the Gospel is spread out before the nations like a field of ripened wheat (see Deut. 14:22-27).

At the Memorial of Blasting, He will sound the shofar and gather His Bride from the four ends of the heavens (see Matt. 24:31).

On the Day of Atonement, all of Israel will look upon the One they have pierced and will mourn for Him in a spirit of repentance. In that day, "all Israel will be saved" (see Zech. 12:10; Rom. 11:26).

During Tabernacles, the Lord will separate the wheat from the chaff;

He will gather His wheat into the barn, but the chaff He will burn with unquenchable fire (see Matt. 3:12).

At the Feast of Purim, the anti-Semitic agendas of Haman will be exposed, and he will be impaled on the gallows he built for Mordechai, and for all the Jewish people. As Esther, the true Church will arise and plead for the life of the Jewish people, those of her Savior's lineage, from whom she was birthed (see Esther 4:12-14).

On Hanukah, the Lord will burn with zeal, and will cleanse and rededicate His Temple; He will remove the abomination that stands where it does not belong, on Jerusalem's holy hill (see Zech. 14:2-9).

And what will be said of Shabbat? The Lord created all things in six days, but the seventh day was the Lord's. Mankind has had 6,000 years upon the earth, to exercise authority and dominion. The seven-thousandth year is the Lord's, called "The Millenium." For six days, man has ruled the earth and has done what was right in his own eyes. But on the seventh day, the kingdoms of this world will become the Kingdom of our Lord and of His Messiah (see Rev. 11:15).

There remains, then, a Sabbath rest for the people of God; for anyone who enters God's rest also rests from his own work, just as God did from His (Hebrews 4:9-10).

THE LORD'S FINAL WORD ON PREPARATION

I have completed the writing of this book, and this morning, I waited on the Lord for His heart on this closing chapter. I was physically unwell as I waited, but He was faithful on this last day of April, 2008, to show me His heart one more time. I love Him!

I see a tiny butterfly with white wings, fluttering its wings rapidly in flight, flying into the sunlight, into the open skies.

She has been prepared on the earth. She has been nurtured and sheltered in her cocoon of metamorphosis.

She was prepared on the earth, and this is where her transformation took place.

When it was time, I gave her wings, and she took flight, and she beat her wings rapidly with tremendous speed and energy; she flew to Me.

No one knows the day or the hour. So precise is My timing that I have reserved it for Myself," says the Lord, "known only to Me. I have preserved the secret of her development within the cocoon, within the chemistry of suffering, of waiting in silence in the darkest place, the darkest hour, the chemistry and metamorphosis of resting alone with Me, of trusting Me to bring to the moment of completion, preparation, and readiness to fly.

It must be My time; it must be the time of ripeness and readiness. If you do not wait upon Me in your cocoon of silence, you will not find Me. You will not be made whole or perfectly prepared and changed.

You will not know Me in My creative transformations, and you will **not** be made ready to fly to Me when I quickly and suddenly call out to you from My canopy in Heaven, from My prepared Bridal chamber in the skies, in the Son of Righteousness. You will not be able to struggle out of your dark cocoon when you hear My thunderous cry for you echo through the heavens, from one end of the earth to another.

You will hear, but will be unable to respond, so dark and tight is the place you are in, so constraining and without the Light of the World awakening your senses.

You will be as one who dreams, stuck, unable to move, unable to open your mouth and cry like a newborn baby cries as it opens its mouth and breathes its first breath in the bright and loud and spacious and open place. You will not have your white wings, and it will seem foreign and strange to you in the darkness of that dream when you hear My voice echo through the atmosphere, "**Come up here!**"

You will watch from a distance, unable to move or respond to the sound of My voice.

If you enter the cocoon too late, the process is too long, and you will not be ready; you will be unprepared.

It is critically important **when** the caterpillar enters the dark and constraining place, the transforming place. She knows when to enter the secret place and wait.

Enter **now**! Enter your secret place **now**, Church, **now**. You have eaten and prepared your Body for a long season of transformation.

I see a light, small butterfly, flapping so fast, its wings are a blur of motion. She is flying into the Son of Right-eousness, never to crawl on the earth again, never to return to the dark, moist place of seclusion, the discomforts and pains of this world.

Fly away to Me; fly to Yeshua. It is finished. I will take you to be My own if you will let Me prepare you and transform you.

The dead will hear My voice and will be awakened as out of a dream; they will fly away home.

Tell My Bride **now**, today, even this hour is the one to enter the chamber of stillness. If you do not enter it in time, the process will be too lengthy, and you will not be ready to move when I call you.

Come!!! I call you to Me! **Amen**.

May these many words I have sown be a blessing to your holy calling and destiny, precious reader. May the Lord add to them His Spirit and His heart of unfailing love.

Amen!

"I Am the Broken Piece!"

The Passover Haggadah for Believers in Yeshua

Instructions for Preparing the Seder

Initial Instructions for Leaders:

In a larger congregational Seder, each table would have an assigned leader. However, there must also be a primary leader or couple to conduct the whole group Seder. The primary leader will also be the table leader at his or her "head table." The "head table" is the table from which the "host" conducts the Seder. There will be guests at the head table also, as in a wedding. You will see below that the table settings at the head table are slightly different from those at the other tables. This host person or couple will read the "Leader" parts in the Haggadah, and will give instructions to the table leaders as the Seder progresses. Therefore, the primary leader must be very familiar with the Haggadah before leading a Seder.

There are also reading parts for the participants. This is marked, "Reader 1, Reader 2," etc., in your Haggadah. Readers can be assigned ahead of time, or people can just take turns reading, going around the room. Table leaders can read the "reader" parts, but not the "leader" parts.

There are also seven dramatic long readings, which are in-depth teachings and prophetic material. These are entitled, "First Reading," "Second Reading," etc. Five of these occur before the meal, and two occur after the meal. The primary leader may read them or could assign these powerful readings in advance. He should assign them to people who can read well in a strong voice, and with much meaning and feeling. If possible, they should have a chance to look them over before the Seder. The power and anointing on these passages could be lost if someone stumbles through them without expression.

Since these long readings are very sweet and poignant, you might choose to play soft, anointed CD music in the background while the reader is reading these particular narratives. This is optional. The music should be instrumental, without words to distract from the reading, and should be gentle and worshipful. If it has a Hebraic sound, that could enhance the readings quite a bit. Someone would have to be prepared ahead of time with the CD, the track numbers, a CD player, and a pre-arranged list of which song would go with which reading. In addition, the song would have to be "faded out" as the reading is finishing. When the reading is over, you need the music to gently stop.

The Seder Has Three Parts:

1. The first part of the ceremony, which lasts almost one hour. After this part, you can dispose of the small ceremonial plate that was on top of your dinner plate. You can eat all of your ceremonial foods before clearing away the small plates to make room for dinner. You won't need another ceremonial plate for the shorter ceremony after the dinner.

2. The dinner. Many groups like to have a "covered dish" Seder, meaning that participants bring a dish. If you bring hot foods, it could be stressful to try to keep them hot while the first part of the ceremony is going on. Someone is always running back to the kitchen to check on the food and missing the wonderful, anointed ceremony. You can do hot dishes, but you might try a covered cold dish supper... it is easier, and we have done this in many churches very successfully. Food suggestions are below.

3. The closing ceremony includes the afikomen, which becomes the bread of Communion. The third cup of personal redemption becomes the Cup of the New Covenant in Yeshua's blood. So we remember His death in this moment of Communion after the supper. We eat and drink it together in solemn consecration and love for Yeshua.

The Table:

You can decide whether to use disposable dishes, silverware, and cups, or real utensils to be washed. In a large group Seder, each table would have:

1. Dinner settings for all, with two cups at each place (one for water, one for grape juice or wine), and a smaller plate on top of each dinner plate, on which to serve ourselves the ceremonial foods from the central plates

2. One small bowl of salty water for the whole table to share (sprinkle enough salt into the water so that it tastes like tears).

3. Two bowls in the center for 1) horseradish (red is preferred, if you can find it), enough to be shared around the table, and 2) charoset (see recipe below), enough to be shared around the table

4. A plate for enough pieces of matzah (about ¼ sheet of matzah) for each participant at the table

5. A plate for enough small sprigs of parsley to be shared around the table to dip in the salt water

6. Only the table leaders will need this at their setting: four large white paper or cloth napkins, which are layered and wrapped around three large, whole pieces of matzah from the box. There is a bottom napkin, matzah, the next napkin, matzah, the third napkin, matzah, and the fourth napkin goes on top. Then gently fold the top edges around the packet of matzah. If you would like, the resources at the end of the Passover chapter show you where to purchase a special cloth holder for these three symbolic pieces of matzah, called a Matzah Tash. You can buy one, or just use the napkins as described above.

7. One copy of the Haggadah for each participant.

Young children who cannot read do not need one, and people can share if there is a shortage of copies. When the Seder is over, collect the Haggadahs so that you do not have to make all these copies again next year.

Only the Head Table Would Have:

1. A central Seder plate for the symbolic foods (if no specially purchased plate is available, a regular plate can be used)

2. Two candlesticks for the initial welcome, to be lit early in the ceremony (you can purchase special candlesticks from one of the resource Web sites, or just use candlesticks you own)

3. The items on the central Seder plate are the following five items (everyone seated at the head table will be taking some of the foods as the ceremony progresses before the meal) :
   a. Horseradish (red is preferred, if you can find it), enough to be shared around the table
   b. Charoset (see recipe below), enough to be shared around the table
   c. Enough sprigs of parsley for each one at the head table
   d. Pieces of matzah for each one at the head table
   e. A cleaned, roasted, or boiled dry chicken bone, representing the shank bone of the lamb (you can use the same bone every year for generations!)

4. A special extra cup sits on the head table only, called "Elijah's Cup." Fill it with some grape juice or wine

before the Seder begins, even though Elijah will not actually come and drink it (this is explained in the Passover chapter!). If you wish to buy a special "Kiddush Cup" from the resource Web sites, you can use this special cup for Elijah's cup. Or you can just use a regular cup.

5.   One copy of the Haggadah for each participant

6.   The Primary Leader at the head table would also have a three-matzah packet in napkins or a Matzah Tash, as described above.

If you are conducting a family Seder around one table, there would be one table leader, and everyone else is a participant. The table leader would also be the primary leader, since there is only one table. Everything else above would be the same for a family Seder.

Set-up Time:

Getting the tables ready, including making the three matzah packets for each table leader, will take at least an hour for a large Seder, if the leader has three or four helpers. Most of the items could be placed at the tables as early as the morning of the Seder meal (which always takes place in the evening). The bowl of salt water on each table, all table settings, cups and plates, candlesticks, and extra plates in the middle of each table for ceremonial foods, can all be done early.

However, the following foods should remain refrigerated until just before beginning the Seder: horseradish, charoset, and parsley. To save time later, the smaller bowls of horseradish and charoset for each table can be made up early in the day and refrigerated. This way, in the evening, you can just remove the bowls for each table from the fridge and place them on each table, rather than having to fill the bowls at the last minute.

Pitchers of water can be placed on each table before the ceremony, and grape juice for each guest can be poured just before the service, so it is not sitting out all day. This last-minute set-up takes at least a half-hour with helpers, so allow extra time.

How Much Grape Juice Do We Need?

Even though the Haggadah says that we drink four cups of wine, we usually do not do this. We serve each guest one cup of juice at the beginning, and when it says, "Drink the first cup, second cup, etc.," we merely take one sip, not the whole cup. This saves a lot of grape juice and keeps people from filling up with too much juice. If someone runs out, there should be extra juice in the kitchen for a refill. After dinner, some will need their cups refilled for the third and fourth cups.

Because the ceremony before the meal takes about an hour, families with young children should give them some food before they come, or the children might get too hungry while waiting.

Since the leader has so much responsibility, you should assign a separate person to take care of the covered dish supper. This person would handle the sign-up sheet for foods to be brought, and would delegate various people to help with serving and the large job of cleaning up (paper plates help a lot). Make sure the leader does not try to do it all. It is way too much for one person or even one couple. Delegate everything possible to helpers, or it will become too stressful, and you will not truly enjoy Passover, as the Lord wants you to. (I have done these for many years, and I can testify that you need a lot of help to do this and still enjoy it!)

Reading the Hebrew:

If you don't know anyone who can pronounce the few Hebrew prayers in this Hagaddah, just skip to the English, and "all" read the English together. I hope to be placing on my Web site a recording of myself reading the blessings in Hebrew, so that a leader can hear me and learn them ahead of time. It will be on the "Teachings" page of www.coffeetalkswithmessiah.com.

Songs:

You will see that there are four optional spots to insert worship songs in the midst of the service. These break up the readings with the joy of music. If you have a musician or singer who can lead, he or she could look over the service and choose appropriate songs for each section. Songs about the Lamb of God, the Blood, or being delivered from our enemies would be good themes. If you use CD music, you can choose from some of the awesome CDs and songs found in the resource section at the end of Chapter 6 of *The Prophetic Calendar: The Feasts of Israel*, from which this Haggadah is an excerpt.

You could print out sheets with the words to the songs; these words could be given out separately, or stapled into the back of the Haggadahs. However, if you choose different songs next year, it would be better if they weren't stapled in, so you could re-use the Haggadahs year after year. You could also use overheads for the song lyrics.

On page 14, there are words for a beloved, traditional song called "Dayenu!" meaning, "It would have been enough!" However, the only way you can sing it is if you learn the tune. Go to www.youtube.com/pastor-joshmw. Scroll down the home page till you see "Playlists." Look for the section on "Hebrew and Messianic Music," then click on "Play All." When the first music video starts (not the one you want), look down the list on the right side, and click on "Dayenu—Passover."[1]

Primary Leaders:

Read over the section of the Haggadah which comes right after "Dinner is Served." Decide if you are using option one or two, concerning how the children will search for the afikomen, and whether you will be giving a reward to only one child, or giving a token reward to all the children in option two, so that no one feels left out. You need to remember to get the rewards ready before the Seder begins. It could be a small candy, or a coloring book, or a special Passover toy, found in some grocery stores that carry Passover foods, or even a small amount of money. Anything to make the children feel special for "finding" the afikomen. It is like finding Yeshua, because He considers the afikomen to be His broken body, redeemed back from the grave, and all of us will eat of it shortly after the children retrieve it.

What Foods Are Permissible:

Even though I understand that Gentile believers are free to eat any foods they choose in their everyday lives, it is very important to honor the Passover Seder, which was given to us by the Jewish people. Therefore, I would humbly request that you honor the dietary restrictions listed below while you are celebrating this awesome feast. Some of you might even wish to honor the Feast of Unleavened Bread for the whole week of Passover, as explained in the Unleavened Bread chapter of my book. But at least for this one night, let's be "kosher!"

Do Not Bring:

Pork, ham, bacon, sausage, crab, shrimp, shellfish (or any products with these as an ingredient), bread, rolls, bagels, pretzels, crackers, pasta, noodles, chips, croutons, breadcrumbs, or anything with yeast as an ingredient. Most Campbell's soups contain yeast, so watch out for those "cream of something" sauces.

Please Do Bring:

Salads, olives, tomatoes, all vegetables, raw or cooked, fresh or canned fruit, all cheeses (except blue cheese), cream cheese, jam, hard-boiled eggs, devilled eggs, chicken, turkey or beef, tuna or salmon, rice dishes, nuts, peanut butter, matzah, all cakes made from Passover cake mix. Pies are all right, as long as the crusts do not contain lard, which is pig fat. If you read the ingredients carefully, most bought pie crusts contain lard. You can also bring dried fruit, chocolate, Passover cookies, or macaroons. Please check salad dressing ingredients to make sure they have no yeast.

Recipe for Charoset: (Quantities depend on how many people you are serving.)

    Apples
    Walnuts
    Almonds
    Brown Sugar
    Cinnamon
    Honey
    Sweet Passover Grape Wine or Grape Juice
    You will need approximately equal parts of chopped nuts and chopped apples. Grind both types of nuts

together in the food processor until they are finely chopped, but **not** pasty. Set them aside, and process the apples. You can chop them by hand if you don't have a food processor.

Use about one apple for every three guests. I use Delicious or Gala apples, or any sweet, crispy apple. You can wash them and keep the skin, or you can peel them all. So if you have 30 people, you would use about 10 apples. When the apples are chopped, use an equal amount of apples and the combination of ground nuts.

Put the apples and nuts in a very large bowl. Add cinnamon, brown sugar, honey, and Sweet Passover Grape Wine. If you can't use a small amount of real wine, substitute grape juice (it won't taste quite as good). The amount of these ingredients is proportionate to the amount of apples and nuts. If you are making a batch for about 30 people, you would use at least a quarter cup of brown sugar, and about a tablespoon of cinnamon, about 2 tablespoons of honey, and about a half cup of wine. I just put it in and taste it, so I'm sorry I can't be more precise. You can adjust these amounts according to taste. Just taste it till it's so good, you don't want to wait for the Seder. Mix everything very well. Chill till serving. It keeps in the fridge for about four days, but is best on the first two days.

WELCOME TO OUR PASSOVER SEDER

"I AM THE BROKEN PIECE!"

Leader: We are so joyful and thankful to be celebrating this Feast of Passover together! We give praise and glory to the Lord Yeshua the Messiah, who has redeemed us from slavery and called us "Friends"!

LIGHTING THE CANDLES—WELCOMING THE MASTER OF OUR BANQUET, THE LORD GOD!

Leader: Yeshua is the light of the world. We will welcome Him, as we light the candles that separate this night from all ordinary nights.

"Mother" lights the two candles and recites the blessing ("Mother" can be any woman of God delegated by the leader for this honor):

> *"Baruch Ata Adonai, Eloheinu Melech haOlam, asher kiddeshanu b'mitzvotav, v'natan lanu et Yeshua ha Mashiach v'tzivanu l'hiot Or la goyim."*

All: Blessed are You, O Lord our God, King of the universe who has set us apart by His Word, and gave us Yeshua the Messiah, and has commanded us to be a light to the world.

A Prophetic Calendar: The Feasts of Israel

First Reading: A Banqueting Table

Like an apple tree among the trees of the forest is my lover
among the young men.
I delight to sit in his shade, and his fruit is sweet to my taste.
He has taken me to the banquet hall, and his banner over me
is love (Song of Songs 2:3-4).

Our loving Father has set a place for us, even prepared a table for us in the presence of our enemies. He has spread the wing of His garment over us and covered us with a bridal canopy of unfailing love. As we sit under His shade, we enjoy the choice fruits of summer, the delight and refreshment of a perfect peach.

> *Here I am! I stand at the door and knock. If anyone hears*
> *My voice and opens the door, I will come in and eat with*
> *him, and he with Me* (Revelation 3:20).

Out of all the promises the Lord Jesus could have given to His Church, He extends to us the promise and privilege of coming in and eating with us. The Lord must consider the fellowship of a shared meal very precious, and one of the most intimate offers He could make.

While we normally think of these feasts as Jewish holidays, the Lord actually refers to them in Scripture as "the Lord's feasts" or "My appointed times" (see Lev. 23:1-2). It is true that they were originally given to Israel, but if they are truly His feasts and not merely Israel's holidays, then all of the Lord's children would benefit to know what was in God's heart when He defined these times and seasons.

One of the Hebrew words used for the feasts in Scripture is *mikrah,* which is a holy convocation, a sacred assembly, or even a rehearsal of God's past, present, and future acts. As we study these celebrations, we will see that each one is remembering or foreshadowing an aspect of Messiah's ministry.

Surely, if these feasts testify of Messiah, they belong to all who love

Him. And if they are really about intimacy with the Lord, why shouldn't all believers have the chance to learn more about their significance and how easy they are to celebrate?

All of these biblical celebrations contain deep treasures of understanding. They unveil the Lord's intense desire for fellowship with His people, as living parables. They paint a prophetic picture of the Lord Yeshua's sacrificial and redemptive purposes on the earth, past, present, and future.

Passover remembers the Israelites' exodus from hundreds of years of slavery in Egypt, and the redemption of a newborn nation, a people belonging to the Lord. It was the blood of the Passover lamb that rescued the Israelites from the destroying angel, who struck down every firstborn in Egypt. It is the blood of Yeshua that covers our hearts, rescuing us from a hideous and eternal "living death" [end first reading].

Optional Worship Song

Reader 1: We celebrate the Passover every year in the spring, at sunset on the fourteenth day of Nisan, and we begin the Feast of Unleavened Bread for the next seven days.

The Christian date celebrating the Lord's resurrection *should* always coincide with the third day after Passover (or perhaps on the first Sunday after Passover). Sadly, these two holidays have been artificially separated as if they bear no connection to one another. But they *must* stay connected!

All:

> And when your children ask you, "What does this ceremony mean to you?" then tell them, "It is the Passover sacrifice to the Lord, who passed over the houses of the Israelites in Egypt and spared our homes when He struck down the Egyptians" (Exod. 12:26-27).

> On that day, tell your son, "I do this because of what the Lord did for me when I came out of Egypt." This observance will be for you like a sign on your hand and a

317

reminder on your forehead that the law of the Lord is to be on your lips. For the Lord brought you out of Egypt with His mighty hand (Exodus 13:8-9).

Reader 2: The telling of the story is so much a part of Passover, that as we eat our ceremonial foods, we read from a special booklet that is only used on this holiday. This traditional booklet is called the *Haggadah*, which means, "the telling." It provides an orderly structure of explanations of why we eat symbolic foods and observe other customs.

Reader 3: We call this ceremonial meal the *Seder*, which means "order." In addition to a fabulous meal, we eat special foods that symbolize various elements of the story. These special foods and customs are not found in any other ordinary meal in our year. This night must always be set apart from all other nights.

Reader 4: Each of these foods not only has meaning in the original context of the Exodus, but also has a richer meaning in the context of the Lord Yeshua's final Passover meal, or "last supper."

Reader 5: *Matzah* is flat, unleavened bread; this represents the hasty departure of the Israelites when they escaped, which meant that they had no time to let their bread rise.

Reader 6: There are *four cups* of sweet wine or grape juice; each cup has a biblical meaning relating to the story of the Exodus.

Reader 7: *Parsley*, which represents the spongy hyssop plant, was used to paint the doorframes with the blood of the lamb. We dip the parsley in a cup of salt water and eat it. The salt water represents the tears that our forefathers and mothers wept while in slavery. The green vegetable also represents the hope of springtime, which comes after the time of weeping.

Reader 8: The *shank bone* of a lamb is on the Seder plate, representing the slain lamb, which used to be eaten at the Passover meal. Many Jewish families no longer eat lamb at this dinner, for reasons we will cover in our detailed view.

Reader 9: *Horseradish* is the best approximation of the bitter herbs commanded by the Lord in the Exodus instructions. It symbolizes the bitterness of slavery.

Reader 10: *Charoset* is a sweet mixture of apples, nuts, wine, and cinnamon. It stands for the mortar used to make bricks for Pharaoh's structures, and also the sweetness of the promise of freedom.

Reader 1: The *afikomen* is a mysterious broken matzah. In addition to eating matzah with our meal, there are three special pieces of matzah that are wrapped in a cloth. During the ceremony, the middle piece is broken in two, and one-half is hidden. Later in the service, the hidden piece is found and becomes the *afikomen*. This symbol has no obvious connection to the Exodus, but it contains amazing New Covenant symbolism concerning the body of the Lord Jesus.

Leader: When believers in Messiah celebrate Passover, we tell the story of humanity's redemption. One night, Jill (the author of this Haggadah) couldn't sleep, and she was singing a praise song to the Lord. Although this took place in the season of the fall feasts, the Lord showed her a vision of Yeshua on the Cross; she saw the word PASSOVER written across His torn body, in huge letters that stretched from His left hand to His right. Yeshua is the Passover, and He was crucified on the very day, and He died at the very hour that the lambs were being slain for the Passover meal (see Exod. 12:6; Luke 23:44-46).

All: The telling of the Passover is an unbroken chain. We will still be recounting it in Heaven (see Rev. 15:3-4). Even the Holocaust could not silence this stubborn witness of God's deliverance. Shall *we* keep silent, or will the true Church join in singing the song of Moses and the song of the Lamb?

SECOND READING: REDEEMED FROM SLAVERY

We reap what we sow. Joseph was sold by his jealous brothers into slavery, and within several generations, their descendents were ruthlessly enslaved in the very nation where their innocent brother had suffered cruel injustice (see Exod. 1:6-10). The Israelites were afflicted with hard work in the fields, irrigating crops, and building the treasure cities for Pharaoh's aggrandizement. The center of our Passover narrative is that "they made their lives bitter with hard labor and cruel bondage" (see Exod. 1:11-14).

Pharaoh also practiced genocide, by commanding that the baby Hebrew boys be killed at birth. He would later reap what he sowed, for God would exact from him the firstborns of Egypt. In fact, well before the ten plagues, the Lord warned Pharaoh, "Israel is My firstborn son" (Exod. 4:22-23). Pharaoh would pay with his own son's life for not allowing God's firstborn son to go free.

Under Messiah's arms of love, the Father has many adopted sons and daughters from the nations, but Israel is His firstborn son. Harming Israel is costly to the nations, more costly than they can bear.

The backs and blood of slaves carry the economic prosperity of any nation heedless enough to enslave them. Our nation is no better than ancient Egypt, for we too were guilty of ruthlessly oppressing an innocent people for hundreds of years, unto death, poverty, degradation, and demoralization. May God, in His great mercy, take away the guilt of our bloodshed, and may we witness the full restoration of the African-American people to their God-appointed blessings, destiny, and nobility. Amen.

Can any nation prosper indefinitely on the exploitation of slaves, if there is a God in Heaven? When the Hebrew cries reached the ears of the God of Heaven, He spoke to His servant Moses:

I have indeed seen the misery of my people in Egypt. I have heard them crying out because of their slave drivers, and I am concerned about their suffering (Exodus 3:7).

This feast celebrates Israel's original redemption from slavery in Egypt and her birth as a freed people, a new nation under God's covenant. The miracles that accompanied the Exodus were so staggering that nothing like them has ever been seen on the earth.

On the tenth day of the first month, called *Nisan*, every Israelite family chose a perfect little lamb and took care of it until the fourteenth day. Then at twilight, the father of the household slaughtered it and put its blood on the doorframes of their house.

After nine painful plagues came upon Egypt, the most devastating blow was yet to fall: the swift destruction of every firstborn of Egypt. It was precisely the blood over the Israelite doorways that would cause the destroying angel to pass over their homes. The innocent always die for the guilty.

And what can be said of the Righteous One, who was hanged on a tree, accursed on our behalf, and wretched? He did this to remove the filth and deserved punishment of the twelve billion souls who have sinned upon the face of earth from the beginning until this very day.

We in the New Covenant were purchased back from enslavement to our own rebellious and sinful natures and are commanded to display God's holiness, provision, and protection. As ancient Israel was destined to be a light to the nations, we are also to be a light to those still in darkness. The invitation to apply the Lamb's blood to our personal doorposts has been extended to all people and nations, until this very day. Passover is our own personal atonement and rebirth, through the Lord [end second reading].

The Four Cups

Reader 3: Throughout the Passover, we drink four cups of wine. Each cup has a biblical message and originates from the following passage:
All:

> *Therefore, say to the Israelites: "I am the Lord, and I will bring you out from under the yoke of the Egyptians. I will free you from being slaves to them, and I will redeem you with an outstretched arm and with mighty acts of judgment. I will take you as my own people, and I will be your God. Then you will know that I am the Lord your God, who brought you out from under the yoke of the Egyptians. And I will bring you to the land I swore with uplifted hand to give to Abraham, to Isaac and to Jacob"* (Exodus 6:6-8).

Reader 4: "*I will bring you out*" involves the Lord physically or spiritually rescuing us from the cage, prison, or tormenting darkness we were trapped in when He found us.

Reader 5: *"I will free you from being slaves"* speaks of a change in legal status from slave to freed people. The Israelites were still slaves when they escaped from Egypt, and we are not legally free at the moment the Lord pulls us out of our prison.

Reader 2: *"I will redeem you with an outstretched arm"* refers to the financial transaction that transfers our ownership from satan to God. He bought back the Israelites from slavery and death with the blood of the perfect lamb. He purchased every soul on the earth from the enemy with the blood of His beloved Son. He was the only one whose blood could purify the ocean of our accumulated filth, due to His perfect obedience, sinless life, and suffering.

Reader 6: *"I will take you as My own people, and I will be your God, and I will bring you into the land of promise"* is really a three-fold, final *"I will."* Once we are brought out, freed, purified, and legally purchased, God is able to take us into His Holy place, into His arms of love.

Reader 7: Each of these four cups represents these four realities. The first cup is called the "Cup of Sanctification," in which we are set apart for the Lord. This cup introduces the consecrated atmosphere of Passover, separating this meal from all other ordinary meals, and setting our hearts apart for our Beloved.

Reader 8: The second cup is called, "The Cup of Freedom," or, "The Cup of the Plagues." It remembers our release from slavery and the suffering of Egypt.

Reader 9: The third cup comes after the meal and is called, "The Cup of Redemption." A human life is infinitely valuable and cannot be purchased with money or gold. Only blood can purchase a living soul, into whom God has breathed and imbued His own image.

Reader 10: The fourth cup is called, "The Cup of Praise." The Seder meal concludes with great joy and gratitude, and we sing spiritual songs to our Father God and our Redeemer, Yeshua the Messiah.

Blessing Over the First Cup of Wine:

Leader: This first cup is called the "Cup of Sanctification," with which we are now set apart for the Lord.

Baruch Ata Adonai, Eloheinu Melech HaOlam, Boray P'ri HaGafen.

All: Praised are You, Lord our God, King of the universe, who creates the fruit of the vine.

All drink the first cup together.

Leader: We now thank the Lord for our life and sustenance. *Baruch Ata Adonai, Eloheinu Melech HaOlam, Sh'hechianu, v'kiyamanu, v'higi'anu laz'man ha zeh.*

All: We praise You, Lord our God, King of the universe, who has kept us alive, sustained us, and brought us to this festive season.

Optional Worship Song

Blessing Over the Dipping of the Green Vegetable

Leader: The parsley represents the hyssop, which was used to place the blood of the Passover lamb upon the doorposts and the lintel of the Jewish homes in Egypt. The salt water represents the tears shed in Egypt because of their suffering.

Baruch Ata Adonai, Eloheinu Melech HaOlam, Boray P'ri HaAdamah.

All: Praised are You, Lord our God, King of the universe, who creates the fruit of the earth.

All dip their parsley in the salt water and eat it now.

THIRD READING: THE AFIKOMEN— YESHUA IS THE BROKEN PIECE:

There is a mysterious practice that has become a part of the traditional Seder, which is still not fully understood by non-Messianic Jewish worshipers. It is widely accepted that this practice did not exist at the time of Yeshua's ministry.

It is very likely that this ceremony was initiated by believers in Yeshua; it was carried into the nations by Jewish believers at the time of the dispersion (A.D. 70) and became common practice in Passover Seders everywhere. Not all Jewish families are aware of its significance, but to believers in Yeshua the Messiah, the symbolism of this ceremony is wonderfully obvious.

Each table leader has a packet of matzah, containing three pieces wrapped in a napkin (or in a special bag made for this ceremony called a *Matzah Tash*).

During the ceremony, the leader removes the middle matzah and then breaks it in half. He hides it somewhere in the house, so that after the meal, the children will search for this missing piece. The child who finds it will bring it back to the leader, who will then make sure it "fits" with its other broken half, and will give the child a "payment" for the piece. Thus, the two pieces become one whole again, and a price is paid to ransom back the missing piece.

The rabbis have several possible interpretations of the three pieces. One is that these pieces represent three tiers of the Jewish population: the priests, the Levites, and the general people of Israel. Another interpretation holds that the pieces stand for God, the mediating priest, and the people of Israel.

Believers in Yeshua assert that the middle piece represents the mediating priest. He is the only one who can serve as both the High Priest and the sacrifice itself. He stands between God and man in the place of intercession and in the place of sacrificial atonement.

Yeshua was rejected and broken; His body was wrapped in a linen cloth and hidden away. After some time has elapsed, He is found and made whole again; He is raised to life. This broken one has ransomed back many from their brokenness, and we are also made whole, along with Him (see Heb. 9:15).

What is even more interesting is the word itself, *afikomen*. It seems to be the only non-Hebraic word found in the Seder. It is a Greek word, which the rabbis have concluded means "dessert," since it is eaten after the meal. However, according to biblical scholars Kevin Howard and Marvin

Rosenthal, this word is a form of the Greek verb *ikneomai*, and can best be translated, "I came."[2] Others have translated it, "the one who has come," or "that which comes after."

During the writing of *The Prophetic Calendar: The Feasts of Israel* (the book by Jill Shannon, from which this Haggadah is an excerpt), Jill was asking the Lord if she had found His heart in the writing of the Passover chapter. At that time, she received this awesome word from Him, concerning the afikomen:

> I AM the hidden treasure, buried in the folds of cloth and the layers of Matzah. I AM hidden; though they eat My body, I AM hidden from their eyes. I AM the pearl, the treasure, the One broken and waiting to be discovered by the youngest child. This signifies that only one with the heart of a child can find Me and recognize Me, hidden in the room.
>
> It is a surprise party. Normally, the guest of honor is surprised when the other guests jump out and greet him. I AM the guest of honor in the ceremony of the afikomen, and when I jump out, they will all be surprised. I was here all along, waiting, in their very Passover. It was always Me, broken, buried, raised to life, but waiting to be discovered by the leaders of My banquets, by the leaders of My Jewish people, even their Sanhedrin.
>
> When they find the afikomen, they find Me. Then that which was broken will be made whole. They will hold up the whole piece with the missing half restored, restored and whole again. How can they find God without Me? I AM the missing piece, the broken piece, the hidden piece, the discovered piece, the redeemed-by-a-child piece, and the reconnected piece to the original piece from which I was broken off.
>
> We will be made whole again; do not fear. This is My heart for the story of the afikomen. Tell My flock what I have told you [end third reading].

Leader: Each table leader should now remove the middle matzah from their napkin packet (or *Matzah Tash*). All table leaders now hold up the middle matzah for the following readings.

Reader 3: Notice that the matzah is striped, due to the markings cause by rapid baking in high heat.

Reader 4: "The chastisement for our peace was upon Him, and by His stripes we are healed" (Isa. 53:5b NKJV).

Reader 5: See that the matzah is pierced. To prevent it from rising in the oven, the bakers pierce it many times.

Reader 6: "But He was pierced for our transgressions, He was crushed for our iniquities" (Isa. 53:5a).

Reader 7: The matzah is unleavened bread. It cannot corrupt or spoil.

Reader 8: "Therefore my heart is glad and my tongue rejoices; my body also will rest secure, because you will not abandon me to the grave, nor will you let your Holy One see decay" (Psalm 16:9-11).

Reader 9: The matzah is called "the bread of affliction." The Israelites ate it in the desert as they fled from their captors. There was no time to let their dough rise.

Reader 10: "Surely he took up our infirmities and carried our sorrows" (Isa. 53:4a).

Reader 1: Each table leader will now break the middle matzah in half, wrap one-half of it in the middle napkin, and hide this piece in one of two ways: In a home setting, it can be hidden in another room, which the children will search later; if this is a community Seder in a crowded dining room, the leader will simply hide it under his own plate.

The leaders at each table break the middle matzah in two, wrap half in the middle napkin, and hide it under their plates. In a home setting, the leader can tell the children to close their eyes while he hides it somewhere in the dining room, or he can hide it somewhere else in the house, where they will be allowed to search for it after dinner. The other half is placed back into the matzah packet between the two other pieces. This half will also be shared with the table after dinner.

Optional Worship Song

The Second Cup—Recounting the Story

Leader: The second cup is lifted up during the story of God's breaking of Pharaoh's stubborn pride with many afflictions. Before we actually drink this second cup, we remember how much the Egyptian people suffered during the ten plagues, and we will be dipping our fingers into our wine ten times, placing the wasted drops like blood on our napkins, as we recite and remember each miserable plague. The meaning is that some of our wine of joy is diminished, as we see the suffering of our enemies. How a nation suffers needlessly when its leaders come into collision with the God of Israel! This cup is sometimes called, "The Cup of Freedom," or "The Cup of the Plagues."

As we now recite each plague, dip your finger in your wine and place a drop on your napkin for each plague.

All: Our cup of joy is diminished. We remember the ten plagues: Blood...Frogs...Lice...Flies...Cattle...Disease...Boils...Hail... Locusts...Darkness...the Slaying of the Firstborn. Who is like You, O God Almighty? Who is like You, awesome in praises, working wonders? The Lord shall reign forever and ever! How many gifts God has bestowed upon us! How many wonders has the Eternal done for us!

Leader: It is amazing to note that the ten plagues are very similar to the trumpet and bowl judgments found in Revelation. We see waters turned to blood, locusts, painful sores, hail mingled with fire, darkness and the destruction of vegetation, crops, and marine life. As Moses confronted Pharaoh with God's power, so our King Yeshua will confront the antichrist with supernatural judgments. In both cases, the evil tyrant hardens his heart, rather than repenting.

The following traditional song can only be sung if the leader has learned the tune and can lead the guests in singing it (see Introduction for the Web site where the song can be learned). They sing slightly different verses than the ones I printed below, but if you learn the tune, you can use these words. If you don't know the tune, or find the Hebrew difficult, you can skip to the next part of the service.

(Optional) Sing "Dayenu"— "It Would Have Been Enough"

Verse 1:

Had He brought us out of Egypt, only brought us out of Egypt, had He brought us out of Egypt, *Dayenu!*

Chorus:

Dai, dayenu, Dai, dayenu, Dai dayenu, dayenu, dayenu (2X)

Verse 1 in Hebrew:

Ilu ilu hotzianu, hotzianu mi Mitzraim, mi Mitzraim, hotzianu, *Dayenu!*

Verse 2:

Had He brought us into Israel, only brought us into Israel, had He brought us into Israel, *Dayenu!*

Verse 2 in Hebrew:

Ilu natan natan lanu, et ha Eretz Yisrael, et ha Eretz Yisrael, *Dayenu!*

Verse 3:

Had He given us Yeshua, only given us Yeshua, had He given us Yeshua, *Dayenu!*

Verse 3 in Hebrew:

Ilu natan natan lanu, natan lanu et Yeshua, et Yeshua natan lanu, *Dayenu!*

All:

Dayenu! Dayenu! Dayenu already!

FOURTH READING: A GOD OF DISTINCTIONS

On the night of the slaying of the firstborn, the Israelites walked out of Egypt as a redeemed people. They were pursued as escaping slaves, but when Pharaoh's armies floated up onto the shores of the Red Sea, the Hebrew slaves were indeed a free people. Israel was as a newborn baby in the desert, covered with blood and with an uncut umbilical cord, where no other nation would care for her or show her pity (see Ezek. 16:4-5).

Passover showed that the Lord made a distinction between His people and those who were not His people, by the application of the lamb's blood to their doors. The Lord also made a distinction between the firstborn and all the other offspring in a family. This separation extended to man and beast, even to the birth order of livestock and pets. We see the Lord's intelligence, personality, and purposefulness all through Scripture, as He made supernatural distinctions between people again and again, proving that nothing happens in a random or uncalculated manner.

When the New Covenant was established in the greatest Passover the world will ever know, the same ancient seal and symbol of distinction and of God's protection could be seen. We see a lamb, its blood and deliverance; we see death pass over the sealed ones. But now, the Lamb is a man: an innocent man; a perfect man; a humble and generous man; a Jewish man. He is filled with healing power and good deeds, and utterly undeserving of a criminal's agonizing death. This man's blood covers the doorframes of our hearts, with a mark only visible to the eyes of Heaven.

When the hour of judgment and separation comes, one population will be spared, and another group will not be spared. There will be no protection or provision, apart from the covering blood of the sinless One.

> Then those who feared the Lord talked with each other, and the Lord listened and heard. A scroll of remembrance was written in His presence concerning those who feared the Lord and honored His name.
>
> "They will be mine," says the Lord Almighty, "in the day when I make up My treasured possession. I will spare them, just as in compassion a man spares his son who serves him. And you will again see the distinction between the righteous and the wicked, between those who serve God and those who do not" (Malachi 3:16-18) [end fourth reading].

Blessing Over the Second Cup of Wine:
Leader: This is the cup of deliverance and freedom.

Baruch Ata Adonai, Eloheinu Melech HaOlam, Boray P'ri HaGafen.

All: Praised are You, Lord our God, King of the universe, who creates the fruit of the vine.

Drink the second cup together.

Reader 2: As believers, we have experienced all four cups of wine. The first was the cup of sanctification; we are set apart from this world and consecrated for Him. Even as we drink the second cup of rejoicing over our escape from the prison of darkness, our joy is diminished as we weep over the poor souls who are daily being swept into eternity without the blood of the Lamb to provide a canopy of heavenly safety and rest.

The Four Questions: *"Why is this night different from all other nights?"*
It is customary to ask a child to read these four questions about why Passover is so different. It is actually only one question and four statements of how it is different. Any child who is able to read may be chosen by the leader ahead of time, or spontaneously during the Seder.

"Why is this night different from all other nights?"

"On other nights we eat leavened or unleavened bread, but on this night we eat only unleavened bread.
"On other nights we eat all types of vegetables, but tonight only bitter herbs.
"On other nights we do not dip even once. On this night we dip twice.
"On other nights we eat sitting or reclining, but on this night we recline."

The Symbols of Passover

Leader: Let us continue our celebration with the explanation of the symbols that remind us of our story. What is the meaning of *Passover*?

All: In family groups our people ate the paschal lamb when the temple was still standing. For them, the Pesach was a reminder that God "passed over" the houses of our forefathers in Egypt during the plague of the first-born.

Leader: What is the meaning of *matzah*?

All: Matzah was the bread of affliction, eaten in haste. "And they baked unleavened cakes of dough which they had brought out of Egypt; for it was not leavened, because they had been driven out of Egypt and could not wait, nor had they prepared provisions for themselves" (Exod. 12:39).

Leader: What is the meaning of *maror* (bitter herbs)?

All: It was eaten, they said, because the Egyptians embittered the lives of our people, as it is written: "With hard labor at mortar and brick and in all sorts of work in the fields; in all their hard labor the Egyptians used them ruthlessly" (Exod. 1:14).

Reader 1: Today, we also remember those whose lives are embittered by persecution and martyrdom at the hand of lawless governments and the violence of radical groups. We will wish for them to remember us when we suffer for our faith as well.

FIFTH READING: THE SUBSTITUTE LAMB

"Take your son, your only son, Isaac, whom you love, and go to the region of Moriah. Sacrifice him there as a burnt offering on one of the mountains I will tell you about" (Genesis 22:2).

Abraham took the wood for the burnt offering and placed it on his son Isaac. The beloved son struggled up the hill, carrying the wood of his own sacrifice on his back. He glanced up at his father, who was resolutely walking toward the mountain, without allowing his eyes to meet Isaac's questioning gaze. Surely his father had thought to provide an animal for the offering. But he only saw the sharpened knife and flaming torch in his father's hands. He would ask about the missing animal.

"Father, the fire and the wood are here, but where is the lamb?"

Although this question was unanswerable, Abraham spoke from a deep reservoir of trust, despite the pounding of his heart.

"God Himself will provide the lamb for the burnt offering, my son."

He built an altar, bound his son, and lifted up his knife to the trembling boy's throat. Seconds before slaughter at the hands of the one he loved and trusted, Isaac was rescued and redeemed from destruction.

The angel of the Lord called out, "Do not lay a hand on the boy. Now I know that you fear God, because you have not withheld from Me your son, your only son."

Abraham looked up and there in the thicket he saw a ram caught by its horns. The ram was Isaac's substitute.

Later, another Son would stagger up the hill, with the wood of His sacrifice on his back. He looked up at His loving Father, but His Father would not meet His gaze. There would be no substitute for this Hebrew son, no last-minute rescue, because He *was* the substitute. They would nail Him to the wood He bore. He was the lamb, who would redeem every death sentence ever to be handed down to sin-infested humanity. God did not spare His son but would use His blood to buy back the world from the merciless and fallen angel of eternal death [end fifth reading].

The Meaning of Unleavened Bread

Reader 3: As Passover represents our personal salvation through Yeshua's sacrifice, the seven days of Unleavened Bread represent a period of cleansing and purification from our old lifestyles and ways. After we have made the faith decision to ask the Lord Jesus to forgive us our sins and to purify us through His blood, He frees us from satan's merciless enslavement and transfers our souls into His Kingdom of light.

Reader 4: We are not only redeemed slaves, but the Lord also takes us to be His own people and seals us with His own Spirit. At this point, we can begin the process of removing the leaven of corruption and malice from our lives. It is our responsibility to cleanse our hands and purify our hearts, although His Spirit nudges us, supports us, and empowers us to do so continually (see James 4:8).

Reader 5: As we are reminded of the unusual and limited foods we can choose to eat this week, we are also mindful that all sexual immorality, idolatry, unholy entertainment, impure language, and addictions must be removed from our actions, words, and even our thoughts. It is a physical object lesson in holiness.

> *Be holy because I, the Lord your God, am holy* (Leviticus 19:2).

Leader: We will now eat the unleavened bread, after we say the blessing. The table leaders should now take out the upper piece of matzah and the half-piece of the middle matzah (not the hidden piece, which will be the afikomen after dinner). Hold these pieces, as we now bless the unleavened bread.

Baruch Ata Adonai, Eloheinu Melech HaOlam, HaMotzei Lechem min ha Aretz u'min ha Shamayim.

All: Blessed are You, O Lord our God, King of the universe, who brings forth bread from the earth and bread from Heaven.

Reader 2: Let the table leaders divide among their table, pieces of the upper matzah and the middle half-matzah (not the hidden afikomen piece) to everyone at the table. We will now eat this piece together. (This is not the communion service, which will come after the meal when we eat the afikomen.) *All eat the matzah.*

Leader: We will now remember the bitterness of slavery in Egypt by dipping a piece of matzah into the bitter herbs and eating it. We also remember the bitterness Yeshua tasted for our redemption. The table leaders can use the bottom matzah, and give it out for this dipping into the bitter horseradish. Children should be careful; it is very "hot." Let us all say together:

All: Blessed are You, O Lord our God, King of the universe who has commanded us to eat the maror.

All eat a small piece of matzah dipped in bitter herbs.

Reader 1: The charoset, the sweet apple mixture, resembles the mortar used to build Pharaoh's treasure cities. It reminds us that even with the bitter, the Lord provides us the sweetness of His love and comfort. Finally, if you need more, take any matzah you have left at the table, and dip it in both the bitter and the sweet and let us eat them together! We will now enjoy our dinner, and come back after we have feasted with our King and with each other!

Dinner Is Served.

Finding the Afikomen—"This Is My Body Broken for You!"

Leader: We have enjoyed our wonderful meal, and are grateful for the hands that prepared each dish! At this time in the Seder, there are two options, depending on where you are holding your Seder, and whether you have only one leader or many table leaders.

Option 1: If this is small, family-style Seder with only one leader, who has hidden *one* afikomen in the house, the children will go and search for it now. The child who finds it will bring it back to the leader, who will receive it and give the child a special reward. He will "ransom" it back from the child.

Option 2: If you are holding a large congregational Seder, and each table leader has hidden his table's afikomen under his plate, then we will not be able to have each child search for it, since everyone already knows where it is, and there may be more children than table leaders. One of the children at each table can show the leader that the hidden piece is under his plate. *Now give a reward that you prepared ahead of time to all the children at the Seder. (You can choose an age cut-off, such as, "All children 12 years old or younger will now receive a reward.)* We can give all the children a reward at this time.

Reader 6: The afikomen that has been hidden away in a white linen napkin and now is taken out again is a clear symbol of the resurrection of Yeshua. It is from this part of the Seder meal that we derive the communion ceremony.

Reader 1: "And He took bread, gave thanks and broke it, and gave it to them, saying, 'This is My body given for you; do this in remembrance of Me'" (Luke 22:19).

The table leader holds up the afikomen and shares it with all the people at his table. Or if there is one leader, he shares the one afikomen with everyone at a small family-style Seder. **Do not eat your piece yet.** *This represents the broken body of the Lord, and we will all eat it together.*

Leader: Let us receive the broken body of Messiah now as we share the afikomen.

Reader 2 *leads in spontaneous prayer for the Lord's sacrifice and broken body. All pray!*

Leader: We all eat it together with gratitude. *All eat their piece, meditating on His sacrifice.*

The Third Cup—"This Is My Blood Shed for You!"

Leader: The third cup is called, "The Cup of Redemption."

All: "For the life of a creature is in the blood, and I have given it to you to make atonement for yourselves on the altar; it is the blood that makes atonement for one's life" (Lev. 17:11).

Reader 1: This third cup, after the supper, is the one that Yeshua connected with our personal redemption in His blood, which was about to be offered to God. In the original Passover, this redemption cost all of Egypt its firstborn son. In the greater covenant of eternal redemption, the cost was God's firstborn Son. The price of a human soul is more costly than we could bear, so the Righteous One bore the cost in His flesh and upon His soul.

Reader 2: "I have eagerly desired to eat this Passover with you before I suffer. For I tell you, I will not eat it again until it finds fulfillment in the kingdom of God" (Luke 22:15-16).

SIXTH READING: THINKING OF OTHERS

The Lord Yeshua sincerely desired to enjoy this final Passover with His disciples, despite the ordeal He would face in just a few short hours. If it had been me, I would not have looked forward to this last meal, to say the very least. Its pleasure would have surely been spoiled by the stomach pain that accompanies the torment of fear.

But the Lord knew the secret of peace and joy in the face of impending sorrow and pain. He was a humble servant who lived to bless, heal, and rescue others, never thinking of Himself or His personal preferences. And so, even at that final dinner, He was not thinking about what His enemies were about to do to Him. He was thinking about how He could bless His friends during their last precious hours together. Yeshua was determined to squeeze out every last drop of teaching, affection, warnings of what would come, and even the washing of their feet, before the unthinkable would become reality.

As He staggered up the hill with His cross, He was still thinking of others and not of Himself. The women of Jerusalem mourned and wailed for Him, but He told them, "Daughters of Jerusalem, do not weep for me; weep for yourselves and for your children" (Luke 23:28-29). He was thinking about the city he loved, and what the merciless Romans would inflict upon it within one short generation.

His father Isaac had watched God provide a lamb at the last minute, which saved him from slaughter. But now there was no last-minute rescue for this beloved Son of Abraham, no other lamb to take His place on the altar of love. He was the lamb, and there was no other way to make atonement in the Holy Place. Oh, Yeshua, how tempting it must have been for You to get out of it. If You had chosen to be rescued, what would Your Father have denied You? But You set Your face like a flint and became the Lamb, so that we could be Isaac, the rescued one.

"In the same way, after the supper He took the cup, saying, 'This cup is the new covenant in My blood, which is poured out for you'" (Luke 22:20) [end sixth reading].

All: This third cup has become our Salvation. His Name is Yeshua, which means "salvation" in Hebrew. Each time we drink this cup, whether at a Passover Seder or in a commemoration of "the Lord's Supper," we remember the price He paid to purchase us for God, to buy back a people for Himself. We will never understand the cost, not even when we reach Heaven.

Leader: Let us refill our cups for the third time this evening. This is the Cup of the New Covenant in Yeshua's blood.

Reader 1: Paul wrote, "In the same way, after supper He took the cup, saying, 'This cup is the new covenant in My blood; do this, whenever you drink it, in remembrance of Me.' For whenever you eat this bread and drink this cup, you proclaim the Lord's death until He comes" (1 Cor. 11:25-26).

Leader: *Baruch Ata Adonai, Eloheinu Melech HaOlam, Boray P'ri HaGafen.*

All: Blessed are You, O Lord our God, King of the universe, who creates the fruit of the vine.

Leader *now prays spontaneously over the cup of Yeshua's shed blood, which has removed our sins and reconciled us to the Father.*

After the prayer, all drink the third cup, meditating on His sacrifice.

SEVENTH READING: THE CUP OF ELIJAH

There is a beloved tradition toward the end of the Seder, called the "Cup of Elijah." Throughout the meal, a special cup filled with wine is set aside on the table, designated for the visitation of the prophet Elijah. This custom is based on the messianic promise in Malachi 4:5-6.

> *See, I will send you the prophet Elijah before that great and dreadful day of the Lord comes. He will turn the hearts of the fathers to their children, and the hearts of the children to their fathers; or else I will come and strike the land with a curse* (Malachi 4:5-6).

This doctrine was in the minds of the Jewish disciples as they were coming down from the Mount of Transfiguration, where they had just seen the prophet Elijah with their own eyes. They asked Yeshua, "Why then do the teachers of the law say that Elijah must come first?" (see Matt. 17:10).

The Lord answered them, "To be sure, Elijah comes and will restore all things. But I tell you, Elijah has already come, and they did not recognize him, but have done to him everything they wished" (Matt. 17:11). The disciples then understood that Yeshua was referring to John the Baptist, or more accurately, the "Immerser."

John was not Elijah himself, and he plainly testified that he was not Elijah (see John 1:19-21). Even so, when the Lord Jesus was teaching about John's ministry, He referred to this same anointing and mantle of prophetic preparation that resided in John.

The ceremony of Elijah's cup is a blessed reminder that the prophet Elijah will return to earth, just as Malachi prophesied. The Scripture will be fulfilled, and it is commendable that we carry this affirmation of God's Word into the Passover Seder, and across our generations.

However, as Jill was writing the section of the Passover chapter on Elijah's Cup, she asked the Lord to show her His heart concerning this particular tradition in the Seder. The following is the word that He gave to Jill.

> How I wish it were My cup they would set out on the table! For one greater than Elijah is standing in their midst! The very Host and Living Sacrifice stands before them, dressed in My robes of celebration, robes of ceremonial honor, and they act as if I'm not even in the room. Instead, they look for Elijah, who is not waiting to drink the cup with his people, Israel. He is waiting to come in the zeal of the Lord of Hosts, to burn like a firebrand the message of repentance into the hearts of a stubborn and hardened people.

> Surely, Elijah will burn in the hearts of the remnant of Israel, the survivors of the nations where they were scattered. But I have already come! They do not need to open the door of their houses and look for Me. I am standing in their midst in this celebration, which is Mine, and it is the door of their hearts I AM knocking on. This is the door Israel must open. The door of their hearts they must open to Me, the Host of the Seder and the Lamb they have eaten without understanding. This is My heart for Elijah's Cup! [end seventh reading].

The Fourth Cup—The Cup of Praise

Leader: The fourth cup is called, "The Cup of Praise." The Seder meal concludes with great joy and gratitude, and we sing psalms and spiritual songs about the wonder of our Father God.

And we have tasted the cup of praise. There is joy, glory, and praise to be experienced in this life, as we live out the righteousness, peace, healings, intimacy, and freedom known only to citizens of the Kingdom of God.

Leader: *Baruch Ata Adonai, Eloheinu Melech HaOlam, Boray P'ri HaGafen.*

All: Praised are You, O Lord our God, King of the universe, who creates the fruit of the vine.

All drink the cup of praise.

Leader: We have concluded our celebration with praise! Let us pray for the salvation of the Jewish people, both physical deliverance from their enemies and spiritual recognition of Yeshua, the Jewish Messiah!

Reader 1 *prays for the Jewish people.*

Optional Worship Song

All: AMEN!

RECEIVING ETERNAL SALVATION

If you have doubts about where your soul stands with God, or have never made a heartfelt decision to accept the salvation and atonement offered by Yeshua's (Jesus Christ's) sacrifice, then this section of the book is written expressly for you.

The God who created the heavens and the earth, as described in the Book of Genesis, calls Himself by numerous titles and names. His covenant Name is the Hebrew name "YAHVEH," best translated, "the God who *is* and *exists*, apart from created things." He also calls Himself our Father and our King. He is the God who is called "The Father" in the writings of the New Testament.

The prophet Isaiah tells us that "all of us like sheep have gone astray; each has turned to his own way" (see Isa. 53:6). There is not one who has been born on the earth who has not sinned and fallen short of the righteous standards of a pure and holy God.

When the Lord God saw that mankind would be forever cast away from His presence due to our sinful thoughts, words, and deeds, He sent a part of Himself from Heaven's glory to become flesh and blood, exactly like His earthly children. This part of Himself was always His Son, even before the creation of the universe. King David declared that God has a Son in Psalm 2, which was written one thousand years before Yeshua was born! This Man is the only person who has never sinned in thought, word, or deed, out of all who have ever lived.

When this Holy Son was born of a Jewish virgin in Israel and became a human child, His given name was *Yeshua,* which in Hebrew means "Salvation." We translate His name into many tongues, and in English, it is rendered, "Jesus." He will answer to His name in *any* language!

In the part of the Bible that is called "the Old Testament," the blood of animals was a necessary sacrifice to cover the sins of the people of Israel. Only blood can atone for sin, according to the Book of Leviticus. However, the blood of animals was not of sufficient value to permanently remove sin from us. Therefore, the Son of God offered Himself as a spotless, sinless offering for the guilt of each and every one of us.

The Lord Jesus gave His life voluntarily. It *seems* that others took His life, but it was the Father's will and the Son's agreement to allow this great suffering and death to take place for our sakes. On the third day, He was raised from death to life, and this physical resurrection opened the gates of eternal life to all who follow Him with all of their hearts.

When we die, or when Yeshua returns to take His people and judge the world, we must face the righteous Judge. He has established the scales of eternal justice such that *no one* will be justified apart from the atoning death of His Son, Yeshua. No matter how "good" one's life is, no matter what religious tradition one lives under, both Jew and Gentile will be cast into hell for his or her personal sins unless they are made righteous and perfect by Yeshua's death and blood. *There is no exception to this heavenly decree.* Therefore, our only hope is to humble ourselves and accept the resurrected Lord Yeshua the Messiah and His death as our personal covering, righteousness, and entrance to Heaven. (*Messiah* means "Anointed One.")

When we pray to the Father to receive the forgiveness and atonement of His Son, the Holy Spirit of God comes to dwell in our spirits, and He never departs from us after this moment. In Hebrew, the Holy Spirit is called the *Ruach ha Kodesh.* He is the part of God who is able to be everywhere at the same time, who searches and knows our hearts at all times, and who counsels and teaches us God's will in our lives. He always glorifies the crucified and risen Lord Yeshua, and always speaks truth that is in perfect agreement with everything written in the Bible, both Old and New Covenants.

When we pray to receive Yeshua, we are also agreeing to lay down our rights, control, and ownership of our lives. We are not "free" to deliberately indulge ourselves in any sinful word, thought, or lifestyle. If He is not Lord of our lives, we have not understood who He is and what He has done. *To receive Yeshua, the cost is our right to govern our own life and destiny.* He has bought us with the price of His own blood, and if we want to hold onto our own rights, we cannot truly accept His purchase of our souls with His blood.

Please count the cost before you pray this prayer because it is very serious business to make Jesus the Lord of your life. Almost all of the biblical writers were martyred for the Lord's sake; it is common in other nations today. However, the reward we will receive in Heaven and the peace we receive on this earth so far outweigh these hardships that they will not be remembered when we see His face, smiling at us with favor and approval.

If you would like to receive the Lord Jesus now, and be absolutely sure that your soul will be accepted as righteous when you face Him very soon, pray the following prayer (or a similar prayer) from the deepest place in your heart:

Dear Lord God, Creator of all things, I humble myself before You as a sinful person. I know I have sinned in my thoughts, words, and deeds, and am not worthy to enter Heaven based on my own righteousness or worthiness.

I know that You have always loved me, and have sent your Son Yeshua (or "Jesus") to die as a substitute for the punishment I deserve. I accept the sacrifice of His sinless blood that He shed for me on the Cross as the atonement for my sins. I believe that You raised Him from the dead on the third day, that He now lives in Heaven, and that I will be raised to life because of His victory over death. I ask for Your Holy Spirit to enter and fill me and change my life from this moment. I voluntarily surrender my rights and control of my life and choose to make You Lord of my life and destiny. I want to be with You forever in

Heaven, and I know that Yeshua's death and resurrection is the only way I can enter Your Holy Presence.

Thank You for so great a salvation and the free gift of eternal life. I love You, Lord. In Yeshua's name I ask this. Amen.

If you have sincerely prayed this prayer, you are now a new person, *reborn* in your spirit into His life of holiness, righteousness, and love. Begin to read the Bible every day, both Old and New Testaments; it is especially important to read the Gospels of Matthew, Mark, Luke, and John to learn about Yeshua's ministry on earth. Begin to pray to Him every day. Talk to Him as you would talk to a friend, but with much love, reverence, and respect for who He is. Find a church or Messianic congregation where the people *truly* love Yeshua and live in the power of His Holy Spirit. They will help you to grow in your new faith. The Lord will be with you, now and forever. *Never deny Him,* no matter what wicked men say to you or do to you, and you will receive eternal life.

If you have received the Lord Yeshua after reading this book, please write to me: jill@coffeetalkswithmessiah.com or go to www.sidroth.org for more information.

Endnotes

CHAPTER 1

1. Dr. Robert D. Heidler, *The Messianic Church Arising!* (Denton, TX: Glory of Zion International Ministries Inc., 2006).

2. Heidler, *The Messianic Church Arising!*, 53-62.

3. Ibid.

4. Jacob R. Marcus, *The Jew in the Medieval World.* (Cincinnati, OH: Hebrew Union College Press, 2000), 104-106.

5. For additional information on the pagan origin of the name *Easter* and its related celebrations, see Dr. Heidler's book above.

6. Marcus, *The Jew in the Medieval World*, 104-106.

7. Sid Roth, *The Race to Save the World* (Lake Mary, FL: Charisma House, 2004); www.sidroth.org.

8. Michael L. Brown, *Our Hands Are Stained With Blood: The Tragic Story of the "Church" and the Jewish People* (Shippensburg, PA: Destiny Image, 1992); www.icnministries.org.

9. Ken Curtis, Beth Jacobson, JoDair McAleese, Diana Severance, Ann T. Snyder, *Glimpses*, no. 84 (Worcester, PA: Christian History Institute, 1996).

10. Choo Thomas, *Heaven Is So Real!* (Lake Mary, FL: Charisma House, 2003).

11. Jill Shannon, *Coffee Talks With Messiah: When Intimacy Meets Revelation* (Theodore, AL: Gazelle Press, 2007). Chapter 10 provides more teaching on Romans 11.

12. Ibid., 102.

13. Heidler, *The Messianic Church Arising!*

CHAPTER 2

1. Biblical examples taken from Exodus 11:5-7; Judges 6:36-39; Daniel 3:22-25; Second Samuel 17:34-50; Esther 5:14-7:10; Matthew 24:40; Ephesians 1:13; and Revelation 13:16-17.

2. Zondervan NIV Study Bible, eds. Kenneth L. Barker and Donald W. Burdick (Grand Rapids, MI: Zondervan, 2002). Commentary on Luke 23:44-46.

3. Kevin Howard and Marvin Rosenthal, *The Feasts of the Lord* (Orlando, FL: Zion's Hope, Inc., 1997), 61.

4. Flavius Josephus, *The New Complete Works of Josephus,* trans. William Whiston (Grand Rapids, MI: Kregel Publications, 1999), 873-880, 906.

5. Zondervan NIV Study Bible; commentary on Matthew 23:5.

6. Messianic Vision, headed by Sid Roth, contains a variety of resources for Jewish and non-Jewish believers, as well as for traditional Jews who wish to learn more about Yeshua the Messiah. See http://www.sidroth.org.

7. Lonnie Lane, "The Holocaust and Uncle Moshe." Article found on Messianic Vision Web site; see http://www.sidroth.org under the section of articles entitled, "Jewish Roots."

8. Jill Shannon, *Coffee Talks With Messiah: When Intimacy Meets Revelation* (Theodore, AL: Gazelle Press, 2006), 106-111.

9. Michael L. Brown, *Our Hands Are Stained With Blood: The Tragic Story of the "Church" and the Jewish People* (Shippensburg, PA: Destiny Image, 1992); www.icnministries.org.

10. Messianic Jewish Resources International's online store is at www.messianicjewish.net (go to the tab on "Biblical Festivals and the Jewish Calendar.") Their phone number is (800) 410-7367. The Web site for Jews for Jesus is at www.jewsforjesus.org (go to the online store, then "Judaica," then either "Sabbath" or "Passover," depending on which items you want.)

Chapter 3

1. Rabbi Solomon Ganzfried, trans. by Hyman E. Goldin, *Code of Jewish Law* (Spencertown, NY: Hebrew Publishing Company, 1998). For detailed instructions about leavening and Passover preparations, see volume 3, pages 23-33.

2. Morris Epstein, *All About Jewish Holidays and Customs* (Jersey City, NJ: KTAV Publishing House, Inc., 1970), 89.

Chapter 4

1. Kevin Howard and Marvin Rosenthal, *The Feasts of the Lord* (Orlando, FL: Zion's Hope, Inc., 1997), 78.

2. Pastors Curt and Anita Malizzi, Hopewell Christian Fellowship, Telford, PA. Full sermon, "Jesus, Bread of Presence" was preached on 3/9/08. Much more is available at www.hopewellchristianfellowship.com.

3. The traditional blessing given at all meals before the breaking of bread. This may have been the blessing prayed by the Lord Yeshua before He distributed the multiplied barley loaves to the crowd.

CHAPTER 5

1. Kevin Howard and Marvin Rosenthal, *The Feasts of the Lord* (Orlando, FL: Zion's Hope, Inc., 1997), 202.

CHAPTER 6

1. Kevin Howard and Marvin Rosenthal, *The Feasts of the Lord* (Orlando, FL: Zion's Hope, Inc., 1997), 106-107.

2. For more information on the Gathering of the Eagles repentance conferences, led by Nita Johnson, go to www.worldforjesus.org.

3. This revelation was shared by Sadhu Sundar Selvaraj in a teaching at Jireh Church on October 27, 2007; www.jesusministries.org.

4. Jill Shannon, *Coffee Talks With Messiah: When Intimacy Meets Revelation* (Theodore, AL: Gazelle Press, 2007). The "Terror Test" is found on page 42.

CHAPTER 7

1. Mahesh Chavda, *The Hidden Power of Prayer & Fasting* (Shippensburg, PA: Destiny Image Publishers, Inc., 1998).

2. Jacob Neusner, *The Mishnah: A New Translation* (New Haven, CT: Yale University Press, 1988), Yoma 3:3B, 268.

3. In this prophetic word, the Lord is making several references to Zechariah 3, in which we see a high priest named "Joshua," which in Hebrew is very close to "Yeshua," the name of Jesus. He represents Israel's sin and cleansing, but as we see in verses 8 and 9, Joshua also represents the great High Priest Jesus, who would come and stand in the gap for us, with our sins covering Him. Then the Father removes all of our filth from Him, because He overcame death and became the scapegoat for all humanity.

CHAPTER 8

1. Zondervan NIV Study Bible (Grand Rapids, MI: Zondervan, 2002); commentary on 2 Chron. 5:3, p. 627.

2. Kevin Howard and Marvin Rosenthal, *The Feasts of the Lord* (Orlando, FL: Zion's Hope, Inc., 1997).

3. International worship leader Paul Wilbur revealed that it was to the Sanhedrin that Yeshua was speaking this prophetic word; this was the ruling council of seventy-one elders, primarily Pharisees and Sadducees. To order these teachings from Paul Wilbur, go to www.wilburministries.com and look for "Sixty Minutes with Sid Roth—The Best of Paul Wilbur"—a teaching on the return of the Sanhedrin after 1700 years and its significance for the Lord's return.

4. Robert Heidler, *The Messianic Church Arising!* (Denton, TX: Glory of Zion International Ministries, Inc., 2006). Dr. Heidler has compiled five types of the Tabernacle, found on page 206. For the purposes of this book, I have augmented these types, and acknowledge with gratitude his outstanding concept and compilation.

5. Howard and Rosenthal, *The Feasts of the Lord*, 202.

CHAPTER 9

1. Flavius Josephus, *The New Complete Works of Josephus*, trans. William Whiston (Grand Rapids, MI: Kregel Publications, 1999), 345-346; also see Second Kings 25 and Second Chronicles 36:11-21.

2. Menelaus served from 172 B.C. until his execution in 162 B.C. Second Maccabees 13:3-8, from *The Apocrypha*, trans. by Edgar J. Goodspeed (New York: Vintage Books, 1989).

3. 2 Maccabees 5:13-14; Ibid.

4. 1 Maccabees 1:20-24;44-63; Ibid.

5. 1 Maccabees 1:54-60; Ibid.

6. Josephus, *The New Complete Works*, 404.

7. 2 Maccabees 6:30b; Ibid.

8. 2 Maccabees 7:14; Ibid.

9. 2 Maccabees 10:6-8; Ibid.

10. "Preface," *The Apocrypha*, trans. by Edgar J. Goodspeed.

11. Josephus, "Introduction," *The New Complete Works*.

12. Kevin Howard and Marvin Rosenthal, *The Feasts of the Lord* (Orlando, FL: Zion's Hope, Inc., 1997), 202.

13. For more information, see http://www.coffeetalkswithmessiah.com.

14. For Messianic resources and information, you can go to this Web site: http://www.messianicjewish.net. Click on "Webstore" and then "Biblical Festivals and the Jewish Calendar." For two other Web sites with many helpful resources from a "traditional" Jewish perspective (non-Messianic), including listening to Hanukah songs online, recipes, and the dreidel game, go to: http://www.jewfaq.org/holiday7.htm or http://www.chabad.org/holidays/chanukah/default_cdo/jewish/Chanukah.htm.

15. Marvin Rosenthal, *The Pre-Wrath Rapture of the Church* (Nashville, TN: Thomas Nelson, Inc., 1990).

16. Mike Bickle, International House of Prayer, Kansas City, MO: www .ihop.org. Go to mp3 teachings, or CD sets, and look for the series on the Book of Revelation. The mp3 teachings are each listed and purchased separately, by date.

CHAPTER 10

1. Zondervan NIV Study Bible (Grand Rapids, MI: Zondervan, 2002); commentary on Esther 2:5.

2. Zondervan NIV Study Bible (Grand Rapids, MI: Zondervan, 2002); commentary on Esther 2:23.

3. As heard on a teaching of Nita Johnson, World for Jesus Ministries, 2006; www.worldforjesus.org.

4. Zerubbabel is listed as one of Yeshua's ancestors in both Matthew 1 and Luke 3. This would indicate that Yeshua's ancestors were among the returning exiles. However, neither of these NT genealogies lists the same sons of Zerubbabel as those named in First Chronicles 3:19. Nevertheless, it is likely that the Lord's ancestors had already returned to Israel by Esther's reign.

5. Sid Roth, *Time Is Running Short* (Shippensburg, PA: Destiny Image Publishers, 1990).

6. Robert Stearns: www.eagleswings.to.

7. Barry and Batya Segal: www.visionforisrael.com.

8. Kevin Howard and Marvin Rosenthal, *The Feasts of the Lord* (Orlando, FL: Zion's Hope, Inc., 1997), 202.

9. The Hebrew name for King Xerxes was Ahashverus, as the Lord has referred to him in this word.

CHAPTER 11

1. This word study, as well as the concept of a "date day" in the next section was heard on a teaching tape by Jack Zimmerman: "The Sabbath: A Messianic Jewish Perspective," MJAA/YMJA Conference, 2005.

2. Robert Heidler, *The Messianic Church Arising!* (Denton, TX: Glory of Zion International Ministries, Inc., 2006).

3. Jacob R. Marcus, *The Jew in the Medieval World* (Cincinnati, OH: Hebrew Union College Press, 2000), 104-106.

4. Heidler, *The Messianic Church Arising!* This book has a wonderful teaching on the Sabbath, found on pages 86-96.

CHAPTER 12

1. Sid Roth, *Time Is Running Short* (Shippensburg, PA: Destiny Image Publishers, 1990), 15-18.

2. Jill Shannon, *Coffee Talks With Messiah: When Intimacy Meets Revelation* (Theodore, AL: Gazelle Press, 2007). Chapter 10 provides in-depth teaching on the Jewish regathering to their land.

3. Maurice Sklar, "Visions from the Dallas, Texas, Revival" (May-June, 1985); www.mauricesklar.com.

4. Shannon, *Coffee Talks*. This teaching parable on Ruth and Boaz is found in greater depth in Chapter 10 of *Coffee Talks*. It is partially reproduced here, with gratitude to Gazelle Press.

APPENDIX

1. This Web site is sponsored by Pastor Joshua Wallnofer of Klondike Baptist Church in Pensacola, Florida. Their group participated in music videos with Philadelphia Biblical University Institute of Jewish Studies. It is a moving video and will also teach you the song.

2. Kevin Howard and Marvin Rosenthal, *The Feasts of the Lord* (Orlando, FL: Zion's Hope, Inc., 1997), 61.

About the Author

JILL SHANNON is a Messianic Jewish Bible teacher, author, and singer/songwriter. Growing up in a Reform Jewish home, she accepted the Lord in 1973. In the 1980s, Jill and her husband immigrated to Israel, learned Hebrew, and gave birth to three children. During these years in Israel, she endured hardship and received vital lessons; after returning to the United States, the Lord began to reveal His glory to Jill in a journey of intimacy. Her testimonies are shared in her first book, *Coffee Talks With Messiah: When Intimacy Meets Revelation,* published by Gazelle Press, 2007.

Jill currently speaks and writes about experiencing God's glory, holy living and intimate friendship with the Lord, the biblical Feasts, Israel, and the Church. Jill also composes and records worship songs, available on her CDs: *A Part of Me, Beckon Me* and *Remember Me.* She presently resides outside of Philadelphia, Pennsylvania, with her husband and two daughters. She also has a married son and daughter-in-law in Pittsburgh, PA.

To listen to clips from Jill's music, order CDs or copies of her books, or download Jill's free biblical teachings on mp3 files, visit Jill's Website:
www.coffeetalkswithmessiah.com
To contact Jill for speaking engagements or book interviews, e-mail: jill@coffeetalkswithmessiah.com or write to:
Coffee Talks
PO Box 26175
Collegeville, PA 19426

Additional copies of this book and other
book titles from DESTINY IMAGE are
available at your local bookstore.

Call toll-free: 1-800-722-6774.

Send a request for a catalog to:

Destiny Image® Publishers, Inc.
P.O. Box 310
Shippensburg, PA 17257-0310

*"Speaking to the Purposes of God for this
Generation and for the Generations to Come."*

**For a complete list of our titles,
visit us at www.destinyimage.com.**